We have no contr
our choices we get to find our own way. My way was baseball. This book illustrates some of the same hardships I endured and overcame living in Callahan, Florida. Regardless of what I have seen or what I have done those trials and tribulations were my playground for success. This book will inspire you to make right choices and have faith in God's plan for you!

Howard Kendrick
L.A. Angels

What sets this book apart is the honest and valuable sharing that Dr. Danielle Russell gives to the reader. This book is a remarkable story of what God can do when you put Him first. Dr. Russell's powerful story is destined to bless the lives of many. Praise God for the publication of the story of this sanctified wife, mother, and physician.

Weptanomah Davis
Today's Minister's Wife
First Lady First Baptist Church Highland Park Landover, MD

Dr. Russell delivers her message as a smooth and easy flowing memory that places you in her childhood. Masterfully, she paints imagery with sights, sounds, customs, culture, and dialect, of warmth but also of adversity, that instantly make you a member of the family, loving her nine feisty aunts, a myriad of cousins, and especially, Aunt C, Papa, Nana, and even Old Man J, through their flaws, eccentricities, and other flavors of humanness. With astonishment, you look back with her, over her circumstances, and wonder how she got over.

Dr. Nadene Houser-Archield,
Prince George's Community College, Largo, MD

Sanctified & Still Standing!

Sanctified & Still Standing!

God's Greatness Revealed
throughout a Life Full of Challenges

Dr. T. Danielle Russell

Tate Publishing & Enterprises

Published by Tate Publishing & Enterprises, LLC
127 E. Trade Center Terrace | Mustang, Oklahoma 73064 USA
1.888.361.9473 | www.tatepublishing.com

Tate Publishing is committed to excellence in the publishing industry. The company reflects the philosophy established by the founders, based on Psalm 68:11,
"The Lord gave the word and great was the company of those who published it."

Book design copyright © 2008 by Tate Publishing, LLC. All rights reserved.
Cover design by Stephanie Woloszyn
Interior design by Jacob Crissup

Published in the United States of America

ISBN: 978-1-60604-187-1
1. Inspiration: Motivational: Autobiography
2. Biography & Autobiography: Religious/Medical
08.06.03

Dedication

Dedicated to my wonderful husband, Albert, without you this would not be possible. To the most adorable son in the world, Donovan, and my beautiful baby girl, Genesis; you are my jewels. Mom, you are my inspiration. Dad, thanks for being my biggest fan. Written in memory of my closest cuz, Jason, my young angel. Thank you, God, for giving me the courage to step out on faith and write this book.

Acknowledgements

First, and foremost, thank you, God, for not letting me rest until I completed the work You had for me to do. I know that I am not done yet. This is only the beginning.

I would also like to thank all of my family members and close friends for encouraging me to go forth with this vision. I initially did not have the courage to write this book, but seeing the excitement in each of your eyes when I told you what God wanted me to do gave me that reassurance and boost that I needed to go forward.

I would really like to thank Tate Publishing for investing your time (and money) into completing this wonderful project. Dr. Tate, you and your staff have truly been sent by God to help young authors reach their full potential.

And, of course, I would like to thank all of my readers for purchasing my book. I pray that it will be a blessing to each and every one of you, and that you will recommend it to someone else that you think could benefit from the words on the following pages.

Be blessed!

Foreword

There are times in our lives when we are faced with decisions that, depending on the choice that is made, will alter the course of our existence. Many times, I think that God puts us into situations to bring out the best in us. He places us into the cauldron of life to purify us, to purge us and to draw out of us the greatness that He placed into us from the beginning. Danielle Russell has been in life's furnace. She has faced adversity. She has been to the bottom of the barrel...and she survived! There were times in her life where she could have easily thrown in the towel, yet she persisted and her faith kept her. She understood that even when you are backed against a wall, God will make a way. When it seems that there is no way out, God won't move what's in front of you, He'll remove the bricks from the wall that's behind you and provide an escape from situations that seem insurmountable. This book is a tale of faith, doubt, hope, despair, life, death, and how Danielle, with God's help, navigated the highways of life and sidestepped disaster after disaster. It will make you laugh and make you cry. It will challenge you to look at your own situation and thank God for the options that He gives us rather than complain about how bad you have it.

The African-American existence as seen through the eyes of a young black girl can be quite complicated. You have so many roles to play, some desired and others totally undesired. When you live your life according to who everyone else wants you to be, it is very easy to lose sight of who you really are. *Sanctified and Still Standing!* illustrates this perfectly. Danielle not only refused to let anyone define her, she played the game according to her own rules. The complexity of our existence is what makes us into the people that we are. Rather than let her circumstances dictate her outcome, Danielle instead used her circumstances to motivate her and fuel her escape from a dismal existence in rural Florida. Reading this book will no doubt give you a new appreciation for the grace of God and how He continues to watch over us and how He allows us to remain under His three P's (Protection, Peace, and Providence). You will enjoy every second that you spend with Danielle as she walks you through her life. You will also realize that no matter how much we think we have it together, we are all just works in progress.

Danielle and I have been married now for the past seven years. We have had to endure both good and bad. Thankfully, most of it has been good. God has blessed us immensely and is continuing to do so. We both have a rich background to draw from, and we've both seen things and done things that we shouldn't have. She has chosen to open her life up to the world. This book reminds me of a scripture in Hebrews 4:13. To paraphrase this scripture, it says that nothing is unseen to Jesus (the Word) and all before Him are laid bare (naked). In other words, we cannot hide anything from God. Neither can we hide anything from ourselves. When we are honest with ourselves and honest about where we came from, God can use us because we are not ashamed to let people see us for who we are. It is amazing how many people identify with you when you are honest—people that have been waiting for the right thing to be said so that they could know that they are not alone in their struggle. Danielle's story will make some angry. It will make some shout for joy. Most of all, it will allow someone out there to know that they are not alone and that God is always faithful regardless of what the situation looks like.

Dr. Albert E. Russell
Husband, Friend, Lover, Confidant

Introduction

To everyone referenced in this book, it was not written with the intent to hurt or harm anyone. God gave me the vision to write this book at three o'clock in the morning around February of 2005 to discuss various events that took place in my life. Each of these events helped to shape me into the person that I am today. If you recognize yourself in this book, it is because you have made a very special impact on me in some way. I remember hearing one preacher say that letting someone else see the scars of our past may show them what God has brought us through and help prevent them from making some of the same mistakes we have made. All of us have pasts and have made many mistakes, some large and some small. The key is to learn from our mistakes, develop a testimony from the lesson(s) that we have learned, and help bring someone else closer to God by sharing our testimonies. I heard another preacher say that God's glory is in our story.

All of us have a story to tell. Don't be ashamed or afraid to tell your story. Someone may be waiting to hear about how God took you out of your mess and turned your life into a blessing. That same preacher also said that if God can trust you enough to test you, He can also trust you enough to bless you. We need to learn to welcome every test God allows the devil to bring our way knowing that God is all powerful and able to bring us through each and every one unscathed. This book is a testimony of how God took a little black girl from a little country town called Callahan, Florida, and led me on to do bigger and better things to further glorify Him. It does not matter who you are, where you are from, or what your family background is. All that matters is who you belong to (God) and that you make up your mind to follow the path that He has set before you.

It is so easy to get caught up in everything that is going on around you, and believe me, I grew up around a lot of crazy things. It is very easy to let those things side track you from what it is that God has planned for you. The devil wants to take each and every one of us out. He wants to physically kill us so that we cannot fulfill God's will to bring more people into God's army. We have to be strong and put *all* of our faith and trust in God and know that we are His children. The devil cannot do anything to us that God does not allow, and as long as we are within God's will He is not going to allow Satan to take us out. But the key is *staying within His will.* When we step out of His will and have premarital sex, use drugs, lie, steal, cheat, talk bad about our neighbors, that's when bad things happen to us. That same pit you try to dig for someone else you may find yourself falling into. And guess what, it's *our* fault. God gives us clear instructions in His Word, and a lot of times we conveniently forget what He said. Don't do that. Be obedient, for the wages of sin is death, but the gift of God is eternal life. I pray that this book will touch, uplift, encourage, comfort somebody and let everybody know that it's not where you're from that matters, but where you end up. I pray that I will see each of you walking on those streets of gold living in that mansion that God has promised to all of us who follow His will.

Lord, please bless my brain and my fingers as I write this book. Amen.

Genesis

Rise, Shine, Give God the Glory!

"Get up, girl! You ain't gon' make me late again this week!" my mother screamed as usual urging me to get up out of my comfortable bed to get ready for Sunday school.

"Aw, Ma, just five more minutes," I pleaded.

"Five more minutes, my behind. You better get up so you can get cleaned off and dressed so we can get out of here," she stated as she pulled the covers off me.

"But can't I stay home with Daddy today?"

"Girl, I ain't gon' tell you no more. You better get out of that bed before I come knock you out of it!"

"Oh, all right then! Shoot!"

"What did you say?"

"Nothin', gosh," I said under my breath.

I knew just how far I could go with my mom. She was just a little thing, five feet two inches and about one hundred pounds, but she had a strong backhand. And I always seemed to want to push her to her limit before backing off. I really think that I got that from her side of the family. Although, she was never that way with her parents. As the middle child of twelve children born to my nana and papa, I must say she was probably the most respectful and respected of them all.

Of the twelve children there were ten girls and two boys.

Ten *girls!* I can only imagine what it was like growing up in that household. And I can use one word to describe all of my aunts. *Feisty!* You had one choice when dealing with them. You could choose to either be on their good sides or their bad sides. And I can tell you from watching the men roll in and out of their lives, the bad side is not where you wanted to be.

I remember hearing stories of one of my aunts taking a machete to the throat of one of my ex-uncles while they were in Germany. She didn't cut him, though. Apparently he had enough sense to know that she wasn't playin'. Needless to say it was over between them after that.

Another one of my aunts messed around and got herself involved with this guy who was very abusive and controlling. I heard he was so mean that after whoopin' up on her one time he tried flushing her head down the toilet to drown her. That ended after she put a pistol to his head. She didn't shoot him. He, also, was smart enough to realize she'd had enough.

Another one of my aunts, boy, she was way too smart to let any single man put restraints on her. Dark chocolate with just the right amount of sweetness. She had all of the men in Nassau County tryin' their best to get with her. And she would play along with 'em, too. Just for a little while. I think she got bored pretty quickly, though, because before long she was on to the next one. I heard a couple of those fellas tried to force her to settle with them. One tried locking her up in a room on the second floor of his house. She showed him, though. She jumped out the window and scaled down the wall. She had a bunch of scrapes on her hands and broken fingernails, but she was okay. She came home talking about how frightening the experience was. But it didn't slow her down. The next day she had found someone else. Another fella tried forcing her to run away with him. He was just goin' to have her *all* to *himself.* But she showed him, too. She jumped from the car as they were driving up US 1. "Stop, drop, and roll, baby. That's what they do on TV so they don't get hurt when they jump out of cars," she said. I always thought that was what you were supposed to do when you were on fire. But what did I know? I was only a little girl. And, hey, maybe she was on fire. Needless to say, she survived with only a few cuts and bruises and was on to her next big adventure.

She met this one guy, though, who I think she really was crazy about. He was a good-lookin' Puerto Rican she had met at one of the clubs she frequented. I think she was with him for several months. I remembered his name for a long time after they broke up. I think this fella may have been able to keep her. She even allowed herself to get pregnant by him. *What?!* we all thought. *You're going to settle down and have a baby?* She was as proud and happy as she could be. "This is going to be a pretty baby," she said. "Half Puerto Rican and half black with long pretty hair." And my aunt *loved* to do some hair. She knew it was going to be a girl. She probably already had a name picked out for her by the time she told us she was pregnant, but I don't think she ever told anyone. She was so happy. She stopped running the streets and spent most of her time with Mr. Puerto Rican. She got herself a steady job at McDonald's in Callahan. She was doing well until one day she started having severe cramps in her lower belly. She went to the bathroom and noticed that her underwear was soaked with blood. While she was urinating she heard a splash in the toilet. She looked down and there was her little red sixteen-week-old fetus floating in the water. Even though she was devastated, her maternal instincts kicked in, and she rescued her dead baby from the water and wrapped it in a paper towel. She then got someone to take her to the ER to be checked out. They told her she was fine, that all of the products of conception had passed, and sent her home. They kept the fetus for examination which revealed nothing abnormal. The examination did, however confirm one thing. It was a little girl. I don't think that my aunt was ever the same after that. How could something so beautiful, that she wanted so much, be taken away from her? *Maybe I don't deserve happiness,* she thought. Shortly afterward, she moved on from Mr. Puerto Rican to whoever she felt was best suited to take her pain away. Even if only for one night.

I remember one night while I was asleep on the daybed in a little room right off the kitchen in my nana's trailer, my aunt came home with another one of her beaus. They were in the den, which I could see from where I was sleeping. I heard them giggling and kissing which woke me up. It had to be about two or three o'clock in the morning. I don't think she knew I was in there sleeping. It was dark, so all I could see was her silhouette. Even though I was only about ten or eleven, I knew they were in there doing something they should not have been. The next morning while we were sitting in the living room, I told my nana what I had seen. "Oh, you got yourself a real live theater show, didn't you?" my nana said. When my aunt came home, my nana cussed her out real good. It didn't stop her, though. My aunt kept right on doing what she was doing. It seemed as though she had a new man every day. I don't think she was brave enough to bring any more guys up in my nana's house, though. At least not that I know of.

This aunt reminded me a lot of one of my mom's older sisters, my aunt C. Aunt C also lived a *fast* life. She was one of the sweetest people in the world, but she *loved* her booze and she *loved* her men. Aunt C was a beautiful red-boned chick with curves for days as well as long, thick pretty hair. Could no other woman in Callahan hold a stick to Aunt C. Aunt C did settle down, though, with Uncle H. Uncle H was a tall, athletic man that she knew from around town. They were married for several years. I don't think it was a good marriage, though, because I heard that they were both tippin' out on each other. And neither of them liked being cheated on. They stayed at each other's throat like cats and dogs. But the crazy thing was that neither wanted to let the other go for fear of someone else having them. That never made any sense to me. Finally, though, Aunt C got tired of the beatings Uncle H put on her, and she packed her bags and left, leaving behind her two sons and one daughter. She didn't go far.

Just up the street to live with another man. Callahan, Florida, ain't but so big.

Aunt C continued her fast life. Drinking and partying. Not a care in the world. At least that's how it appeared. I think deep down inside she really did want a man to treat her like a princess. Make her feel special. What woman doesn't? That's when she met Old Man J. Old Man J was probably about thirty years her senior and was about as dingy of a man there was. However he provided Aunt C with a roof over her head and all the beer she could drink. Old Man J had several missing teeth and walked with a limp. I could not *believe* this was her new beau. To each his own. And Old Man J was *mean!* I don't think there was a nice bone in his body. He must have been nice to her, though, at some point.

Well, Aunt C and Old Man J kicked it for a while. But Aunt C still wanted to go to the club and have her fun. Old Man J didn't like the fact that he couldn't completely control her. He wasn't very fond of going to the club anymore. After all, he was an *old* man. Soon Old Man J began to suspect Aunt C was cheating on him because she was always out. Aunt C avidly denied any of his allegations but he just would not let loose. Aunt C was about thirty-five years old at the time.

It was probably about mid-June 1982, and Aunt C had some shocking news. "I'm pregnant!" she exclaimed. *You're pregnant for that Old Man J,* I thought. She seemed thrilled by the thought of having another child. Maybe she felt this child would fill the void she had been trying to fill by running the streets and drowning herself in beer.

"What you gon' do with another child?" one of my aunts exclaimed.

"Raise it. What you think!" Aunt C replied.

"Well, whatever! You a fool for havin' a child for that *nut!*" my other aunt retorted.

Everyone in Callahan knew Old Man J was a little crazy. We would soon find out just how crazy he was.

It was a beautiful day in early July 1982. It seemed like the entire family was in my grandmother's backyard for a BBQ. All of my cousins and I were running around playing and having fun.

"Tag, you're it!" one of my younger cousins exclaimed as she ran away from me.

"Uhn, uhn. I'm gon' git you back!" I yelled as I chased after her.

My mother walked out of the back door with her infamous pan of baked beans. Everyone loved her baked beans. She put just the right amount of sugar and butter in them. *A lot!* She even laid the strips of bacon across the top. I *loved* her baked beans. Just as she sat the pan of beans on the outdoor table, we heard the most frightening sound I had ever heard in my young life. *Pop, pop!* I had never seen my mother run as fast as she darted out of the backyard towards the noise. "Ma!" I screamed as I took off right behind her. Our journey did not take us far as the noise had only come from two houses up from my grandmother's house. This was the house that Aunt C lived in with Old Man J. As we approached the yard, we saw Aunt C lying face down in the dirt.

"He's still got the gun in his hand!" someone yelled. Old Man J was still standing in the doorway with a smoking .22 caliber pistol in his hand aimed directly at Aunt C as she lay helpless on the ground.

"I don't care! He's just gon' have to shoot me! That's my sister lying on that ground!" my mom yelled as she jumped over the ditch into the yard to care for her sister.

"Ma!" I screamed again looking at Old Man J still aiming the gun in their direction.

My mom reached Aunt C, dropped to her knees, and turned her over. Dirt covered Aunt C's entire face. Aunt C tried to speak but was unable to because as soon as she opened her mouth blood began to bubble out of both her mouth and her nose. My mother rocked her back and forth trying to comfort her, but she knew it was too late.

"Do you accept Christ as your Lord and Savior?" my mother hurriedly said as if Aunt C's life depended on it. A puzzled look came across Aunt C's pale face. "Do you accept Christ Jesus as your Lord and Savior!" my mother anxiously exclaimed. A peaceful and understanding look came across my aunt's face. After that she knew exactly what my mother's intentions were and what her question meant.

A gentle smile came across my aunt's angelic face as she gently nodded her head to say, "Yes." She then began to cough and her entire body shook as the blood filled her airway. A few seconds later my aunt C was lying dead in my mom's arms. Old Man J then lowered his gun and went back into the house and sat down as we waited for the police to come take him away. His job was done. And in a way my mom's job had been done as well. She truly believed Aunt C had confessed her salvation before she took her last breath.

It seems like it took forever for the police and the ambulance to get there. When they finally did arrive, they pronounced my aunt C dead on arrival, and the police hauled Old Man J off to prison.

The next evening we were at our house attempting to proceed with our daily lives as usual. After dinner I had taken my bath and was getting ready for bed. I came out of my bedroom after putting on my nightgown and noticed my mom standing in the dining room with a stunned but happy look on her face.

"What's wrong, Ma?" I asked.

"Nothing, sweetie," she replied.

"Why you looking like that?"

"Because," she said hesitantly, "your aunt C was just here."

"What?" I asked confused.

"A breeze just came through the window and the wind smelled just like her. I think her spirit just came and walked right through me. It was like she was trying to tell me that she is okay."

"Oh," I said obviously confused and sort of freaked out. "I didn't know they could do that."

I left my mom standing in the dining room with her arms folded across her chest rocking from side to side as if she was hugging herself. I slept sort of uneasily that night because the only thing that I could think of was that we had a ghost in our house. *What if she is angry that we didn't get there sooner to save her?* my young naïve mind thought. *I hope she doesn't try to take it out on me.*

The next few days, I sort of paused every time a breeze came through the window. I sniffed to see if I smelled any familiar fragrances that reminded me of Aunt C. Thank the Lord I didn't.

We later found out that Old Man J admitted to arguing with my aunt earlier in the day about the paternity of the child she was carrying. Old Man J could not allow himself to believe that he was the father because he had such a strong suspicion that my aunt had been unfaithful given her past history. He also thought that he was too old to make any more babies. In a drunken rage, he accused her of sleeping with every man in Callahan and that any of these men could be the father of her baby. My aunt adamantly denied his false accusations. She was apparently fed up with the entire obnoxious situation, had packed her bags with the few belongings that she possessed, and was preparing to leave Old Man J and move back next door with my nana. This set off a rage in him that could only be calmed by one thing.

He apparently had found an old .22 caliber pistol in the fireplace the night before. Aunt C noticed him playing with it but thought there was no way he would ever be able to get it to work. *Plus,* she thought, *he'd never shoot me. I'm carrying his baby.* I guess he fooled her good. Somehow Old Man J was able to rig the gun to fire two shots. Unfortunately, my aunt C learned the hard way. Never underestimate the abilities of a crazy person who thinks he has been pushed to the edge. We later found out at the autopsy that Old man J was in fact the baby's father. In fact, he was the babies' father. That's right. Babies! Aunt C was five months pregnant with two beautiful baby girls.

Old Man J received one count of second-degree murder and was back out on the streets in two years. I guess two dead black babies did not account for much back then because he wasn't even charged for their murders. I think the courts felt bad for him and let him off easy because number one, he was *old* and number two, even they were able to see how *crazy* he was. They probably didn't think he had much time left on this earth anyway. And do you know he actually had the nerve to move back to my grandmother's neighborhood? *Crazy!* However, even though they hated him, my family decided to let God deal with him on Judgment Day. He only lived for about two more years after he got out, anyway.

That's one July I'll never forget.

One of the saddest things about my aunt C's death was the fact that she left behind four children—three boys and one girl. The girl, my cousin Aretha, was the oldest. She was a very pretty girl, but I think that she never really thought that much of herself back then. One of the things that she picked up from my aunt C at a very young age was her love for the opposite sex. She was around eleven when we found out she was pregnant with her first child. Eleven years old. I cannot imagine what that must have been like. I remember the night that she went into labor. My mom had just gotten off work from Winn-Dixie.

"Aunt Gail, I keep peein' on myself!" she yelled from the bathroom.

My mom went into the bathroom, "Girl, you ain't peein'. Your water just broke. We gotta get you to the hospital!"

My mom, grandma, and Aretha all rushed out of the house and headed to the hospital in Jacksonville. My grandma was in the backseat with Aretha trying to keep her calm.

"I don't think I'm gon' make it!" Aretha yelled.

"What you mean you ain't gon' make it?" my grandma asked.

"It feels like the baby is comin' out!"

"Let me see!"

My grandma checked between Aretha's legs. "Gail, you better pull over. This baby's head is already out!"

"Oh, Jesus, help us!" My mom pulled the car over and jumped into the backseat in time to deliver Aretha's baby boy.

"What do we do now?" my mom said.

"I don't know. Is he breathin'?" Nana asked.

"I don't think so," my mom said. "We got to hurry up and get to the hospital!"

My mom handed the baby to my grandma and they rushed to the hospital. Unfortunately when they got to the hospital there was nothing that could be done. Aretha's little baby boy was pronounced dead.

They kept Aretha in the hospital for two days. When she came home, there was no mention of her experience. After a couple of weeks she was right back out in the streets doing the same things she had been doing before.

When she was thirteen or fourteen she was pregnant again; this time with twins. Unfortunately these babies died at birth as well. Twin girls. She went into labor a little early with them. She made it to the nearest hospital in time for this birth; however, Twin A was stillborn. Twin B was born alive but in unstable condition due to her prematurity. The hospital that Aretha delivered at did not have a neonatologist, so they tried to Life Flight Twin B to a hospital with a neonatal intensive care unit. Unfortunately she did not survive either. Cousin Aretha had three dead children by the time she was fourteen years old. I have no clue who the fathers were or if she did either.

I think that after this pregnancy the doctors must have gotten her on some good birth control. Either Depo or Norplant, because Cousin Aretha did not get pregnant anymore as a teenager, and I know she did not revert to celibacy.

As you can tell, I have a pretty interesting family. I love them all to death. Like I said earlier, you can choose to either be on their good side or their bad side. Me, I always did my best to stay on the good side. I was a very quiet child, so I got to sit around and listen to all of their stories when all of the other children had to go outside and play. I must say, my aunts all learned from the best, because none of my aunts were nearly as feisty as my grandmother, my nana. My nana had to be feisty, though, to deal with my papa.

Neither my nana nor my papa was much bigger than my mother. My nana was about five feet four inches, and my papa about five feet six or seven inches. He probably weighed no more than one hundred and thirty pounds soaking wet. My papa was as dark as he could be with deep blue eyes. A black man with blue eyes. How 'bout that? He was a hard working man, but he *absolutely loved him some gin!* "My, my, my. That's some good gin!" he would exclaim after each sip. Breakfast, lunch, and dinner. It was all about the gin. I honestly cannot remember very many times when he was sober or not holding a bottle in his hand. I think he even slept with that bottle. And every day it was the same thing. As soon as Papa came home from work, everybody knew what time it was. "You lazy fools. Get ya'll tails up out my doggon' house! I work all day and all ya'll do is sit around here on your lazy behinds. Where's my dinner? Ya'll some bad behind chil'ren! Look at this mess. Git the heck outside!" It went on for hours. My grandmother did her best not the say anything back, but eventually I could tell that he had struck a nerve because she would start yelling and cursing right back at him.

"Shut your ol' drunk tail up!" she'd reply.

I have to admit. Sometimes it was pretty funny. My grandfather was usually so drunk that all he could do was sit on the couch and run his mouth. He would eventually tire himself out and fall asleep.

My grandfather's people came from a small town called Kingstree, South Carolina. Kingstree was smaller than Callahan with lots of farmland. He never really talked much about his parents. He never really talked much about himself at all. I remember going to South Carolina with my grandfather once when I was about six years old. I think we stayed about two days. I don't remember much about the visit. I do remember running around outside of a big old white wooden house with my new-found cousins.

"Let's play hide-and-seek!" one cousin yelled.

"Okay!" we all replied. We all ran to hide as one boy cousin counted.

"One, two, three, four..." we heard him count. I ran to hide behind a large floral bush. I noticed everywhere that I ran one of my other boy cousins followed.

"Go find your own hiding place," I told him.

"No, this is my hiding place," he smiled back. "Give me a kiss!" he said as he tried to grab me.

"Git away from me, boy!" I yelled as I pushed him away and ran off. I was strong for a little girl. He got the picture and left me alone.

Later on that evening, I saw something that I had never seen before in my entire life. Our South Carolina family took a whole pig and roasted the entire thing in a big pit.

"Eww!" I said.

"Girl, what are you talkin' about? That's the best pork you will ever taste," my mom said.

"Whatever," I replied. It always took a lot to convince me of anything. I had to admit, though, it was starting to smell pretty good. However the only thing I could think about was the fact that the head was still on the pig. I sort of had a fear of hog heads.

That was my grandfather's fault. Or should I say that was his goal. You see, my papa had some hogs of his own at their house in Callahan. He kept them in a little pen off to the side of their trailer, sort of off in the woods. I remember helping him slop the hogs. For all of you city people, slopping the hogs is when you take all of the food scraps from the previous day and put them in a huge bucket with some water and feed it to the hogs. You can image how wonderful that smelled. People from the entire neighborhood used to bring over their scraps to contribute to the slop bucket.

When a hog got fat enough or old enough, my papa would then kill it to make his own sausage, bacon, chitlins, and whatever else he could think of. He used every single part of that hog. *Every* part. He even used the hog's head. I know you're probably thinking, *Oh yeah, hog head cheese, souse meat. I've heard of that.* Yes, he used it to make hog head cheese, but that wasn't its only purpose.

You see, my grandfather was one of those old school cats who did not believe that children should be anywhere near the kitchen, let alone in the refrigerator or the freezer. And he had his ways of keeping us out of the freezer.

In Florida, frozen sodas, Kool-Aid frozen in a cup, were a big deal because it was so dog gon' hot all of the time. We were always trying to go in the freezer to make us a frozen soda. My papa used to get mad because inevitably someone would forget to close the freezer door. "You trying to refrigerate the whole neighborhood!" he would yell. "Ya'll some bad kids!" he would say as he shook his head. "I'll fix ya'll though."

One day one of my cousins wanted to fix herself a frozen soda. She had gotten her some Kool-Aid and put it in a Styrofoam cup. She even got fancy and added some mixed fruit to it. She was all proud of herself. She got her cup and went to open the freezer to put it in. "Ahh!" she screamed as she opened the door.

"What's wrong with you, girl?" one of my aunts asked. My cousin just stood there as my aunt approached her to see what had startled her so. As my aunt approached the freezer, she let out a huge laugh, much to my cousin's dismay. Of course my curiosity got the best of me, so I had to go over and take a look for myself. I will never forget what I saw. Two huge eyes and a snout were staring back at me.

"Papa told ya'll he was gon' fix you for goin' in and out of that freezer. One day ya'll gon' listen," my aunt stated.

She was right. After seeing that hog's head in the freezer, I don't think that I ever went into that freezer again without being told to do so. Even then I was very cautious.

"Ain't no hog head in there, is it?" I would always ask.

Well, back to the pit. That pig smelled so good and everyone was acting like it tasted so delicious to them that I did end up tasting it, and it was very tasty I must say. It was the juiciest and most well-seasoned pork I had ever eaten. I guess, once again, my mom did know what she was talking about.

I loved my papa. He took me and my younger cousin, Flaggy, wherever he went. We made frequent trips with him to the drive-in liquor store and to one of his friend's house who liked to make turtle soup. My papa was always catching turtles and taking them over to her house.

I loved my papa so much that one day I think I saved his life. Or maybe at least saved his skin. He and Nana had been arguing again as usual. This argument seemed a little more heated than usual. My nana was very angry.

"You better shut up!" she yelled.

But of course he kept on talking. The next thing I noticed was my grandmother walking out with a big cup full of a tea-like substance.

"Keep on talkin' and I'll pour this whole cup on top of your head!"

"No, Nana!" I yelled as I jumped in between them.

When she saw me standing there she calmed down and lowered the cup. "Please, don't hurt Papa," I pleaded.

One of my aunts grabbed me and said, "Girl, you crazy. Do you know what that was in that cup?"

"Yeah, tea," I said naively.

My aunt laughed and said, "Girl, you are lucky. That wasn't tea. That was pot ash."

"Pot ash. What's that?"

"Acid. That stuff could've taken the skin right off of you."

"Oh," I said as I suddenly got nervous.

For the rest of that day all I could think about was what if my grandmother hadn't stopped when she did. What if she had attempted to pour that pot ash on Papa and it had gotten on me instead? I would have been scarred for life. *That's the last time I step in to try and stop a fight.* It's always the person trying to help who ends up getting hurt. I must say, though, my papa was very grateful.

After many years my mom told me what pot ash really was. It was some sort of acid mixture that my papa used on the hogs. My mom said that the week before he was going to kill a hog he would start feeding it a diet consisting of only corn and a little bit of pot ash. Supposedly this cleaned the intestines out really well. I guess this was a good thing because we loved us some chitlins, and I suppose cleaning the hog out before he killed it made it a lot easier to get clean chitlins.

Like I said, my papa was a very hard-working man. No matter how drunk he got, he always got up the next morning and made it to work on time. He worked at a paper mill in Fernandina Beach, Florida. He worked there for over thirty-four years. His life seemed entirely too short to me, though, because he died when I was only eleven years old from a heart attack. I heard that he awoke from his sleep one night with shortness of breath and chest tightness. He thought it was his asthma flaring up, so he kept puffing on his inhaler. This didn't help. Actually, it probably made things a little worse because it caused his heart to beat faster, possibly depriving it of even more oxygen. My grandmother held his hands as the EMTs were taking my papa out of the house on a stretcher.

"These some bad kids," he managed to say in between breaths.

Those were the last words my grandmother heard him say as they loaded him onto the stretcher. My grandfather died from his heart attack before the ambulance arrived at the hospital. The date was September 10, 1987. Needless to say, the house was never the same after that day.

. . .

"Danielle, are you ready yet!" my mom yelled from the living room. "We need to go so that we can get there before Sunday school starts!"

"I'm coming, Ma!" I said as I finished spraying moisturizer onto my Jheri curl.

Everyone was wearing Jheri curls back then. I, however, always managed to spray way too much moisturizer on my hair.

"Shoot!" I exclaimed as the moisturizer began to drip all over my neck and the back of my dress. I grabbed a towel and tried to blot some of the moisturizer out of my hair.

"I'm leaving!" yelled my mom.

"Here I come!" I said as I ran out of the bathroom into the living room to meet my mom.

"Bye, Daddy," I said as I kissed my dad on the cheek.

"Bye, sweetheart," he replied. "See you after church."

"Okay."

Finally, we were off for another full day of Sunday worship.

In the Sanctuary

By Faith Pentecostal Church was a small red brick church on White Road in Callahan. It was less than ten minutes from our home. It was a church where the pastor, Pastor Mac, and his family made up the majority of the members. I think Pastor and First Lady Mac had about nine or ten kids. Five handsome boys and four or five pretty daughters. They also had a boatload of grandchildren, all of which attended By Faith. One of their grandsons played the drums at the church, and I loved the drums. Or should I say I loved me some him. He had this way of sucking on his bottom lip that I always thought was *so* cute! I would always spend the entire church service sneaking peaks at him to see if he was looking at me. He never seemed to notice me, though. I never thought that I was pretty enough for him anyway. Plus I was way too quiet and shy to ever talk to a boy.

We arrived at church just in time. I rushed off to my Sunday school class in the choir stand, and my mom went to her class in the back of the church. Despite my reluctance to get out of bed in the morning, I actually enjoyed attending Sunday school classes. This was my time to shine! Back then I had one of those memories where you would only have to tell me something one time and I was able to repeat the entire thing back to you word for word. Therefore I was always the class representative when it was time for our class to stand before the church and go over what we learned that morning.

"Danielle, you want to review the lesson for us today?" Mrs. Beth would ask.

"Sure," I would say.

Mrs. Beth had been my Sunday school teacher for as long as I could remember. Out of all of Pastor Mac's daughter-in-laws, she was always my favorite. She was so patient and kind. She was a great teacher. And, to top it off, she was drummer boy's mother. I loved Mrs. Beth.

"Today we learned from the book of Matthews," I began. "We talked about Jesus and one of the parables He told. The parable was about a king who had planned a wedding but none of his guests wanted to come. The servants that he sent to remind his guests of the wedding were even beaten and killed..."

I completed the entire parable word for word, detail by detail.

"...The Pharisees didn't like Jesus and they were always trying to trap Jesus, but Jesus always outsmarted them. I learned from this parable that whenever Jesus calls, you better be ready because you never know what you might miss out on," I ended.

Everyone stood to their feet to applaud me. "Very good!" Mrs. Beth exclaimed. As I returned to my seat, my mom and one of my cousins gave me a big hug.

"I'm so proud of you," my mom said.

"Thank you," I replied. I felt like I was on top of the world.

I then peeked over to see if drummer boy was looking at me. He was. A slight smile came across his face. I looked away quickly as a sense of embarrassment overtook me. *He saw me looking at him.*

I loved the attention that I got for being "smart." People always told me that I was going to go far in life, and I believed it to. I spent many days at home watching *The Cosby Show* knowing that one day I was going to have a family like that of my own. Growing up in Callahan, I didn't see very many well-to-do black families. Everyone was struggling just like the next man. There were a couple of black families that seemed to have everything together. My family wasn't one of them. We were pretty much struggling to make ends meet. And I don't even think that the problem was that my family members *couldn't* do better. I just think that they were content with having just enough and didn't want to put forth the effort to get more. Maybe they were afraid of failing, but I'm not sure. One thing I do know is that if you never try, then you never fail, but you also never make any progress.

Regardless of how poor we were, though, my mom always made me feel that I was just as smart and important as the next person. She had me doing almost everything that she could do when I was very young. I was cooking, cleaning, writing, spelling...I was doing everything. My dad always thought that she was making me grow up too fast, but my mom thought that "If she can understand it, she can do it."

By the time I was three years old, I was saying my ABCs, counting to one hundred, and tying my own shoes. My mom felt that I was ready for kindergarten. I remember sitting outside of Callahan Elementary School in the car holding my empty Miss Piggy lunch box while my mom went inside to speak with the principal.

"I'm going to see if I can get you into school," my mom said.

"Yeah!" I exclaimed.

My mom left me in the car while she went into the school. I sat there opening and closing my lunch box as I listened to the radio. It seemed like this was taking forever. About a half hour later, she came back to the car with a look of frustration and disappointment on her face.

"I just don't understand this place. You can do everything that those kindergarteners are required to do and even more, and they say because you're not five yet you can't start school. Oh well. At least we tried," she said as she gave me a slight smile and rub on the cheek. She then cranked the car and we drove away.

Oh well, I thought to myself. When we got home, I put my lunchbox back in the cabinet where it sat for another year and a half.

Going to school was something that I could not wait to do. Unfortunately, since the Callahan school system did not allow early entry, I had to find something to do to bide my time until I turned five. My parents kept me occupied by teaching me new things at home. I learned math and how to spell. My dad also kept several different pets at the house, which kept me busy. We had several types of dogs, a rabbit, and a couple of birds. I had fun caring for them, but something always seemed to happen to them after a couple of months, then a new pet arrived.

I had several fond memories of childhood to include birthday parties in which my cousins and family friends from up the dirt road would attend. We also took a trip to Miami to see my aunt. We went to the wax museum in St. Augustine, which I thought was really fun. We often went to American Beach in Fernandina, which was where all of the black folks went to swim and hang out.

Aside from my fond memories, I also had some not so fond memories. One of my not so fond memories included something that happened to me one day when I had gone to the bathroom. I can't remember if I had actually used the bathroom or not, but when I went to wipe my bottom, to my surprise I felt something down there that was wiggling around. I had no idea what it was, but I knew that it was not supposed to be doing that. I screamed as loud as I could and ran into the living room with my mom. I remember it was a cold winter evening because my mom had the kerosene heater burning.

"What's wrong with you, girl?" my mom asked.

"Something is moving in my butt!" I said with a look of terror on my face and tears forming in my eyes.

"What?" my mom asked. "Bend over and let me see."

I pulled my pants down and bent over. The next thing I knew my mom was pulling something out of my behind. She was pulling and pulling and pulling...It seemed as if she was never going to stop pulling. Finally when she had gotten it out I saw her toss something long and squirmy into the furnace.

"Ma, what was that?" I asked still with tears in my eyes.

"Girl, you had a tapeworm!" my mom exclaimed.

"I had a worm in my butt?" I asked astonished. "How did I get a worm in there?"

"Lord, who knows? I gotta get you some stuff to drink to make sure there aren't any more in there," my mom stated.

I don't know what I drank, probably some turpentine or something, but it sure was nasty. And it sure made me poop a lot. Every time I pooped, I checked to see what was in it. For a good while my poop contained some little corn-looking structures. My mom told me those were probably little eggs or something from the tapeworms. I finally stopped seeing those things in my poop after a few days. My mom told me I was okay then.

Time continued to pass and I finally turned five. *It was time for me to go to school!* The night before my first day of kindergarten, I was so ecstatic. I did not sleep well at all. I was finally a big girl getting ready to do my thing. Boy, was I happy.

"What's my teacher's name again, Ma?"

"Mrs. Smith," she replied.

"Oh yeah, Mrs. Smith. Do you think she is nice?"

"Yes, dear. She is very nice. Now you just remember to pay attention and only talk when she tells you to."

"Yes, ma'am," I replied.

"Now go to sleep. You don't want to be too tired in the morning. And don't forget to say your prayers."

"Yes, ma'am. Our Father, who art in heaven. Hallowed be thy name…"

I tossed and turned that entire night as I anxiously anticipated my first day of school. At some point I finally drifted off to sleep, but it seemed that five minutes later my mother was waking me up to get dressed.

Unlike on Sunday morning, I eagerly jumped out of bed, washed my face, and brushed my teeth. I hurriedly gobbled down a bowl of Cocoa Puffs. My mom and dad had saved up and brought me some nice new school clothes. I put on a cute yellow floral sundress with a pair of red jellies sandals, and we were off. My mom drove me to school for the first couple of weeks until she felt I was comfortable enough with riding the bus.

Callahan Elementary School was exactly how I had imagined. It was a well-kept red brick school with shiny hardwood floors. Everything was on one level. It had high ceilings and glass casings holding numerous trophies and awards along the main hallways. There were kids everywhere heading toward their classrooms. There were also several parents there making sure that their children knew exactly where they were supposed to be. There were several teachers, the principal, the school counselor, and the school secretary standing in the hallways directing parents and children to the correct classrooms. That first day my mom walked me to my classroom, and even though I was a big girl now, I was very grateful.

"Which way do we go to get to Mrs. Smith's classroom?" my mom asked one of the teachers.

"Down the hallway to the right, down the steps through the double doors to the outdoor rooms. She is in room 12-B."

"Thanks!" we replied.

My mom and I walked down the hallway together hand in hand. As we passed by the various classrooms, I looked inside of them at the many older kids who had already made their way into their respective rooms and were seated at their desks. Some kids unpacked their book bags while other kids hugged or slapped high fives with classmates who they hadn't seen all summer.

I wonder what my class is going to be like, I thought as we walked down the steps and approached the double doors. When we got outside the sun was shining brightly. In front of us was a long covered sidewalk with classrooms along the right side. At the very end of the sidewalk was a fence, and on the other side of the fence was a huge playground. *Oooh, I can't wait to get out there.*

So far, school was everything that I expected it to be. And we hadn't even gotten to my classroom yet. "Here it is, Ma—12-B!"

We opened the door and went inside. The classroom was very nicely decorated. Different posters with ABCs and 123s hung on every corner. There were also posters with all of the rainbow colors and various animals. I was familiar with everything in the classroom. We even had a little hamster cage in the corner.

"And who do we have here?" a short, thick white lady with brown curly hair stated.

"This is my little Danielle," my mother proudly replied as she rubbed my head.

"Well, you come right on in, Danielle. I'm Mrs. Smith."

"Hi, Mrs. Smith," I said as I extended my hand toward hers. Mrs. Smith took my hand and guided me into the classroom. She assured my mom that I was in good hands. My mom then gave me a big hug.

"I'll see you at two-thirty," she said. I nodded my head to let her know that I was okay. She then gave me and Mrs. Smith a smile and walked out the door.

"Come on in, Danielle, and have a seat at one of the tables." I chose a seat near the front of the room. My mom told me that the smart people always sat in the front in order to be able to hear the teacher better and see what she wrote on the chalkboard.

My class consisted of about twenty kids. Out of the twenty, only two of us were black. At the time I didn't even notice because I did not know there was a difference between black people and white people. My mom says that I thought that I had just stayed out in the sun too long. That was why my skin was darker than everyone else's.

I loved going to school. Before long I had made plenty of friends in my class and was known as pretty much the smartest kid there. Mrs. Smith taught the class ABCs and 123s, but my parents had already taught me that stuff. She also taught us how to tie our shoes. I already knew how to do that, too.

Because I already knew all of the stuff Mrs. Smith was teaching, I think I got bored pretty easily while inside of the classroom. Because of this I often got in trouble for talking *way* too much. No matter how hard I tried to be quiet and stay focused, someone would always do or say something to get me started. And once I got started I did not know when to stop.

"Danielle, is there something that you want to share with the entire class?" Mrs. Smith asked.

"No, ma'am," I said.

"Well, what in the world is so important that you feel the need to disrupt the class?"

"Nothing, ma'am."

"Well, the next time it happens you'll be taking a trip to the principal's office."

"Yes, ma'am."

I always got caught talking. No matter how many other people were talking, it seemed like Mrs. Smith always caught me. On my report card, I would always get all satisfactories except in conduct.

My mom didn't like the fact that I got U's in conduct. "Girl, what did I tell you about talkin' so much?"

"Sorry, Ma, but it ain't always my fault. The other kids always talk to me first and then I get in trouble."

"I don't want to hear it. You just better do what you are supposed to do."

"Yes, ma'am."

Of course, I didn't stop getting in trouble completely. I even got paddled a couple of times. After each paddling, the principal would always send a notice home to my parents letting them know that I was paddled and why. The first time that I got paddled, I took the note home to my parents. My dad saw the note first. I thought that he would feel sorry for me and comfort me. *Oh no*, that's not what happened. He grabbed his belt and whooped my behind. When my mom got home and saw the note, she grabbed her belt and whooped me again. Three whoopins in one day. *What kind of mess is this?* After my second paddling, I got smart. When I got home, I ran to the backyard, balled the notice up, and threw it in the woods. No way was I going to allow myself to get two more whoopins that day.

After finishing kindergarten, my conduct improved a bit. I flew through elementary school with no problem. My parents always kept me ahead of all of the other kids. My dad was teaching me my times tables and division while the other kids were still learning to add.

Talking to the other kids in class I realized that a lot of them were involved in other activities outside of school. Some of my friends were into gymnastics; others in Girl Scouts. Still others were taking dance classes or playing little league ball.

"Daddy, I want to take dance class. Penny is taking dance classes, and she says it's fun."

"It's fine with me, but you better ask your mother."

"Okay!" I said excitedly.

I asked my mom that evening, and she was thrilled that I wanted to take dance lessons. She always wanted to take dance classes when she was younger, but she never got to. She took me down to the community center and signed me up the next week.

"Okay girls, let's begin," my dance teacher instructed. "One, two, three, tap. One, two, three, tap." I enjoyed tap and ballet classes. After each class, I would run home to show my parents what new things we had learned. I thought that I was pretty good and looked kind of cute in my leotard and stockings.

I had been in tap and ballet classes for about two months. I was sort of becoming bored with it by then. I was becoming interested in this little league thing that I kept hearing about.

"Ma, I don't want to dance anymore. I want to play tee-ball."

"What, girl? I've already paid my money for those classes and you want to quit. Why should I let you play tee-ball? What if you change your mind about that in two months? That will be another twenty dollars wasted."

"Ma, I promise I won't change my mind this time. I really want to play tee-ball."

"Oh, let her play. I'll pay for it," my dad chimed in.

"Oh, okay. But you better stick with it. Ain't nobody got all this money to waste every time you decide you want to do something and then lose interest halfway through."

"Yes, ma'am. Thank you, Daddy!" I said excitedly. I could not wait to go to school the next day to tell all of my friends that I was going to be playing tee-ball, too.

• • •

After Sunday school was over, morning worship began. The service started at eleven o'clock. Of course, not everyone came to Sunday school, so more people had trickled into the sanctuary. The main families were, of course, the Mac family, various members of my extended family, several unrelated elderly members, and a few other families who had come out of Jacksonville. There were probably no more than fifty members total, with the Mac family taking up about thirty of the fifty.

Regardless of how few members were present, our church services always seemed to be filled with the Holy Spirit. It seemed like everyone in the sanctuary was shouting or speaking in tongues or at the altar tarrying. And this could go on for hours at a time. I usually just sat in the pew with my cousin Rashawn just looking at everybody. It was interesting to see who was going to catch the Holy Ghost next and who was going to pass out on the floor and who stayed passed out the longest. There was this one lady in our church who would always start shouting while holding her baby. By the time someone was able to pull the baby away from her, the poor baby would be yelling her little frightened head off. The ushers or other volunteers from the congregation would grab arms trying to keep the shouting individual in the center so that he or she would not hurt themselves. If a woman passed out one of the ushers would bring a white sheet and put it over her lap to keep her legs covered. People would be fanning each other as if they were trying to cool the Holy Spirit down.

The people at By Faith knew how to have church!

By Faith had some pretty strict and conservative traditional beliefs. According to Pastor Mac, women should not wear pants, should not cut their hair, nor should they wear makeup or earrings. Members should not go to the movies for fear of corruption by the devil by all of the evil displayed upon the screens. Also, you were to be in church all day Sunday, Wednesday night, Friday night, and choir rehearsal on Saturday. We had tons of revivals, special programs, and church conventions to attend.

I, of course, did everything that they said women should not. I was always cutting my hair, my ears were pierced, I wore jeans, and a lot of times my jeans were tight-fitting with lots of holes cut in them, and I loved going to the movies with my dad. I guess I was just the church heathen. But everyone treated me like I was a little angel. That is, everyone but my other grandmother who I called Mudea, my father's mother.

Mudea was a heavyset, very light-skinned lady with lots of moles on her face and soft, long curly hair. Mudea did not play. Especially when it came to that church. If she ever caught me talking in church or chewing gum I would get the most evil look or a sharp pinch on the thigh. "You better be quiet, girl!" she would whisper very loudly. I did not like being in trouble with Mudea. However, it always seemed like I was.

Mudea kept my cousin Rashawn and me a lot while our parents were at work. Both of us were only children until Rashawn's mom, my dad's twin sister, Aunt E, got married and had Rashawn's two brothers and one sister. Still Rashawn and I were the oldest, so we were always together. He appeared to be Mudea's little angel, though, because no matter what we did *together* I was always the one to take the blame and get the whoopin'. Rashawn and I used to fight a lot. Of course I was stronger, being athletic and all, so I used to always win. Because he always ended up with more scars, I always ended up with more beatings.

I remember one day Rashawn and I were playing on Mudea's porch and my friend Denitra came to hang out with us. The three of us were playing Wheel of Fortune. Denitra and I were laughing about some stuff that had happened at school earlier that week. I noticed Rashawn tossing some marbles my way. I thought that he was just playing so I tossed the marble back. The next thing I knew Rashawn had his hands around my throat trying to choke me.

"Get your hands off of me!" I yelled. He kept trying to choke me as we rolled on the floor. Finally I was able to loosen his grip and push him off me. I then started swinging at him punching him in the head, chest, whatever I could reach. He was, of course, punching me back. He finally pushed me down on the floor knocking over the majority of my grandmother's plants. I guess he got tired or finally realized what was going on because he got up and sat in the rocking chair like nothing had happened. I wasn't through yet, though. I was burning up. I got up off that floor, walked straight over to Rashawn, and *pow!* I slapped him so hard across his left cheek that I saw a tear roll down his face.

"What was that?" Mudea yelled.

"They out here fightin'," Denitra commented.

Mudea ran out on the porch just as Rashawn was yelling "Stop, Danielle. Get off of me!"

I didn't see Mudea walk up behind me with that long switch in her hand. *Womp! Womp!* "Girl, what is wrong with you hittin' that boy like that? Have you lost your mind?" she yelled as she tore my behind up.

"No, Mudea, no! He hit me first!" I pleaded while I tried to protect my legs.

"Shut up! You ain't grown! You ain't got no business hittin' nobody!"

My grandmother beat me all across the porch and under one of the tables. Finally I got tired of being hit so I grabbed the switch from her and broke it in half. She then hit me a couple of times with her hand, but the good thing about her being a big woman was that she got tired quick.

"Wait till your daddy gets home! Go to the back room!"

"Yes, ma'am," I said as I wiped the tears from my face and ran to the back room. For some reason she allowed Denitra to stay a little while longer, so she came to the back room where I was.

"I hate her. She always takin' up for Rashawn. He hit me first and he didn't even get a whippin'. I ain't never comin' over here again!"

Denitra just sat there, stunned, not knowing what to say.

Eventually she said, "Well, I'm going to go home for dinner. I'll see you in school on Monday."

"All right, then. See ya later," I said.

I was angry for the rest of the day at my grandmother. She always showed favoritism toward Rashawn. When my daddy came home, I told him exactly what happened scene by scene.

"Daddy, I don't ever want to go over there again. It just isn't fair that Rashawn didn't get a beatin' too."

"Well, sweetheart, it sounds like you did give him a beatin'. Just get some sleep. It will be better tomorrow."

I guess, I thought to myself as I got ready for bed.

I managed to avoid Mudea's house for a couple of days, but before long I was right back over there as usual. Rashawn and I had made up and were best cousins again.

"I'm sorry," he whispered.

"Don't worry about it," I said nonchalantly. "I'm sorry for leaving that huge bruise across your face."

"It's okay," he said.

After that, Mudea had me in the kitchen, as usual, helping her bake some type of cake or shucking some corn, hulling some peas, washing dishes, or something. *I can't wait to grow up and get away from here so I don't have to do all of this mess,* I always thought. *Why am I in here working like a dog while Rashawn is sittin' in there watching TV? This sucks.* I never thought that I would appreciate any of the stuff Mudea was "teaching" me, but eventually I did. She taught me a lot about cooking and cleaning and being a young lady. She also taught me a lot about responsibility and caring for older people given the fact that she was ill a lot and often required a lot of assistance with her daily activities. I would often have to help her get in and out of the bathroom. I would even have to help her with her baths. I would do her hair and even clip her toenails. It was a lot of work, and I honestly did not appreciate having to do it at the time. Little did I know that caring for people would eventually become a huge part of my life.

Mudea had five children: two sons from her first marriage—one in Ohio and one in Jacksonville—then my dad and his twin sister, Aunt E, and their older sister, Aunt M, from a second husband.

Aunt M was a very special person. She was single, no children, and had a great job working for Prudential Life Insurance. She was always getting promotions and transferring to all of the major cities in Florida. Miami, Orlando, West Palm Beach; she lived everywhere. And she always drove a nice car and had a nice house. Sometimes I wished she would adopt me and take me with her wherever she went. I loved my Aunt M. She would always take me school shopping or take me to get my hair done. She always wanted me to look like a little lady. Going to Aunt M's house was always a big deal to me. The cities that she lived in were exciting, and her houses were always so nice. That was the kind of life I wanted to have when I grew up. Plus, a husband and about four kids.

I always wondered why Aunt M was never married. She was a nice-looking lady with a lot to offer a man. Maybe she was too busy with work to settle down. I don't know. I do remember her having a few male friends, but never one that she introduced as her boyfriend. Nonetheless, Rashawn and I wanted to be successful just like Aunt M when we grew up.

Aunt E was always one of the sweetest people God placed on this green earth. Everyone that ever met Aunt E always complemented her sweet demeanor. I don't think I can recall a moment when Aunt E ever lost her temper. Even with four kids, she always remained calm. In fact the only time I've ever really heard her raise her voice was in church whenever she would catch the Holy Ghost. "Thank you, Jesus! Thank you, Jesus!" she would say real fast as she shook her head and swung her right arm real fast from side to side.

Aunt E worked in the cafeteria as the dessert cook in one of the schools in Jacksonville. And boy, could she bake the best cookies and cakes our taste buds could handle. She met and married Uncle W when Rashawn was five years old. Shortly afterward came the other three children.

Aunt E had Rashawn outside of marriage, which, of course was a no-no in the Holiness church. I heard that in the beginning she told people that Rashawn's father had forced himself on her. However, I don't think that they ever filed any charges against him. Because of all of the craziness, many years passed before Rashawn had any type of a relationship with his father. I think this had a whole lot to do with the way Rashawn's life played itself out.

Never Shall Forget

After each Sunday morning service, we would all gather in the fellowship hall for Sunday dinner. I just loved me some Sunday dinner at church. We always had fried chicken, baked chicken, ham, homemade macaroni and cheese, mashed potatoes, rice, gravy, green beans, collard greens, biscuits, corn bread, yellow cake with white icing, chocolate cake, pies, lemonade, sweet tea...You name it and we had it. The ladies in that church really knew how to throw down in the kitchen. The ladies of the church divided themselves up into committees, and each committee would take turns preparing Sunday dinner. Whenever my mom's or Mudea and Aunt E's committee cooked, I would always volunteer to help prepare plates so that I could fix what I wanted on my own plate. I really did enjoy helping serve the food, though.

After the benediction, usually around two o'clock, everyone would rush out of the church trying to be one of the first ones in line. The elder members would take a seat as the younger members served them. The fellowship hall was rather small, so the older people usually sat inside while all of the kids sat around outside eating and talking. Sometimes after we finished eating, someone would initiate a game of tag and all of us would start running around the churchyard.

"Stop running in ya'll good clothes!" someone would yell, spoiling our fun.

Then we would all settle down and sit on the front steps of the church and continue our conversations.

"Danielle, you ready to go home?" my mom would ask even though I knew this wasn't really a question.

"Yes, ma'am. Bye, ya'll. See ya at five thirty."

As we headed home, my mom would always hum or sing one of the songs we had sung that morning during service.

"Did you enjoy service today, Danielle?"

"Yes, ma'am. Ma, why Ms. Laurie always be rubbing her hands in people heads while she shoutin'?"

"I guess that's just the way the Holy Spirit uses her," my mom answered.

"I hope she doesn't ever come and do that to me," I said. My mom just shook her head.

Ms. Laurie was one of Pastor Mac's daughter-in-laws. She was a very nice lady. However, whenever she caught the Holy Ghost I always wanted to run away from her because she would go around grabbing people by their heads and shake their heads back and forth and speaking in tongues until they started shouting, too. It was kind of scary. Sort of like she was putting a spell on them. Every Sunday she would be grabbing and shaking somebody's head. And she was one of those people who would catch the Holy Ghost while holding on to one of her babies. I always wanted to ask her if she wanted me to hold her baby at the beginning of service because I knew she was going to shout if nobody else did.

Yes, By Faith was filled with the Holy Spirit.

• • •

We arrived home from church around three thirty. My dad was sitting on the couch as usual watching football. That was his Sunday worship. And as usual my godfather was right on the couch along with him.

"Hey, Daddy. Hey, God-daddy," I said as I gave each of them a hug.

"Hey, sweetheart. How was church?" my dad replied.

"Good. You should have come with us."

"Maybe next time," he replied.

I knew he was just saying this. My dad never went to church with us. I don't think I remember a time when he ever did. And I never understood why not. Especially since my mom states that's how she initially fell in love with my dad—because he was so involved in the church.

My mom started attending church when she was a little girl. Out of all of her siblings, she was the only one who felt the need to go to church. My nana attended the Baptist church around the corner, but she didn't force her kids to go to church with her. My mom went with her, though.

She met my dad at school. She was fourteen; he was eighteen. My mom was a cheerleader. My dad was a star basketball and baseball player. After each of the games, my dad would walk my mom home. My dad courted my mom throughout her high school years. My mom started attending By Faith as a teenager after being invited by Aunt E and one of her cousins who my mom was good friends with. It was there that she noticed how involved in the church my father appeared to be. Always there. Very active. She says he knew the Bible like no other boy she had ever seen. And she loved that about him. A handsome, smart, athletic, God-fearing man. What more could you ask for? He was the one.

When my dad finished high school, he was offered a scholarship to attend art school. My dad could draw just about anything. Despite that, he decided that he wanted to move to New Orleans with his half-brother and work there. I mean, who wouldn't want to live in New Orleans? Nonstop partying. Plenty of jobs. The perfect place for a young man to live. He got a job working at a restaurant on Dumaine Street. He was doing pretty well there. He lived in New Orleans for about a year before he got himself into something that caused him to have to leave New Orleans pretty quickly. It was years before I learned the real story.

When my dad returned to Callahan, my mom was there waiting for him. By this time she had graduated from high school and was preparing for college. My mom was super smart, graduating in the top five of her class. She was offered a full scholarship to attend the University of Florida that she was thinking about accepting. She never quite made it there, though.

She loved and missed my dad so much that she decided he was the one she was going to give away one of the most precious parts of herself to. Her virginity. *One time won't hurt anything,* she thought. Never did she imagine that she would get pregnant with me after only the first time. *No way!*

My mom was seventeen years old when she got pregnant with me. After she found out she was pregnant, she moved in with my dad, Mudea, Aunt E, and Rashawn. My mom told me that at first Mudea didn't treat her very nice.

"How do we know this is Elroy's baby?" she would ask my mom.

"Because he's the only one I've been with," my mom would say.

"Um, hum. We'll see."

My dad was always Mudea's baby, and I think she didn't like the fact that another woman was getting some of his attention. I don't think that my dad ever had any doubts that he was my father, though. If he did, that uncertainty certainly vanished after the first time he laid eyes on me.

I was born April 19, 1976, at Humphries Memorial Hospital in Fernandina Beach, Florida. My mom was eighteen years old when she had me. My parents decided to get married the following June.

The early years were tough for my parents. For the first few months, they continued to live in the house with Mudea until my mom got tired of being treated like she didn't belong.

"Elroy, we have got to get a place of our own," my mom told my dad.

The first three years of my life, my mother was a stay-at-home mom. She gave up everything to raise me while my dad worked at a paper mill in Yulee, Florida. My dad bought us a little white wooden house from this older lady named Ms. Smith. It wasn't much, but it was our own house. It had three small bedrooms, a living room, a kitchen, one bathroom, a porch, and a nice-sized yard for me to run around and play in. It was an old but nice, cozy little house. I was able to have my own dog and everything.

My first dog's name was Trixie. I loved Trixie. She was a short white dog with brown or black spots. She was the only dog that I remember my mom allowing to stay indoors. I actually think that Trixie came with the house, so she was already house broken. Trixie was my best friend. We would often take walks with her. I would run around in the yard and play with her. She was my buddy.

My mom said that she believes Trixie was a gift from God, and she doesn't even like dogs. She says Trixie probably saved my life a couple of times. I often played out in the yard by myself with Trixie. Once, while playing in the yard, a large snake slithered up toward me. My mom said she heard Trixie barking louder and more aggressively than she had ever heard. She said when she got out there Trixie was fighting that snake off with all of her might. My mom grabbed me and we ran into the house. A few minutes later, we saw Trixie burying that dead snake in the yard. Another time my mom said I was outside, and she heard that same type of bark coming from Trixie. When she came outside I had wandered from in front of the house toward the main road. She said Trixie was barking trying to get me to go back to the house but I wouldn't listen. I could have been hit by a car if it wasn't for little Trixie. I thank God for her.

Unfortunately, though, Trixie's life was way too short. One day my mom, Trixie, and I were going for a routine walk. Somehow I ended up on one side of the street and my mom was on the other. I don't quite remember all of the details, but somehow Trixie ended up in the middle of the street when a car was heading straight for her. "Trixie, get out of the street!" I yelled.

"Here, Trixie!" my mom whistled.

Trixie looked very confused and frightened as she looked from me to my mom. She didn't know which way to run. The car apparently never saw her because they didn't even attempt to slow down. When the car hit Trixie, she flew to the side of the road.

"No!" I screamed as I ran toward her. "Trixie, get up!" I said. But Trixie was already dead.

That was my first experience with death. I was probably about three or four years old. My mom tried everything she could to console me, but it was no use. My best friend was dead.

After Trixie, many dogs came and went, but none were ever quite as special. I don't even remember any of their names. I know we had a Doberman pinscher, German shepherd, and a few others. Something would eventually happen to them, though. I didn't care too much after Trixie died.

Our little house was perfect. The holidays, the birthday parties, me running around in my Wonder Woman underwear. It was the greatest. That is, until the rats decided to take up residence. Day by day, more and more of those little suckers popped up. No matter what my parents did, they couldn't control them. There were rat traps all over the place.

"Daddy, there's another one!" I would scream.

"Don't worry, baby. They're just as scared of you as you are of them," he would assure me. They sure didn't act like they were scared. They actually acted like they owned the place and that we were intruding.

"I wish they would all just die," I would say.

We lived in that house until I was about five years old. One night I was awakened from my sleep by something rubbing against my leg. I slowly pulled the covers back. "*Ahh! Ma! Daddy! Ahh!*"

My parents ran into the room to see what was going on. When they entered my room, they noticed the large rat running across my bed, then onto the floor. "I can't take this anymore! We're moving!" my mom yelled.

About a week after that rat climbed into bed with me, we packed our things and moved to Eastwood Oaks Apartments in Hilliard, Florida. I really enjoyed living in that apartment. It was so much nicer than our old house. And there were plenty of children my age for me to play with. My friends and I would go to the pool and roller skate around the neighborhood all the time. And we had cable! That was the life.

One of the most memorable moments I have of living in Hilliard is actually one of my dumbest moments, now that I think back upon it. I was a very gullible child. I always believed in the Tooth Fairy, Santa Claus, and the Easter Bunny. I really believed that they were all real. I remember one Christmas the local fire department took Santa around to the various neighborhoods to hand out candy to the kids. From what I had always remembered was that if Santa caught you awake he would put pepper in your eyes. I did not want to have pepper put in my eyes. When my friends told me Santa was on his way to Eastwood Oaks Apartments I ran to my apartment and jumped in my top bunk bed to pretend that I was asleep in the middle of the day. I think I stayed in my bed for about one to two hours before I would go back outside. I was really afraid. How dumb was that? When I went back outside all of my friends were roller skating and eating their candy. They asked where I had gone. When I told them where I was, they all burst out laughing at me. None of them had gotten any pepper put into their eyes.

When my mom got home from work that night I told her what had happened. "You silly girl," my mom laughed. "Santa Claus is just some white man dressed up in a red suit. He's not real." I don't think I believed in Santa anymore after that day.

• • •

Our five thirty service at By Faith was called WWC. WWC stood for "Willing Worker's Club" It was a short service mainly designed for young adults. During this service we learned the books of the Bible and quoted scriptures that began with different letters of the alphabet each week. This was always one of the services that had the fewest members. I avoided it as much as possible because it always felt like you were being put on the spot, especially if you were one of the few young people at service. A lot of times some of my cousins and I would sneak out of this service and run to the store on the corner to get some Laffy Taffys, Chick-o-sticks, Coconut Long Boys, Sugar Daddys, Mary Janes, chips, sodas, whatever we had a taste for. Of course we had to make sure we saved a quarter to put in the offering plate during the night service. After we left the store, we would take our time walking back to the church. A lot of times WWC was over by then and we would sit around eating our snacks while we waited for the seven o'clock night service to begin. Man, we were in church *all day long!* I would always be struggling to stay awake during the night service. Most of the time it just seemed like a repeat of the morning service except with fewer people and a little more boring. We would finally get to go home at about nine or nine thirty. By then I was completely worn out from all that church.

Draw Me Near

Not much went on in Callahan, Florida, so when the Nassau County Fair came each year, it was a huge event. People from Callahan, Hilliard, Folkston, Yulee, Fernandina, and even some people from Jacksonville would come down to go to our fair. Sometimes some of the women in my family would get together and rent a booth to sell fish dinners and desserts. I, of course, would always be volunteered to help prepare the meals. I would have preferred to run around the fair all day, ride the rides, and see who was there. It seemed like someone was always putting me to work on something. *Why couldn't I just be a kid and have fun all of the time?* It seemed like I was always stuck in the kitchen with Mudea making pound cake, nut bread, fruit cake, shucking corn and peas, or cleaning some collard greens. I appreciate having done that stuff now because most people who eat my cooking are surprised at my skills, but back then I dreaded it.

The fair usually came sometime in October. Just like any other fair, Friday and Saturday nights were the most fun. My friend Candy and I usually went together on these nights. We would try to look cute for the boys from Hilliard and Folkston, even though we were not really into boys yet and if any of them tried to talk to us we would just keep walking. We liked it when they tried, though. It made us feel pretty.

My favorite ride at the fair was the Loop-de-Loop. I would ride that roller coaster over and over again. I also liked the Tilt-a-Whirl, squirrel cages, and the bumper cars. We would, of course, buy the bracelet that allowed us to ride as many rides as we wanted to.

Life was good for me in Callahan, Florida. When I was six, my dad bought us another house in Callahan. I was sad about leaving my friends in Hilliard, but very excited about moving into a bigger house. It wasn't really a house. It was a trailer that had a brick living room and bedroom built on to the front. Part house-part trailer homes were big in Callahan. I didn't care, though, because it was nice and I had two acres of yard to run around in. It also had a fig tree in the front yard and a huge mulberry tree in the backyard. Needless to say, in the spring we had some really good pies and preserves.

I thought our new house was perfect. My mom seemed really happy there for a while. She and my dad seemed to be doing okay at first. However, eventually I could tell that she was really getting tired of my dad never going to church with us. In fact, not only was he skipping church to hang out with my god-daddy and watch football, but every time we came home from church our house was filled with men and marijuana smoke.

Aside from the drugs, my mom began to hear rumors about my dad messing around on her. My papa would often tell my mom that he had seen her car parked in front of this lady named Miss Lola's house.

According to almost everyone in Callahan, Miss Lola was a pretty sleazy and nasty lady. All I knew was that she had the nastiest looking fingernails I had ever seen. They were extremely long and curled under at the tips. I never knew how she wiped her butt good with those nails. My mom told me to never eat any food from her house if I ever went over there because her hands were probably not very clean.

My mom says she used to work at a nursing home with Miss Lola. She says that no one ever knew this but one day she walked in on Miss Lola while she was taking care of one of her patients. The patient was a young white male who she believes had Cerebral Palsy because he had severe contractures in his arms and legs. She says when she walked into the room she saw Miss Lola allowing this young male to rub and kiss all over her breasts. She said it was the nastiest thing she ever saw. She didn't even say anything. My mom just walked out of the room and acted as if she never saw what happened.

My mom didn't want to believe that my dad would be low enough to mess around on her with Miss Lola until she saw her car parked in front of Lola's trailer one Sunday. She said that we often ended up having to walk to church because my dad would say that he had some place he needed to go with her car. It was one of these Sundays that she saw her car in front of Lola's trailer. She said she grabbed me and we turned around and went right back home. They had a huge argument when my dad got home. My dad denied that he was messing around with her and said he had just stopped by for something. Of course, my mom did not believe him.

Right next door to us lived the son of the man my dad bought our house from along with his wife. Randle and Lara were a couple of the nicest white people I knew. I would often go over to their house and hang out with Lara, as well as Randle's younger sister Lisa. They had a record player that I loved to play with. My mom said that she often saw my dad and Lara talking outside, laughing and carrying on. She said it happened so often that it began to seem a little inappropriate. One day after my dad had picked my mom up from working at Winn-Dixie and dropped us off at home, he quickly disappeared while my mom was in the shower. She asked me where he had gone and I had no clue. She looked out of the window and noticed that Lara's car was gone as well.

"Come on," she said to me as she grabbed the flashlight in

one hand and my arm in the other. We began to walk up the road in the dark looking for my dad. We didn't have to go far. A little ways up the road, we saw both my dad's and Lara's cars parked on the side of the road.

"Stay here," she told me as she approached the car.

My mom said that when she got to the car she saw my dad and Lara going at it. Kissing and touching each other.

"Elroy, what are you doing!" she yelled.

Before she realized what was happening, my mom attempted to slap Lara across her face, but my dad grabbed her arm. Why did he do that? My mom took that flashlight and beat my dad across his chest real good.

"Vanessa, Vanessa, Vanessa!" my dad yelled.

Finally she snapped back into reality and realized what she was doing. Once she calmed down, she gave my dad and Lara an evil look, she grabbed my arm, and we headed for home. By that time Lara had hastily jumped out of my dad's car and hurried home before my mom had a chance to get revenge on her.

My mom says that later that evening while they were lying in bed she saw how swollen and black and blue my dad's chest was. She then began to feel sorry for him.

"Elroy, please answer me just one question."

"What is it?" my dad replied.

"If I had not gotten there when I did, would you have slept with her?"

My dad had this astonished yet puzzled look on his face. He paused for a very long time before saying anything. Finally after appearing to be searching for the perfect answer he said, "I don't know. Maybe."

Why did he give such a stupid answer? My mom felt that this obviously meant he cared nothing for her feelings.

"Do you realize you bring out the worst in me?" she asked. "If I had had a knife in my hand this evening, you would be dead and I would be in jail right now all because you can't be faithful to me.

I don't like the person that you are turning me into, and I don't think that us staying together is such a good idea anymore."

At that moment, my mom realized that she had to do something to get us away from my father and out of Callahan. She didn't know yet what it was going to be, but she knew she was going to have to make some sacrifices in order for us to have a better life. We had to get out of Callahan.

I really enjoyed living in that little country town. I had lots of friends, family, and really not a care in the world. By the time I was eight years old, I was known as one of the best softball players in Callahan. Everyone wanted me on their team. I played several different positions including pitcher, left field and center-field because of my speed, and then short stop and second base. Softball was my life outside of school. My best friends, Candy and Jenny, and I were usually always on the same team. We were all really good. We rarely lost a game. I also continued to excel at school and was eventually tested for the gifted program. I didn't make it into the program the first couple of times I was tested because I only scored in the 120s on the IQ test, and I think you had to score in the 130s to get in. I still don't understand how you can score someone on their interpretation of ink blots. But anyway, eventually I scored in the 140s and got in. I think that by then I had just gotten used to taking the test.

Well, like I said, life was good for me in Callahan, Florida. That is up until I turned eight years old and my mom told me of her big idea. "...If I join the army, they will give me a five thousand dollar bonus, and I will be able to save up money to send you to college!" she said with such excitement and enthusiasm. I did not want to hear anything about my mom leaving home. I think at first I may have thought it was a good idea because five thousand dollars was more money than I could ever imagine us having, but when I really thought about it, I was crushed. My mom was leaving us.

"I don't want you to go!" I cried.

"It will only be for six weeks. That's how long it will take for me to get through basic training. After that you and Daddy can come and stay with me."

"But I don't want you to go!" I kept saying.

"Sweetie, I am doing this to try and make a better life for you," she said as she gave me a big hug. My mom didn't cry much, but I think that night she had a few tears swelling up in her eyes. I think she turned away from me before they fell, though.

When the preacher at our church found out that my mom was joining the army, he told her that it was the devil who was leading her to do such a thing. Regardless of what he said, my mom had already made up her mind, and once she makes up her mind to do something, God Himself would have to come down from His throne in heaven and strike her down to force her to change it. My mom has always been a very determined lady.

Kumbaya, My Lord

One day a few of my cousins and I went with my uncle Calvin over to his father's house across the trestle. He had a big piece farmland. Lots of space for us to run around and play on. We all decided to go for a walk down this long road just to see what was down there. This was my first time going to the farm, so I went along with everyone else. My girl cousin Carey and I walked up front while the boys walked behind us. I was about seven years old at the time.

"I'll bet she'll do it," I heard my cousin Darnell tell my cousin Tommie.

"Do what?" I asked.

"Tommie wants you to go in the chicken coop with him," Darnell said.

"For what?" I asked.

"So ya'll can play house."

"Play house? What do you mean play house?" I asked naively.

"He'll show you," Darnell said with a chuckle.

"Okay," I said not knowing any better.

When we got back to the house, we all went into the chicken coop. Before I knew what was happening Tommie had pulled my shorts down and was on top of me. He was about eight years old. Darnell was in the background telling Tommie what to do. Darnell was about eleven or twelve.

"Danielle, you spread your legs, and Tommie you put your thing in between her legs." We did what he said for a few minutes and then we stopped.

"Trudy, you want to come and get some?" Darnell asked. Trudy was Darnell and Tommie's little brother.

"No! And I'm gon' tell that ya'll was in here hunching!"

At that point I began to get scared so I pulled my clothes up and ran out of the chicken coop. *If Trudy tells my mama I'm gon' get in trouble*, I began to worry.

"Trudy, please don't tell, please don't tell," I begged. Finally, he agreed not to tell. I felt a whole lot better.

Several months went by and Trudy kept his word. He didn't tell.

One day as I walked over to my papa's sister Aunt Elise's house I noticed Trudy sitting in front of my mom, my cousin Mickie, my other cousin ET, and my aunt Elise. I then saw everybody turn and look at me with this look of astonishment on their faces.

"Danielle!" my mother yelled. "You get over here right now! Were you and Tommie hunching?!"

"Yes, ma'am," I said frightened.

She then went and grabbed a switch and proceeded to give me one of the worst whippings of my life. After she whooped my behind she went down to my aunt Pecola's house, grabbed Tommie, and whooped him, too. When we got home, she told my dad what happened and he whooped me as well.

I'm not sure if I really understood what I was getting whipped for because at that time I had no idea what "hunching" really meant or why it was a bad thing. I honestly had no clue until a couple of years later when one of my friends tried to explain to me where babies came from.

Oh no, could I be pregnant? I thought to myself after she told me that babies were produced by a man getting on top of a woman and "doin' it." I stood in front of the mirror and looked at my chubby belly. *Could there be a baby in there?* I wondered. I then sucked my belly all of the way in until it looked completely flat. I left the bathroom and found my mom in the kitchen.

"Ma, when you were pregnant, could you suck your belly in like this?" I asked as I sucked my belly in.

"No, chile," my mom replied.

Whew! I thought. *I'm never hunchin' again.*

Little did I know that the little event in the chicken coop that occurred when I was seven years old would come back to haunt me.

When I was about twelve years old, this older boy named Jimmie started liking me. I noticed every time I walked from my grandmother's house to my aunt Pecola's house he would be sitting outside in a lawn chair with my cousin Tommie staring at my butt. One day I saw the two of them giggling about something. Apparently Tommie told Jimmie about our little hunching episode. However he neglected to mention that it occurred when we were extremely young, way before he was ever able to actually have an erection. He made it seem like we had recently had sex.

Of course after hearing this, Jimmie really wanted to get with me because he thought he was going to get some. I had no idea Tommie had told him about this. Jimmie and I talked for a few weeks. He would call Nana's house for me, and we would talk a little bit on the phone. One night he and his older brother called the house. His older brother was dating my older cousin Aretha. He asked Aretha if we could meet them on the corner by the shop.

The corner was where all of the older people hung out to smoke, drink, do or buy drugs. My cousin said sure, so we left and met them on the corner. Of course, I was so shy I really did not say anything while we were there. We just stood around a burning tire as Aretha and Manny talked.

"You like my brother?" Manny asked.

"I guess," I said.

"Well he likes you."

I was really flattered, but I was way too shy to show it.

Manny and Aretha talked for a few more minutes and then we left to go back to Nana's.

The next day when I got off the bus from school at Nana's house, I noticed my aunt Leen in the car talking to my dad. I had no clue what they were talking about. I just waved hello and went in the house. When my dad came into the house, he was very upset.

"Leen told me that you snuck out the window last night with Aretha to go meet some boy! What were you thinking?"

"Daddy, I didn't sneak out no window. We walked out the front door."

"Don't lie to me, girl. You already in enough trouble!"

"But Daddy, I ain't tellin' no tale."

Saying the word *lie* was just like cussing if you were a little kid, so we referred to lies as tales.

Just then the phone rang. It was Jimmie calling to talk to me. *Oh, crap!* I thought.

"Elroy, it's him," one of my aunts said, handing him the phone.

"Hello, is this Jimmie? What did you do to my daughter last night? Did you touch her? I don't want you to even think about talking to her ever again. I am not the violent type, but I will get violent with you if you ever lay a hand on my daughter," he yelled as he hung up the phone.

My dad then grabbed me and said, "Let's go!" I had never seen him this angry before. I thought we were going home, but my dad sped around the corner and pulled in front of Jimmie's trailer.

"Did he touch you?!" he yelled.

"No, Daddy!" I cried.

The more I cried, the louder my dad yelled. I didn't think this moment was ever going to end. I was *so* embarrassed because people were looking into our car trying to see what was going on.

"Did you touch him?!"

"No!" I yelled both appalled and astonished.

Finally my dad decided not to get out of the car and we went home. He continued to yell at me when we got home. He even got a belt and hit it against the floor several times but never hit me. I continued to try to explain to my dad that we did not sneak out of the window. We walked through the front door, stood on the corner, and talked for a few minutes and then returned to Nana's house through the front door. I don't know if he ever believed me, but he finally calmed down. I was on punishment for a few days after that and did not even want to think about boys for a while.

Even though I was probably more afraid of my dad that day than I had ever been, I could understand his anger. Even though I did not sneak out of the window and never had any intentions of doing anything with that boy, he had every right to be mad. I could only imagine the fear he had of his little girl fooling around with some no-good boy from a drug-dealing family who most likely only wanted me for one thing. I was always rather mature for my age, and I had lots of female bodily features that most girls my age did not have. That caused me to get lots of attention from guys who were way older than I was. I was smart enough not to pay their smirks or sexual comments any mind. And I was also smart enough to realize why my dad was so angry with me. I just wished I had been smart enough not to follow my cousin Aretha to the corner to meet with those boys. I mean, what if they had just grabbed me and took what they wanted? Where would I have ended up then? I know that my life and my emotional state would not have been the same if I had ended up being raped. Would I have ended up with a baby or some nasty disease? I thank God that He always looks out for babies and fools, 'cause I was definitely a fool that night. Needless to say, it never happened again.

The next day, my aunt told me that the only reason she told my dad was because she did not want me to end up like my cousin Aretha. She said that I had too much going for myself to let some no-good boy ruin it. I told her I understood, and I thanked her. I knew she was only looking out for me and I had enough sense to appreciate her for that. Besides, she had always been one of my favorite aunts. And she knew what she was talking about. She got pregnant with her first child at the age of fifteen, so she knew all of the trouble that went along with teen pregnancy. I definitely did not want to go down that road.

Well, that chicken coop incident did come back to haunt me. Apparently my cousin Tommie liked the attention he got from Jimmie after lying to him about us having sex in the chicken coop, so he began to tell everyone. *How embarrassing.* Not only was I being labeled as a twelve-year-old tramp, but everyone thought that I was a tramp who had sex with my own cousin. Before long, every black person at school had heard the rumor. I found no peace at school outside of my classrooms. Thank God there was only one other black person in my classes besides me. And he was very quiet and had a huge crush on me.

Changing classes became difficult for me because someone would always come up behind me clucking like a chicken. It got to the point that I started walking behind the buildings in the wet grass to get to my next class instead of taking the sidewalks in order to avoid everyone. My shoes would always be wet and grass stained. I started to hate going to school. However, I never let this affect my grades or my participation in extracurricular activities because I was way too competitive to let those other kids outdo me. In all honesty, it just made me appreciate my white friends and being in all-white classes even more. All of the white kids seemed completely oblivious to all of the rumors about me.

By the time I got to the eighth grade, the clucking became a routine thing that I just learned to ignore. However, as if this was not bad enough, more drama was about to come into my life.

One day while in the eighth grade, I was called to the front office. There sat these two completely strange white people who I had never seen before.

"We're from social services," they said. "We would like to ask you some questions. Do you feel safe in your home? Has anyone hurt you?"

"Yes, I feel safe, and no one has hurt me. There's no one in our house but me and my dad," I said shocked and confused. "Why are you asking me these things?"

"We are here because someone called us stating that your father has been molesting you. We have been following you for the past three weeks investigating the accusations. Is this true? Has your father molested you?"

"No," I emphatically said once again. "Who called you and said that?"

"It was an anonymous call so we don't know. Are you sure that your father has never touched you in a way that made you feel uncomfortable?"

"No," I firmly stated once again.

"Well, why do you think that someone would call us and tell us something like this?" she asked.

"I don't know. I know there are a lot of people in Callahan who may be jealous of us or angry that we don't do the same things that they do like taking drugs or flunking out of school, but I don't know why anyone would do something like this."

The social workers explained to me that they had been following me all over Callahan and taking pictures of me for the past three weeks. They followed me to school. They followed me home. They observed me with my dad. They stated that they had not witnessed anything out of the ordinary. They eventually concluded that the accusations were false and closed the case. To this day, I wonder who was evil or stupid enough to try and get me taken away from my father. There must be someone in Callahan who really hated us to do such a thing. Evil is as evil does. My mom says she thinks she knows who called it in, but now it's just water under the bridge, and we have definitely crossed that bridge and moved on.

My mom was in Korea at the time of the investigation, but as soon as she got notice of what was going on, her unit commander sent her home to check things out for herself. She stated she knew that nothing strange was happening, but she needed to come home to see 'bout her family.

Never Alone

The day my mom left for the army had to be one of the most difficult days of my life. Nothing would ever be the same again.

"It's only for six weeks. Then you and your dad will be coming up to South Carolina for my graduation from basic training. You can handle that," she tried to convince me. She gave me a big kiss and a long hug. I could tell from the way that she hugged me that she was trying to convince herself as well that everything was going to be okay. She knew that she had to make this sacrifice in order to make a better life for the two of us. To her, this was her only option. My mom was twenty-seven years old when she left for basic training at Fort Jackson, South Carolina.

After my mom and dad said their good-byes, she boarded her bus. We sat in the parking lot and watched the bus drive away until we couldn't see it anymore. After that my dad and I just sort of stared at each other. *What are we going to do now?* we thought. The first thing I had to do was stop crying. But no matter how hard I tried, I could not stop the tears from flowing. My mom was gone. How could that be? Up until that point, my mom and I had been pretty much inseparable. Other than work, school, and softball, everywhere that she went, I went as well.

My mom taught me from a very young age that I needed to

be self-sufficient. I can remember being three years old and she had me standing up on a stool learning how to wash dishes and scramble eggs. She never made me feel like I was too young to learn something. She always made me feel like I was a big girl.

After she left, I learned to appreciate all that she taught me. Although my dad was an extremely good cook, there were many times when I was at home alone and had to fend for myself. The few cooking skills that I had as a nine-year-old helped to calm my hunger many days; that is when there was something in the house for me to cook. I ate a lot of sandwiches and soups when my dad had to work late. Most of the time, though, I rode my bicycle over to Mudea's house after school to have dinner.

My dad was a chef at one of the golf clubs at Amelia Island Plantation. He would often bring home gourmet foods, such as lobster, soups, salads, etc. When he had time to cook at home, I was in heaven. He would make fried chicken, macaroni and cheese, stewed pig's feet, collard greens, gumbo, black-eyed peas, peach cobbler...You name it and my dad could cook it. I think I picked up a lot of my skills from him as well. As you can tell, I come from a cooking family. It's a wonder I didn't end up weighing about three hundred pounds. Everybody used to tell me that I was going to end up big like Mudea. That really scared me, so I was always very self-conscious about my weight. I was never fat, though. I'm sure the fact that I was always very athletic had a lot to do with that. Instead of being fat, I was always real muscular and strong. I could out arm wrestle even the strongest boys in my class. I could also outrun them all. No one ever really wanted to play against me in anything. They always wanted me on their team.

I can remember in middle school making many boys very angry and embarrassed because I would outrun them or beat them in arm wrestling. I liked being considered tough. None of the white kids ever messed with me. There was only one white girl who tried me when we were in middle school. Her name was Brandy, and she was about sixteen years old in the eighth grade. She was one of those girls who thought she was tough. She smoked, skipped school, was having sex and didn't care who knew it. She was in my homeroom class and we took gym class together. One day in gym class, my friends and I were talking about this other girl in our class. I don't remember why we were messing with that girl, but she knew we were talking about her. After we left the locker room, she apparently told Brandy that I was joking on her instead of the girl we were actually messing with.

The next morning in homeroom, Brandy was apparently telling everyone that she was going to fight me. I had no clue because I had no beef with this girl and really had not ever paid her any attention. After the bell rang for first period, I noticed this huge crowd following behind me. Brandy was leading the pack talking all kinds of mess about me behind my back. I had no clue what her problem was, so I kept walking. The more I walked, the louder she got and the more obscene words she said to me. It took everything in me not to turn around and knock her in her crooked mouth. But, being the good girl that I was, I kept on walking. Eventually she ran to the front office. About ten minutes into first period, while I was in science class, an overhead page went out calling me to the front office.

Apparently, Brandy went to the office and lied, stating I was talking junk to her and was trying to start a fight with her. The vice principal believed me immediately after I told him what happened. He knew of my reputation as being one of the smartest kids in the school and I had never been in any trouble before. He told me that he was a little suspicious of her given her history and the fact that she had decided to check out of school early again that day.

When I got home, I told my dad what had happened. He commended me for walking away, but told me not to ever be afraid to stand up for myself.

"If she puts a hand on you, you knock her lights out," he said.

"You know I will," I replied. He smiled and rubbed me on the top of my head as usual. This was his way of showing me that he was proud of me.

The very next day, we went to the meat market and guess who we ran into. Brandy was the cashier. I had no idea that she worked there. I told you she was old. You had to be at least fifteen to have a work permit.

"Daddy, that's her," I said when we got the register.

"Who?" he asked.

"The girl who tried to pick a fight with me yesterday."

"Oh," my daddy said with a frown on his face.

When Brandy saw us, she got the most frightened look on her face because she noticed how I was mean-mugging her. She didn't say a word.

"That's a big girl," my dad said.

"She's about twenty years old in middle school," I stated.

"That explains it."

I don't think Brandy returned to school any more after that day. The only other time I ever saw her again was one day in my nana's neighborhood walking down the street with Manny. I was headed to the shop with Aretha to get some candy when we ran into them. When Brandy saw me with my cousin, she looked like she wanted to take off running the other way. She knew she was in the wrong neighborhood then. I didn't even say anything to her. I just gave her a look like, *what's up now?* but she looked down at the ground. Aretha casually spoke to Manny and we kept walking. I could tell Aretha was a little taken aback by the fact that Manny was with someone else. Especially a white girl. That seemed to be becoming the trend in Callahan. In a town with such an obvious division of the races, interracial dating was on the rise.

Manny was known as the biggest drug dealer in Callahan, so we knew what he and Brandy's relationship was all about. Drugs for sex. Why not? She seemed to have nothing else going for herself at the time.

Manny always stayed in trouble in Callahan. I really think that the police were well aware of his entrepreneurship because they were always patrolling around trying to catch him in action. One day I guess they actually caught him in the act of something because they took him down. I think there must have been some type of shoot out or something. All I know is that there were a lot of police cars and an ambulance up the street in front of Manny's trailer. I'm not sure why they called the ambulance because the only one who was shot was Manny, and from what everyone says the cops didn't intend for him to live because after they finished shooting him up they took ink pens and stuck them in the bullet holes. They let him lay there and bleed to death before they put him in the ambulance. They wanted to make sure this menace to society was dead. Instead of calling an ambulance they may as well had just called the coroner. It would have saved the taxpayers a couple of dollars.

I'm Pressing My Way

After all the talk about Manny's death died down, things went on as usual in Callahan. Nothing to do but school and softball.

When I was in the seventh grade, I decided that I didn't want my Jheri curl anymore. I was tired of always having activator stains on my shirts and of people being afraid to touch my hair. I begged my dad to let me reverse my curl. He took me to my grandma's house, and my aunt Vy straightened it out with the hot comb. I was so happy. My hair came down to my shoulders, and I could shake it like my white friends. I thought I was *so* cute! Although, I had no idea how to take care of my hair, and with my mom gone, I really had no help. The cuteness only lasted for a couple of days because with me playing sports, I would sweat so much that it would kink right back up. Eventually one of my aunts put a relaxer in it for me to help keep it straight. I think we did this way too soon because all of my hair started falling out. Finally my aunt M took me to get some braids.

It was around 1988 and extensions were just getting popular. It cost my aunt M one hundred and fifty dollars to get my hair braided. Back then that was *a lot* of money. I think it took about twelve hours for me to get all that hair put in my head. By the time the lady was finished I looked like a black Chinese-

American because my edges were pulled so tight that my eyes were slanted upwards. Talk about a headache. But I thought I was cute, so it was worth it.

The next day, all of the white kids came up to me and wanted to touch my hair. "Danielle, your hair is so pretty. What did you do, let it down?"

"No. I just got it braided and they added some extensions."

"Extensions? What's that?"

No matter how hard I tried to explain to them they still could not grasp the concept of braiding additional hair into someone's head. I finally just gave up and said, "Yes, I let my hair down."

I wore my braids for about three months and finally took them out when I couldn't make them look neat anymore by tying a scarf around my head at night. My braids had been so tight that by the time I took them out, I had no hair around my edges at all. My godmom took me to this hair salon in Hilliard to this lady named Ms. Neet. She looked at my hair and said, "Girl, we're gon' have to put some weave in your hair to give you a cute hairstyle. It will only be temporary while we get your hair back healthy."

"What's weave?" I asked. At that time not many people I knew were having additional hair sewn into their heads. Ms. Neet explained it to me and finally I said, "Okay, just make me cute."

When Ms. Neet got done, no one could tell that I had some-one else's hair in my head. It looked so real. And I was *so* cute!

When I got to school the next day all of my friends com-mented on how pretty I looked. A lot of the black girls who I didn't really socialize with kind of turned their noses up at me. I knew that meant they liked my hair and were going to be trying to copy it when they got home that day. I was really happy that people liked my hair, but I was very self-conscious about the fact that it wasn't really my hair. I didn't know what I would do if people found out that I was wearing a weave.

One day I invited my friend Nicole over to my house to hang out. She and I had been cool for a least a year in middle school.

She was my best friend, so I thought, next to Candy. Little did I know that Nicole had the biggest mouth ever. Nicole could not hold water if her life depended on it. I remember one day Nicole and I were sitting on the wall outside at school and this girl named Dana walked by. Dana and I were kind of cool for the most part, but I think we always had a little bit of a competition going on because we both wanted to be the cutest. Dana had on some skin-tight jeans. "Those jeans look uncomfortable. I wouldn't wear my jeans that tight," I said.

I'll be doggon' if after the next period Dana wasn't in my face saying, "Nicole told me you were talking about me."

I gave Nicole the meanest look I could muster, but I couldn't back down from Dana.

"All I said was that they look uncomfortable, and they do," I said.

"Keep my name out of your mouth," she said as she walked away.

"Whatever!" I said heading to my next class.

I should have learned my lesson about telling Nicole anything that day, but I must have let it go or something because my dumb self let Nicole know that my hair was a weave when we were at my house that day.

"Really," she said, shocked.

"Yeah, but don't tell anybody."

"I won't," she lied.

The next day *everybody* was asking me about my hair.

"Is that your hair? Is that really a weave?"

I was so embarrassed that a few days later, I cut the tracks loose myself and took them out. By that time, I had enough hair to pull into a small ponytail and feather my bangs. That still didn't stop the jokes.

There was this one black girl named Angie who was a year older than me. Angie always seemed to have something against me. I think part of the reason was that I was always getting so much attention because of my shape and she was very fat. She had a pretty face, though. One day when I rode the bus over to Nana's house after school, Angie was in the back of the bus talking about me the entire bus ride. I honestly don't know what she was saying, but I knew it had something to do with my hair. When I got off the bus, she yelled "Rapunzel, Rapunzel, let down your long hair!" out of the bus window.

"Shut up, you old fat cow!" one of my cousins yelled back.

Shortly after that, I heard that Angie got real sick and all of her hair fell out. I think she finally lost some weight, too, but I'm not sure if she kept it off.

My mama always told me that the very thing you make fun of others about can come right back and haunt you. I guess Angie got what was coming to her. Folks better learn to be careful what you try to clown somebody else about. You could be condemning yourself. And you definitely don't want to mess with God's anointed. You're always going to pay for that. And you never know who He's got His hands on, so it's best to treat everyone with kindness and respect. That's what I was always taught.

Shelter in the Arms of God

O ne day after school, I came home to find my daddy sitting in the middle of the living room with an envelope in his hands. He had this incredibly sad look upon his face. It was a look that I had never seen before.

"What's wrong, Daddy?" I asked concerned.

"Come sit down," he said slowly as he patted his knee for me to take a seat.

I sat on his knee, and he struggled to take the letter out of the large envelope. "You see this? These are divorce papers from your mama. She wants to leave me. I don't understand. Doesn't she know that I love her? She up and joins the army, and then decides she wants a divorce. What am I supposed to do? What kind of mess is this?" he said. The more he talked the more upset he became and eventually he broke down crying as he gave me a hug.

I think that I was in total shock, thinking, or should I say, wishing that I was just having a bad dream and that I would wake up at any moment.

As I mentioned earlier, *The Cosby Show* had a huge impact on my life. Claire and Cliff Huxtable had the type of family that I always dreamed of and that I planned to have one day myself. I was going to be a lawyer and I was going to marry a doctor, and we were going to have a bunch of kids and always be happy. I remember one day while watching *The Cosby Show*, one of Rudy's friend's parents were getting a divorce. Her friend was so distraught at the fact that her parents were separating. She felt that her whole world was crashing in. She began to blame herself thinking that she was the reason for the divorce and that made her feel even worse. I remember feeling very bad for that girl and even began to feel sad myself.

I am so glad that my parents are never going to get a divorce, I thought.

Now, sitting on my father's knee, my worst fear had come true. I began to sob uncontrollably. *What had I done to deserve this? My mom leaves and is now halfway around the world in some foreign country I've never even heard of, and now my family is going to be completely ripped apart.*

Lord, why me? It's just not fair.

At that bleak moment, the devil started putting all kinds of crazy thoughts into my immature head.

Maybe I should run away. Maybe that will pull them together. Maybe I should hurt myself really bad. What if I just died? Death would have to feel better than what I'm feeling right now. Why, God? Do you even love me anymore? Does anybody love me? Please don't let this happen! Who am I going to live with? Is there going to be a huge custody battle? Will I have to choose between my parents?

Even though all of these unreasonable thoughts were going through my head, I didn't know what to say to my dad. "We'll be okay," I told him. Even though my mom was divorcing my dad, I felt like she was divorcing me, too, because she had left both of us when she left to join the army. My dad honestly did not do anything to make me feel any better because some of the comments he spoke made me feel even more like my mom didn't love me.

"How is she just going to leave *us* like that?" he stated angrily.

I just couldn't take it anymore. I had to go into my quiet

room and lie down in my bed to process everything that I had just learned. *My parents are getting a divorce! Why?*

I was so angry with my mom that night that I decided to write her a nasty letter letting her know exactly how I felt.

Dear Mom,

Dad just gave me the news about the divorce. How could you do this to us? First you left and now you want a divorce. Don't you love us anymore? It's just not fair. We are supposed to be a family and you are taking that away from us. Right now I hate you. I wish that you were not my mom. A real mom would not do this to her husband and daughter. The devil has really gotten into your head or something. Have you found another family that you like better than us? Well I gotta go.

Your daughter,
Danielle

I sent my letter off the next day. About a week later, my mom called and told me that she had gotten my letter.

"Young lady, I don't know who you think you are writing me a letter like that. Everything that I'm doing I am doing for you. You don't know anything about why I asked for a divorce. You're really too young to understand half of the things I have gone through while married to your father. One day when you are older, I'll tell you more. But girl, no matter what happens between me and your father, you are always going to be my baby and I will always love you."

After talking to my mom, I felt so bad about sending that foolish letter. I could hear it in her voice that the letter that I wrote really hurt her feelings. At that point, I was even more confused. I did not know whose side to be on or what I should do. Over the next couple of weeks, I prayed harder than I had ever prayed before.

Lord, please don't let my parents get a divorce. Please let them realize they still love each other. Please just let this be a dream.

I felt like if I prayed hard enough, God would just completely wipe that part of my life away as if it never happened. I just wanted Him to pull me out of the middle of this mess and put somebody else there who deserved it. What had I done to deserve it? I honestly tried to be good and kind. But sometimes I wondered if it was even worth it. It seemed the more good I tried to do, the worse things got for me. Sometimes I felt as if the devil was trying to get me to lose my mind so that I would go out and just start doing crazy stuff. That would be taking the easy way out, though, and I was not one to do something just because it was easy to do. I always tried my best to walk the straight and narrow.

I also think that I cried more during those weeks than I had ever cried in my entire life. Even more than when my mom left to join the army.

Of course, when Mudea found out what was going on, everyone at By Faith knew and that was the new topic from the pulpit.

"The devil done just took hold of Gail. She done allowed him to break up her marriage," the pastor stated. "We got to pray for God to bring her back home and to protect this child she done left behind."

I felt so alone. Being an only child sucked at times, and I believe this was when it sucked the worst. I had *no one* who knew exactly how I was feeling. I wasn't comfortable discussing my feelings with anyone. I'm pretty sure I went through a state of depression and could have benefited from some counseling, but back then you were just supposed to brush your knees off and get over things. Besides, who could afford a counselor? And anyway, counselors were for crazy people or people who got in trouble.

A few weeks later, my dad told me he was going on a trip to New Orleans to see some old friend of his. He didn't tell me who this person was. All he told me was that he would be back in about a week. *Fine.* I stayed at Mudea's house hating life because once again I was feeling like a live-in maid. Constantly cooking, cleaning, and helping her with her baths. I don't ever think I will forget what Shower to Shower smells like because Mudea would put that on from neck to toe. Being that she was a large woman, she would sweat a lot, so she would put on a lot of powder to try and keep herself smelling fresh. One thing I can say about her was that she was always a clean woman. And she could cook her behind off.

I loved eating at Mudea's house because everything she made was good. Being in the country, we always ate country foods like chitlins with pig ears in it, fried tripe, field peas, butter beans, corn bread, and all kinds of cakes. I always wondered who would have thought to try and eat pigs' intestines and cows' stomachs. Regardless of who came up with the idea, Mudea made it taste good. When she baked her cakes, she would always bake a sample cake in a little tin pan for her to make sure the batter was right and for us kids to indulge in while we waited for the real thing. We all loved her sample cakes and would gobble them up as fast as she took them out of the oven.

When Mudea found out she was hypertensive and a diabetic, it really changed Sunday dinners for us. She took her doctor's recommendations seriously, and instead of using salt, she began using salt substitutes like Mrs. Dash. That really took away *a lot* of the flavor from her food. After that, I don't think I enjoyed eating at her house very much anymore.

Mudea began walking the track and lost a considerable amount of weight. I think she only had to give herself insulin injections for a few months before she was able to manage her diabetes with just her diet and exercise. She told everybody God had cured her of her diabetes. About a year later, Mudea was diagnosed with some type of gynecological cancer. She refused to allow the doctors to operate because at By Faith we were taught that all we had to do was pray and God would heal us of all of our infirmities. Mudea gave a testimony at church one Wednesday night that she had been diagnosed with cancer and asked every-body to pray for her. She laid on that altar for a long time that night as everyone prayed over her trying to drive that evil spirit of cancer out of her body. By the time she got up from the altar, a sense of peace had come over her as if she had taken all of her burdens to the Lord and left them there like she was supposed to. Sometime during those next few weeks, Mudea said that she had had a bowel movement and had passed a large black lump which she believed was her tumor. When she went back to the doctor, they were extremely astonished at the fact that her cancer was no longer there. Mudea just smiled and looked at them smugly and said, "Jesus is the greatest doctor of 'em all." There was nothing they could say to that.

One Day at a Time

At the end of the week, my dad returned from New Orleans. I was so happy to see him because that meant I could go home to my own bed and be free to do what I wanted to do. Mudea always tried to get me to be too much of a girlie girl. I loved running wild outside racing all of the boys and playing whatever sport everyone else was playing. I was very much a tomboy, and Mudea didn't like that one bit.

When my dad returned, he showed me a bunch of pictures he had taken while in New Orleans.

"Who are these people?" I asked.

In the pictures were some strange lady and a boy who looked to be about my age.

"Well, sweetie, this is the reason I went to New Orleans. That boy's name is David. He's your brother."

"What?! My brother. But I don't have a brother. My brother died when he was born."

• • •

When I was three, my mom did have another baby. She had a little boy, but he came out stillborn. They said somehow he drowned in the blood before he came out. I remember sitting in the front row at By Faith when we had his funeral. I don't remember if I was sad or not because at the time I really didn't understand what death meant. Plus, I didn't even know him yet. All I know is that my dad seemed really sad. After the funeral, we all went to the cemetery and my baby brother was buried in a Styrofoam cooler. We couldn't afford a headstone, so my papa planted a pine tree there to mark his grave.

When I got older, my mom told me that about a week before she had my brother she began to have some bleeding while taking a bath. She went to the hospital but by the time she had gotten there the bleeding had stopped, so they sent her home. She said they never even performed an examination on her. A week or so later she went into labor.

She had to have a repeat C-section because of the emergency vertical C-section she had to have with me. She said I decided that I wanted to turn around and go back the other way on my way out. I think I was probably transverse or something. She said I've been stubborn ever since.

Anyways, my brother was born without a pulse, and they were unable to resuscitate him. It was too late. I honestly think that if she had known more at the time, she could have sued her obstetrician for malpractice because when she presented with painless bleeding, they should have automatically performed an ultrasound to evaluate her for placenta previa. That's probably the reason my brother died—because he bled to death not because he drowned in the blood. How can you drown in blood when you don't take your first breath until you are out of the womb?

• • •

Well, after my dad told me that was my brother in those pictures I was really confused. He said the lady in the picture was David's mom. He told me he knew her from when he was in New Orleans before he and my mom got married. He said that David was a year older than I was.

While we were looking at the pictures, my dad picked up the

phone and called David and his mother. He talked to David's mother for a minute and then handed the phone to me.

"I want you to talk to your brother," my dad said.

In the back of my mind, I kept thinking, *I really don't want to talk to these people. This is just too much for me to handle right now.*

Reluctantly I took the phone. "Hello."

"Hi, Danielle. It's so nice to finally get to talk to you. Our dad has told me so much about you."

Our dad? I thought. That sounded extremely weird to me. *Mighty funny he's never told me anything about you.*

"Please don't be mad at him for not telling you about me. Our dad and my mom were very young when she got pregnant with me. When my granddad found out, he threatened to kill our dad if he ever stepped foot in New Orleans again. That's why he had to leave us and has not been back since then. That's also probably why he never told you about us. He's a good person, and you're very lucky to have him there with you. I'm so excited about having a sister. I can't wait to see you in person."

"Yeah, me too," I lied. I could not wait to get off that phone and go to my room.

My room was my sanctuary. I really only had to come out of it to eat because I had a sink and a toilet in there. Whenever I got in trouble, my parents would always send me to my room. I didn't care because I liked being in there away from everyone else anyway. I would sit in there and have conversations with my dolls. I could play for hours by myself and never get bored. I took great pride in my room and always did my best to keep it clean. Every Saturday I would take everything out of my room and give it a thorough cleaning. It wasn't a very pretty room. It was rather small and the sliding closet doors were coming off the hinges. The faux wood furniture was very old and mismatched, and my floral curtains were cheap and dusty, but it was my room. I fixed it up the best way that I could. Most of my friends thought my room was nice because they were just as poor if not poorer than we were. Some of them didn't even have a room of their own.

As soon as we hung up the phone, my dad looked at me with a smile as if everything was all good and a ton of bricks had just been lifted off of his chest. I gave him a phony smile back. He then gave me a hug. After that I told him I was going to go to my room to finish my homework or something. He probably knew that I just wanted to get away because I always either did my homework before I got home or as soon as I walked in the door from school.

When I talked to my mom that week I told her all about what had happened.

"You see? I told you there were a lot of things that you didn't know. And I didn't feel it was my place to tell you about your brother. I figured your dad would tell you when he was ready. Do you remember that picture of the little boy in the photo albums that you would always ask about? The one that we said was one of your cousins? That was David."

That explains why everyone would always switch the subject so quickly when I would ask about the boy in the picture. They never actually lied to me because he was my cousin. He just happened to be a lot more than just a traditional cousin. My mom went on to tell me that my dad did not tell her about David until they were already married. That was one of the many strikes he had built against himself. She then told me that David's mother was actually my dad's younger niece. When my dad was living with his brother in New Orleans at age seventeen, David's mom was somewhere between the ages of twelve and fourteen. She supposedly always looked a lot older than she actually was. Somehow she and my dad ended up having sex and she got pregnant. When my uncle found out, he actually pulled a gun on my dad and threatened to kill him. That night my dad hopped on a bus and headed back to Callahan. He was actually running for his life. He didn't return to New Orleans until thirteen years later when David's mom contacted him and told him that David wanted to meet his father. Of course, my dad didn't really tell me the whole story, as usual.

After a while the whole David issue sort of faded. My dad didn't bring it up anymore and neither did I. They were in New Orleans and we were in Florida, so it's not like we ever saw them. For me the issue faded as quickly as it had evolved. As long as I didn't have to share my space with some stranger, I was fine.

Things were kind of quiet around our house for a while, but that didn't last for long. The devil was always busy bringing new horrors into my life. And then there was Tonya.

When my dad worked at the Paper Mill in Yulee, Florida, he was friends with this white guy named Donald. Donald was married to Tonya, and they had a daughter around my age named Monique. We went over to their trailer a few times to hang out. We all even went bowling together. I liked hanging out with Monique because she was pretty cool.

We began hanging out with them less and less after a while. Pretty soon my dad told me they had moved to Georgia. The next thing I knew Tonya had moved in with me and my dad. Apparently they had been messing around behind Donald's back, and he found out about it and put Tonya out and filed for divorce. He took Monique and they moved to Georgia.

I did not like Tonya at all after that. She always looked so trashy. She was a skinny white lady with brown hair and raggedy teeth. She always wore clothes that were too tight or too short. And she always smelled funny to me. She wasn't clean like the women in my family. She didn't cook, clean, or work. She didn't do anything but lay up with my daddy.

I was so miserable living in that house when she was there. I always stayed in my room when I was home. I really did my best to always have something to do to keep me away from home as long as possible. As long as my dad knew where I was, he didn't seem to care.

Tonya stayed with us for what seemed like forever. But I think it was only actually a few months. During those months, they fussed a lot and then they made up. It was sickening. I think my dad eventually got bored with her and put her out. The last time I saw her was weird. It was about three o'clock in the morning and I had fallen asleep on the couch as I often did on the weekends. It was a Saturday morning. I have never been a heavy sleeper, so when a horn beeped out front and someone knocked on the door I was wide awake by the time my dad reached the front door. I continued to lie still on the couch, though, until he had gone outside. When I got up and looked out of the window, I saw Tonya out front with some other lady. Tonya was holding something in her arms wrapped in a blanket. I could have sworn it was a baby. I closed the curtain and got back on the couch and pretended to be asleep. My dad stayed outside for a good little while before the car drove away and he came back in and went back into his bedroom. He never even mentioned to me that Tonya had been there, let alone what she had come there for.

For many years, I wondered what it was that Tonya was holding in her arms. After I got older, I actually asked my dad about it. As usual he acted as if he did not know what I was talking about. My dad has always had trouble being truthful about the mistakes he has made in his life. I think that has something to do with the fact that he is so emotional. My dad will cry if he is watching a commercial if that commercial reminds him of something in his past. Holding stuff in and never confessing your mistakes and asking for forgiveness really takes a toll on some people. I think that only really evil people can do bad things and go on with a clear conscience as if nothing had ever happened. I have never believed my dad to be an evil person. I have believed him to be someone who is afraid of showing any signs of weakness. I believe for him admitting to being wrong would be admitting to being a little weak at times. If he had only learned to open up to people, I think his life would have been more fulfilling. If only he had stayed in the church and in the Word, his life would have been so much better. Maybe he would have had the happiness and the peace that he has always been looking for.

After Tonya he just seemed to go from white lady to white

lady. And they all seemed to look the same. Skinny, blond hair, blue eyes, big breasts. And they all looked rather trashy to me.

There was one woman by the name of Belinda that he seemed to stay with for at least a year. I was shocked he stayed with her for so long. She moved in with him for a while. I think all of the fun and games ended when Belinda popped up pregnant. My dad put her out stating that the baby wasn't his. Belinda said fine, she would raise the baby on her own. She told my dad that she didn't want him to have anything to do with her son. I think this kind of hurt my dad's feelings when he saw that the little biracial baby boy had a lot of his features. He brushed it off and moved on just like he always did, not talking about it much. I told him that as the father he did have rights and that if he had a paternity test proving that he was the father, she could not keep him out of his son's life. We just left it at that and he never mentioned it again.

I Know It Was the Blood

When I was a little girl, I remember my mom taking me to the pediatrician for a wellness examination. I remember being real embarrassed because I had to pull my underpants down and spread my legs for him to look in my private area. I closed my eyes real tight and kept my hands over my face through the entire exam. I remember him telling my mom that I was already beginning to mature and that I would possibly start my period at an early age. At that age I had no clue as to what he was talking about. I just wanted to get out of that office and away from that man who had just seen my most personal area.

When I was eight, my mom began telling me what a period was. Before she left to go to the army, she told all of my aunts to look out for me to be starting my period when I was about nine or ten. It seemed like every single one of my aunts had to tell me about menstruation. "Just let me know if you have any questions or if you start your period and need some pads," they would say. I was so embarrassed just talking about it.

Well you can imagine how it felt being a ten-year-old with a period. I was one month away from turning eleven in the fifth grade and early one Sunday morning while I was using the restroom I noticed blood in my underwear. I wasn't afraid at all because so many people had talked to me about it that I was well aware of what was going on. I just did not want to tell my dad. So I stuffed almost an entire roll of toilet tissue into my underwear and put on my white dress and left for church. As soon as I got to church, I found my aunt E and told her that I thought I had started my period. She was extremely excited and I couldn't figure out why. She told me that after church she would take me to the store to get some pads. By the time church was over it seemed like all of the women in church came up and congratulated me on becoming a woman.

Gee, thanks, I thought. If this was what becoming a woman was like, I would much rather remain a little kid.

I think I spent more time in the bathroom than in church service that morning because that wad of toilet tissue would not stay in place. Plus I kept soaking through it so I had to change it out two or three times. *This is so gross,* I thought.

My aunt took me to the store and then we headed to my house to share the news with my father. "Congratulations," he smiled. "Why didn't you tell me this morning? Your mom had actually left some pads for you in the bathroom closet."

"Oh," I stated. I then went to my room and lay across my bed.

The next week was pure agony. Cramps and bleeding. Just great. This is what I have to look forward to every month. *Why wasn't I born a boy? Boys seem to have all of the fun.*

To make matters worse, I had to go to school with my period. As far as I knew, I was the only girl in my class with her period. Heck, I was probably the only girl in the fifth grade with a period. One day while at school, I noticed a lot of commotion around the girl's bathroom. There was actually a line of people outside pointing and talking. Being the slightly nosey child that I was, I went over to see what was going on. I went into the bathroom and there was a bloody pad stuck to the wall.

Was that my pad? Did someone know that I was having my period and go into the trash can and take my pad out and stick it to the wall to try and get me in trouble? Is there any way they can test that blood and tell if it is mine?

I was so embarrassed and afraid that I immediately left the bathroom and went back to my class. Why would somebody do that?

The worse thing about having my period for me was that it was just me and my dad. So that meant I had to go into the only grocery store in Callahan where everybody knew my family and buy my own pads. How embarrassing!

Usually I would wear a jacket or something and tuck the pads into it until I got to the counter. I was always worried that some- one would think that I was trying to steal them or something, but honestly I think I would have been less embarrassed about getting in trouble for stealing than I would if one of my friends, let alone some boy that I knew, saw me buying those pads. That would be yet another thing they would have to poke fun at me about.

Sometimes I could get my dad or my great aunt who we all called Granny to go into the store and buy them for me. I really hated being a woman at the age of eleven.

Despite my embarrassment, I managed to survive and con- tinue with my usual daily activities. School and sports.

• • •

When I was in the seventh grade, I decided to play basketball. I was, of course, the starting point guard. I wouldn't say that I was all that great of a player, but compared to the other girls on the team I was pretty good. My specialty was shooting three pointers. I remember one home game I made seven three pointers. We lost that game but everybody was telling me how great I played, so it didn't matter. The thing that I was not so good at was dribbling. Pretty strange for a point guard not to be good at dribbling. My problem was that I was extremely right handed. I could not do much of anything with my left hand, let alone dribble. I would always dribble myself into the right corner and get stuck. It didn't seem to matter how much I practiced I just could not get the hang of dribbling and shooting with my left hand.

Oh well. It's not like I was trying to get a basketball scholarship or anything. My main sport was still softball.

One of the other things that we did a lot in Callahan was attend the West Nassau High School football games. Those games used to be off the hook. Everyone who was anyone would be at those games. The biggest rivalries were Callahan vs. Hilliard and Callahan vs. Fernandina. Those games were always jam packed. We would never go to watch the game though. All we wanted to do was walk around and see who we could see. Even though I wasn't really into boys, it still made me feel good when one of them tried to holla at me. Most of the time I would just keep walking and wouldn't give them the time of day. The reason I did that was because I didn't know how to talk to boys. I was terribly shy when it came to that sort of thing.

I remember in middle school the only other black person in my class was a boy named Sean. Sean and I called ourselves boyfriend and girlfriend for about three months. The entire three months all we did was write each other love letters and pass them back and forth to each other. We were right in the same classes all day long and hardly ever spoke a word to each other.

One day when I was on my way to basketball practice, Sean and this boy named Derrick were walking behind me. I heard Derrick tell Sean that he should try to get a kiss from me. When we got to the locker room entrance, Sean came up to me to tell me bye. When he tried to kiss me, I turned around and went into the locker room. I was so nervous and freaked out, I didn't know what to do. The next day I wrote Sean a letter telling him that things weren't working out between us and that I wanted to break up with him. Everyone told me that I broke his heart, but I was not trying to be kissing on no boy. I figured if I kept telling him no he was going to break up with me eventually anyway.

After one of the football games, I lost track of my cousin who I was sort of at the game with. I was going to ask her if they could give me a ride home since she lived right down the dirt road from me. I walked all over that football stadium, and she was nowhere in sight. It was about nine thirty or ten o'clock and there were not a whole lot of streetlights on the little streets by West Nassau. Everybody I knew had already left. Usually after the games everyone met at McDonald's. Not having much of a choice, I started walking down those dark streets all by myself. I was so scared, but I didn't know what else to do; I had to get home somehow. I walked and ran, walked and ran. I kept looking over my shoulders because I was scared someone was going to jump out of the darkness and grab me. I cut behind the elementary school and walked down the little road that ran in front of the basketball gym. I made it about halfway before one of my other cousins, Patsy, drove up next to me. At first I didn't know who was pulling up beside me so I got scared.

"Girl, what are you doing out here in this dark by yourself?! Didn't you have a ride home?" Patsy was about twenty-five years older than me.

"Well, I was going to try and ride with Kristen, but I couldn't find her after the game. I was gon' try to meet up with her at McDonald's," I said relieved that she was there.

"Well, get in. I'll give you a ride to McDonald's to find her. It's pitch black out here. Somebody could snatch you up, and nobody would even know it."

When we got to McDonald's, I saw Kristen there in her skin-tight cat suit. She was one of those girls who *always* got all of the boys' attention. And she loved it. I had always wished that I was more outgoing like she was, but I was way too shy. She was very popular, too, not just because she was pretty and fun to be around, but that girl could sing her behind off. If there was any event going on at any of the churches in Callahan, you could bet Kristen would be singing at it.

When I finally got home that night, I was so thankful to God that nothing bad had happened to me. God always comes through in the clutch. My cousin Patsy had definitely been a ram in the bush that night because I thought I was going to have an anxiety attack walking down those dark streets by myself.

Just Another Day

When I was twelve, my mom was stationed at Fort Bragg, North Carolina. During that summer, I went for a visit. Since this was my first time going that far away from Callahan, my mom did not want me to ride the bus by myself, so my aunt Vy came along with me. That was one trip that I'll never forget.

I was so excited about getting to see my mom after she had been in Korea for a full year. I had seen her briefly when she came to Callahan because of that stupid molestation investigation, but she was only able to stay for a couple of days after the case was closed. Now I was going to have a full three weeks with my mom. This was the longest time I had spent with her since she left when I was nine.

When we arrived at the Greyhound bus station in Fayetteville, I was so excited. When I finally saw her, I ran to her and gave her the biggest hug.

"Hey, Ma!"

"Hey, baby!" she said as she hugged me back.

She and Aunt Vy gave each other a quick hug and off we went. Since I was not living with my mom, she actually stayed in the dorms. Therefore while we were there we had a room in billeting. It was a nice little room with two beds, a table with two chairs, a nineteen-inch TV, and a bathroom. To me it was very nice because I rarely got to go anywhere and stay in a motel, let alone a fancy hotel.

After we unloaded our things, we went to Burger King to get something to eat. Since it had been a long day, we just decided to take our baths and go to bed. After my bath, my mom told me she was going to go out for a while, but that she would be back shortly. Soon after she left, I fell asleep.

When I woke up it was about ten o'clock p.m. I looked around for my mom, but I didn't see her. Aunt Vy was asleep in the other bed. I had to use to restroom, so I got out of the bed. As I approached the restroom door, I heard my mom laughing. Then I heard a man's voice. Next I heard the toilet flush.

What in the world? I thought. My mom was in the bathroom with some man, and she was using the bathroom in front of him. I was so *angry!* I jumped back in the bed and started crying.

When my mom came out of the bathroom, she noticed that I was upset.

"Girl, what's wrong with you?"

"Nothin'. I need to use the bathroom, and I want to call my daddy."

"Is that what you're crying about?"

"I'm not crying," I sobbed.

"You must think I'm crazy or something. Well, this is my friend Al."

"Hey," I said without even looking up. It was bad enough that I had to deal with my dad and his new girlfriends, but the thought of my mom with another man that she allowed to be in the bathroom with her while she peed made me sick to my stomach.

"We'll just see you tomorrow, Al," my mom said as she walked him to the door.

After Al left my mom asked again what was wrong with me.

"I heard ya'll in the bathroom talking, and then I heard you flush the toilet. I know you used the bathroom while he was in there. You let him see you using the bathroom."

"Girl, I'm in the army. Ain't no privacy in the military. Plus we both work in the medical field. I don't have nothin' he hasn't seen before," she replied.

I wasn't buying it. "Whatever. I'm ready to call my daddy. You said I could call him tonight and it's already ten o'clock."

"Who do you think you are talking to? I am still your mother and you had better show me some respect. Come here and get this phone before I knock you out."

After I talked to my dad, I fell asleep. The next morning, my mom had to go to work, but she had Al come over and take Aunt Vy and I to breakfast. I tried my best to ignore him the entire time, but he kept asking me all kinds of questions. I gave him the shortest answers possible. Finally he gave up and just talked to my Aunt Vy.

I think that I saw Al one or two more times while we were there. For some reason I just didn't care for him too much. Not that he ever did anything negative to me, but I didn't like the fact that he had seen my mom using the bathroom.

The rest of my visit with my mom was rather uneventful. Everything except with my aunt Vy. One day when we were walking to Burger King to get something to eat, she met this guy named Rico. Rico was a young black guy who lived in the dorms up the street from billeting. Later that night we walked over to Rico's room. At first we were sitting down watching TV. After a short while Rico took me up the hall in the dorm and bought me a snack out of the snack machine. After that they put a TV show on that I liked. Then they took a seat behind me at the back of the room. The next thing I knew, my aunt Vy was sitting on top of his lap going up and down trying not to make much noise.

I guess they thought that I was too young or too dumb to know what was going on. I could see the reflection of what was going on in the TV. I just sat there, though, and played dumb.

After they had finished "watching TV," Rico took us back to

our room. I think Aunt Vy saw him a few more times before we left. I made sure that I did not go with them.

I was kind of glad when the three weeks were up because I missed my dad and my friends. Even though Fayetteville was a lot bigger than Callahan, I was kind of bored. I was going to miss my mom though.

I Saw the Light

My seventh and eighth grade years flew by. My routine was pretty much the same as always. School and softball.

My mom came home for her usual visits. The next time she came home, she was no longer with Al, but she had this young guy named Oliver. The next time I went to visit her, she was dating and actually living with this white guy who was a doctor. He was nice enough, but rather quiet. He took me shopping, so I was able to stand having him around. What I couldn't understand was why both of my parents had jungle fever. I can say that there may have been one or two white guys in Callahan that I thought were cute. One of them was this guy named Jeremy. I think every girl in intermediate school was crazy about him though. He was athletic with sandy blond hair and blue eyes. The American dreamboat. I could never actually see myself dating a white guy though.

My mom was always very pretty with a very nice figure, so it was easy for me to see how she always had a boyfriend. Even if she didn't keep them for very long.

As time progressed, I continued to mature. I became more aware of the fact that I was becoming a woman. I started to become more aware of my appearance and my feminine qualities. I also became more aware of the opposite sex. Even though my curiosity about boys continued to grow, I was determined that I would not allow any boy in Callahan to get the best of me.

Things at home seemed to continue to crumble before my eyes. My dad was always either at work or gone someplace else. I was always at home alone, and our house seemed to be falling apart. If you remember, my dad had bought us a trailer with the house portion built onto the front. The way that it was designed was when you walked out of the living room, you walked down some steps and out onto a front patio portion before you actually got outside. Don't get me wrong, compared to our previous house it was extremely nice, but apparently my dad didn't have time to make repairs or keep it up. Over time, I guess the shingles started to wear out in certain areas of our house. Especially in the area immediately above the door that led to our living room. Eventually a big hole developed in our roof. When it rained, initially it just leaked, but as the hole got bigger, the rain just poured through like there was no roof there at all. I tried to put buckets out there to catch the water, but they would simply overflow. It always smelled sour out there. If that were the worst part, I could have handled that, but it got even worse.

In Florida, there are a lot of snakes. Growing up, I saw many snakes in our yard. Usually they were rat snakes out hunting for some food. The scariest ones to me were the black snakes because they crawled so fast. One thing that I found out by that hole being in our roof was that snakes liked to crawl up there. There were many days when I would be walking out of the front door in the mornings on my way to school when I would open the front door and happen to look down and there would be a snake sitting right there. A couple of times, I didn't notice it until I was about to step down on it. Like I said, there were steps leading down from the living room to the patio, so you can imagine how many times I almost broke my neck leaping over a snake and down those steps trying not to lose my balance.

Not only did I encounter a lot of snakes because of the hole in the roof, but there were also a lot of large scorpions out there. I kept my bike on the patio so that it would not get stolen. At least twice while taking my bike off of the patio I noticed scorpions in the corner of the patio. I would scream so loud.

"*Daddy!*"

"What, girl?!"

"There's a snake out here!" or "There's a scorpion!"

My dad kept this really big lacquered stick in the corner of our living room for times just like those. Even though he was frightened as well, he would grab his stick and come to my rescue. He was my hero.

During my eighth grade year, I made up my mind that it was time for me to be with my mom. I was sick of the snakes and scorpions, I was sick of people making fun of me about the chicken coop, and I was sick of having to buy my own feminine products. I needed a fresh start.

At the end of the year after softball season was over, I was going to move with my mom to attend high school. I asked my dad if it was okay, and he told me it was my decision. He said that he knew one day I was going to grow up and need to have a woman's guidance. My aunts had been great for me, but now I needed my mom.

Even though my dad said that he understood, I could tell that he was very sad that I had made up my mind to leave. My mom was extremely excited that I had finally decided to come live with her. It was what she had dreamed about for the past five years. However, she never wanted to force me to come. She said she knew that I would make up my mind and come whenever I was ready. It took five years before I decided I was ready to leave Callahan. I was with my dad after my mom left for the army from the age of nine up until I was fourteen. It was time for me to learn about being a woman.

I was kind of fed up with Callahan and the small town mentality that the majority of its people had. I was tired of people seeming to be happy for you when you were doing well, but appearing even more excited when something bad happened to you. It was as if your misfortune made them feel better about their own irreparable situations. I knew that Callahan was not going to be it for me. I had bigger dreams of better places with more opportunities. Yes, it was high time for me to start over in a totally new place where nobody knew anything about me.

My eighth grade year was a lot of fun. All of my friends were both sad and yet excited for me that I was moving to Fort Benning, Georgia. When softball season was over, I packed my bags and was ready to go.

My dad and I had a lot of pets when I was growing up. One of them was this cat named Turk. I think we got Turk when I was in the seventh grade. He was on orange calico cat, and I named him after the movie *Tuff Turk*. Well, Turk used to follow me everywhere. He even used to sleep in my room. I think when I packed my suitcases he sort of sensed that I was leaving.

It took me about a week to decide what I was going to take with me to Georgia. After I had gotten all of my bags packed, I went into the living room to watch TV for a while. When I got sleepy, I went back to my room to get ready for bed. As I approached my bedroom, Turk shot out of my bedroom door which scared me because I didn't even realize he was in there. When I got to my room and looked at my suitcase all I could do was scream.

"Turk, I'm going to kill you!"

That stupid cat had pooped all over my clothes in my suitcases. I chased that cat throughout our entire house that night throwing everything that I could at him. That cat was running for his life, so I never caught up with him. I had to unpack all of my clothes and wash them about three times to get that funky smell out. I guess that was Turk's way of telling me that he didn't want me to go.

The next day my cousin Pete came to get me in his black Camaro. Pete was also stationed at Fort Benning and had come to Callahan to visit his mom for the week. I didn't really know Pete, so I was a little nervous about riding with him. Even though his car was nice, I don't think he had any air conditioning because I remember it being extremely hot the entire ride up to Georgia. Because I didn't know anything about Pete, I think we rode five hours straight without saying more than five words to each other. I was so nervous that I didn't even speak up when I really had to go to the bathroom. Thank God for a strong bladder. Even though the ride was a little socially uncomfortable for me, I was very appreciative of the ride.

When we arrived at Upatoi Terrace on Fort Benning, I was satisfied with our humble quarters. I think that I was expecting a nice big brick house or something with lots of yard space. Since we were a small family, just my mom and I, we received a small apartment. It consisted of five little rooms: two bedrooms, which were right next to each other; a living room; a kitchen; and a single bathroom. The outside was made out of schoolhouse red bricks. The inside walls were painted cinder blocks, and the floor was plain and simple tile. My bedroom furniture and our dining room table were old, used military issued furniture. There was nothing spectacular about our house, but at least the roof was intact and I didn't have to worry about any snakes falling down on my head. My mom was always a neat freak, so our house was usually spotless and smelled like bleach.

No sooner had I gotten to my new house and put my bags on the floor than there was a knock on the front door. When I looked up at the storm door there was a slightly tall, medium-built, somewhat good-looking man with a tight boxed cut standing there. He pretty much walked in like he owned the place.

"Oh hi, Keith," my mom said as he pecked her on the cheek.

"Danielle, this is my friend Keith," my mom said.

I had been around long enough to know what the true meaning of friend was when it came to my parents. "My friend" was a term for someone who was always going to be in my way when it came to me getting my parent's attention. These "friends" were always at our house, always eating our food, and always trying hard to get into my business.

Later on that first night, Keith took us out to dinner at one of the Chinese restaurants in Columbus. Things were going pretty decently I thought. I didn't talk much and it was mainly because I didn't know anything about Keith. Apparently he took my silence as a sign that I did not approve of him. When my mom had stepped away to go to the restroom, Keith said to me, "I guess you don't really like me that much. Well, tough. You're just going to have to live with it." He said this very slyly with a confident look upon his face. It was as if he knew he already had my mom wrapped around his finger.

I was shocked. I had no clue what to say to that. *How dare he talk to me that way? Who does he think he is?*

I couldn't wait to get home that night to tell my mom what he said. I thought for sure that she would get rid of him after I told her how he spoke to me. Then it would just be my mom and me. I was sick of outsiders trying to come in and get in the way of my relationship with my parents. Whenever my mom or dad had a new boyfriend or girlfriend around, I just felt like a distraction. Like I just did not belong in the picture.

After Keith dropped us off, I immediately said to my mom, "You know what he said to me when you left the table?"

"What?" my mom asked.

"He said that I was acting like I didn't like him and that that was just tough because I was going to have to just live with it."

My mom just laughed, "Oh, girl, he was just teasing you. He's a really nice person."

What! You're just going to brush it off like that?!

"Whatever," I said. "I'm going to get ready for bed because I'm tired." I was very angry at my mom for taking his side.

Her nose must be wide open, as my Mudea used to say about my cousin Rashawn when he seemed interested in a girl. *I can't believe she took his side.* She just brushed me off like what I said was not even important. This wouldn't be the last time she did this with Keith.

When I got to Columbus, it was just two weeks before the

school year was to start. My mom had already filled out the paperwork to enroll me at Spencer High School, home of the Greenwaves. I just had to take my shot record to the school board office and I was good to go. I didn't know anybody in my neighborhood and had no clue about anything in Columbus, so I was real anxious to start school and see what the people were like.

We didn't have much money, so I didn't really get to shop much for new school clothes. But because my mom and I both wore a size six, all of her clothes were new to me, and she let me wear whatever I wanted of hers to school. My mom has always had a nice figure, and back then she liked to wear clothes that showed that off a little. She and I were shaped alike, so her clothes really fit me.

When my first day of school rolled around, I was so nervous. I was very excited about getting to start fresh with a clean slate and not having to worry about people picking on me. However, I was sort of afraid because I had not known anything about anyplace outside of Callahan. I was so nervous I had my mom walk me to my first period class. I was a big grown ninth grader with my mommy walking me to class. And I was not the least bit embarrassed.

It didn't take long for me to make friends. This really nice girl from my first period class came up to me, and we became instant friends. Her name was Dione. She and I hung out a lot when we first started school. We went to the fair together and everything. Her parents were military, though, like mine so she ended up moving away shortly after school started. I was pretty bummed about that.

I also met this sort of hyper yet nice girl named Kanesha. Kanesha was an interesting girl. She loved to talk about *everybody*. And she was *loud*. You could hear her laughing from across the school's campus. I'm not sure if I really liked her or if I just liked hanging out with her because that would keep me from having to be by myself. At times I did feel sort of embarrassed about hanging out with her because she wasn't what I considered cool. She wasn't really athletic and not too many other people seemed to care for her. I really wanted to be a part of the "in" crowd. Especially since I was rather popular back home. People who were good in athletics usually were pretty popular.

Well, my chance to be in the "in" crowd finally came. I somehow met this girl named Lavelle. Lavelle was short like me with a little lighter complexion and a cute shape. She sort of reminded me of myself. She and I hit it off kind of well from the beginning. She told me that she played softball. Well, my heart just skipped a beat because softball was still my favorite thing in the world, and I really wanted to be a part of the team. She took me over and introduced me to the coach, Mr. Mac. Mr. Mac was thrilled about me wanting to join the team but told me that I would have to get permission from my mom and that I would have to sit out a few games since the season had already begun. Of course my mom said yes, and I was soon on my way to the realm of popularity being one of the softball players.

Our softball team, known as the Lady Waves, got much respect. We always had a winning season, and whenever we came to town, people knew we were no pushovers. Coach Mac was like a new father for me. Not only was he interested in my ability to play softball, but he always made sure that my grades stayed up. Softball was *always* secondary. He taught us all about dedication and discipline.

Soon as a freshman I was hanging out with some of the juniors and seniors in my class. Probably only a couple of months into high school, I got what I considered to be my first real boyfriend.

His name was Terrell. When I first saw him at the fair, I dragged Dione all over the fairgrounds following him around because I thought he was the cutest and finest thing I had ever seen. He had no idea who I was or that I was following him. And I had no idea he was going to be going to Spencer, let alone be in my algebra class. When I saw him at school, my heart skipped a beat. Even though I had a huge crush on him, I was still way too shy to talk to him. The only reason we ever started calling ourselves boyfriend and girlfriend was because I met this girl named Tweety who told me that he had been checking me out and wanted to go with me. I shrugged my shoulders like I really didn't care and said, "Okay."

Terrell and I dated for a couple of months. Again, the mainstay of our relationship was that of passing notes. We never talked on the phone. I'm not sure if my mom would have allowed me to talk to boys at that point anyway.

I remember one night I hung out with these two girls who were juniors. They picked me up from home, and we went to a party that one of the girls' boyfriends was having. He played football along with Terrell, so I knew Terrell was going to be there.

I was looking so cute in my black and white polka dot short tight skirt with ankle length white tights with the lace around the bottom. My shirt was one of those shear shirts with half being black and white polka dots and the other half flowers. I was *fly!*

Well, when I saw Terrell, I almost peed myself because this would be our first boyfriend-girlfriend interaction outside of school. I had already made up my mind that I was going to get my first kiss that night. When he came over to speak to me, I did not know what to say. We chit chatted for a bit, nothing important. Finally I decided I was getting cold and wanted to go into the house to the party. Before I left, I closed my eyes and went for it. The entire time I was hoping that my lips didn't end up on his nose, his eyes, or his chin. That would have been terribly embarrassing if I had missed his lips all together. But I didn't. I could tell he was kind of shocked. After the kiss, I turned around and walked off like it was no big deal. Tryin' to be cool like I knew exactly what I was doing. When I got in the house, I had to sit my behind down somewhere to try to calm my nerves. My heart was racing a million miles a minute. I'm not sure if it was because I liked him that much or because that was the first time I had ever put my lips on a boy. Either way, I was proud of myself. I had overcome one of my biggest fears.

My relationship didn't last but for a couple of months with Terrell. Even though he was really cute, I think that I began to get bored with him. I'm not completely sure what the problem was. All I know is that around January of my freshman year I was sicker than I had ever been in my life. Fever, cough, body aches, throwing up. This went on for what seemed like forever. I was out of school for an entire week before I got better. And do you know that boy did not call me one time to check on me and see how I was doing?

Even though I probably would have been extremely nervous about talking to him, I was still pretty upset that he didn't call me. Something had to give.

When I got back to school, everyone asked where I had been and commented on the fact that I had lost weight. I told them that I had bronchitis and had to go to the doctor and get put on antibiotics. Terrell just carried on as if I had never been absent from school at all. I began to wonder if he really cared about me at all.

One day after school before softball practice, we were standing along the wall in the hallway by the lockers. I went up to Terrell and told him that I didn't feel the same way about him and that I wanted to break up. I then walked away. I left him standing on the wall with a very dumbfounded look on his face. On the way out of the locker rooms to the softball field, several of his football buddies came up to me asking why I had dumped their boy. They said he was heartbroken. I just shrugged my shoulders and walked on out to the field. Of course they said I had done him wrong. *Oh well.*

My freshman year at Spencer High School was very interesting. Almost every week there was a huge fight between the boys from Washington Heights and the boys from Cusseta. The winner of the battle would change every week. It was just like one of those high school movies on TV that I always thought were so interesting to watch. Gangs, guns, fights. You name it. Well, I don't think that we actually had gangs. I think they were just a bunch of neighborhood dudes who felt like they had something to prove. I remember one morning while we were walking to the cafeteria from the bus, a Cusseta boy came and busted a Washington Heights boy in the head with a bottle right in front of us. After that boys came running out of the woodwork to fight. People were coming into the cafeteria with blood running all down their faces.

There was a lot of commotion and confusion that morning and a lot of the teachers did not know what to do. The next thing we saw was our principal walking with a couple of cops looking for the perpetrators. A lot of people were suspended that day.

I was one of about five hundred freshmen in my class. Seventy five percent of my school was military. The majority of the other students were from Columbus and a small percentage was bused in from the small country town outside of Columbus called Cusseta. The Cusseta students were bused in to Spencer because their high school had burned down and a new one was being built. About sixty percent of us were black, twenty percent were Hispanic, seventeen percent were white, and the rest were from other countries.

Because everyone knew that Cusseta was such a poor town, pretty much everyone from Cusseta wanted to prove that they were more than just country. A large number of the people who lived in Cusseta worked in the chicken plant. I think a lot of the kids from there pretty much felt that the chicken plant was where they were heading after high school, so rarely did they try to really exert themselves in school. Although they were very athletic, I hardly heard any of their names called on the honor role. Small town mentality. This was the type of thinking I was really trying to get away from. I still thought they were cool and ended up hanging out with a lot of the Cusseta girls because we were all athletes.

Life at Spencer was very interesting to me. Coming from

a small town where everyone knew everyone else, this was different to me. I actually had a choice of who I would hang out with. My first year, I met two of my very best friends, Carlee and Renae. I met Carlee in my gym class. She was this friendly, outgoing, popular girl that all of the guys seemed to have a crush on. She seemed to know everybody. Renae and I started hanging out while playing basketball. She was more of a tomboy who was also pretty popular and got along rather well with everyone. Both Carlee and Renae had siblings at Spencer. Carlee had an older sister who was really pretty. She also seemed to have a lot of boys after her. Renae had an older sister who was dating a guy who was considered to be the biggest troublemaker at the school. She was in love with this guy. Nobody messed with him because he was so erratic and liable to do anything to you. Renae also had a younger brother who was also in my gym class. He was very short but cute. He always went around looking at all of the girls' behinds trying to see who he could get with.

I think that was the goal of all of the boys at Spencer. Get in where you fit in. There must have been some sort of competition on getting with as many girls as possible because hardly any of those guys were faithful. You would see them with one girl this week and another one the next week. And the poor girls would be so heartbroken believing that these little sneaky, lying dudes were really into them.

When I got to Spencer, I wasn't tryin' to hear it. I was going to keep my virginity until I got married. I did not care what anybody said to me, how much they said they liked me, I just was not trying to hear it. Plus, I was still way too shy to talk to a guy in a romantic way, let alone consider even having sex with him. I was going to focus on my schoolwork and my sports and leave those boys where they were. By that time, I had decided that I no longer wanted to be a lawyer like Claire Huxtable. I was going to be more like Cliff and be the doctor.

Just like everything else, the work in high school came very easy to me. Making straight A's was nothing but a thing. I almost did it without any effort. Back then I had a mind like a sponge that could absorb pretty much anything that the teacher said. I really did not take many notes or anything.

I did talk to a couple of guys, but I never let it turn into anything serious. Usually I would break up with them if they tried to get too close.

During my freshman year, I played softball, basketball, and was on the track team. Our softball team did really well that year. We only failed to go to the state championships by losing one game to Columbus High School. We beat every other team in Columbus, Georgia, and the surrounding counties. I was the starting second baseman. It was a little bit of an adjustment to me because all of my life I had played fast pitch softball but in Columbus we played slow pitch. It was weird watching that ball drop down from such a high arch. My timing was way off at first, but I eventually got the hang of it and hit several homeruns. My batting average was always well above three hundred.

I've Got a New Home

When I got to Columbus, one of my mom's first goals was for us to find a church home. We visited a few churches that I thought were so boring that I didn't want to visit them again. I was starting to get discouraged in thinking that we would never find a church in Columbus that reminded me of By Faith. Well, boy was I wrong.

The Sunday that we visited The Bread, I knew that we were at home. There were several teenagers there around my age, and boy was this place filled with the spirit. People were singing, shouting, jumping all around. And over in the corner I saw him. Mr. Organ Player. Mr. Organ Player was the pastor's oldest son. I thought he was one of the cutest boys I had ever seen. Even cuter than drummer boy in Florida. *Oh, I was so over drummer boy.* When he came up to me after church and asked for my phone number, I was more than happy to give it to him.

I think he called me that night. We chit chatted about various things. I basically just answered whatever questions he had. He asked me a lot of questions about myself. I told him I was from Florida and had just moved to Columbus to live with my mom who was in the army. I also told him that I had plans of becoming a doctor. I think from our conversation he could tell that I wasn't someone he was going to be able to play games with.

He didn't call me very much after that. We would always speak at church. He would even talk to me about the other girls he was involved with at the church.

I was cool with pretty much all of the guys at our church. One guy who we called DeeDee had the sweetest voice I had ever heard. That boy could sing! He and I were sort of like brother and sister. He would always come to me and talk about his problems. I really hoped that he would make it big someday as a gospel singer.

DeeDee had an older brother who I was cool with as well. I could tell that he had a serious crush on me, but I was interested in Mr. Organ Player, so I made sure I never gave him the impression that I was interested. I always treated him like a good friend. We even ended up going to my senior prom together as friends because he and I were just that cool.

There were a few girls at our church who I mostly just spoke to at church. We never really hung out together because most of us had completely different personalities. I was a really outgoing person, but I really wasn't as into boys as they were. Yes, I had a few crushes, but that was pretty much as far as it went. With me being so cool with the guys in the church, they pretty much told me about all of the girls there that they had messed with. As soon as a new girl walked into that church, they would pounce. If she was weak enough, she would end up being another one of their prey. That was how I found out that Mr. Organ Player would never be anyone that I would allow myself to be serious about. He was the biggest playa out of all of them. He would always be known to me as Mr. Organ Playa, and I had learned from watching the women in my life who had been played that I was not going to allow myself to be a statistic.

I think the fact that I had such a huge crush on him, yet knew so much about how he was with girls really made me angry. He and I did not get along very well after I found out what he was really all about. I think the pastor was always trying to get the two of us to like each other because he could tell that I was someone who was going to make something out of myself, but I was not stupid enough to allow myself to really fall for him. He was not about to use me and then go around bragging about it.

The funny thing about the girls they would mess with was that they would be the main ones up in the choir stand leading the songs and pretending to have the Holy Ghost. They would go from being laid up with some guy on Saturday night to stepping on my feet while shouting on Sunday morning. I remember one Sunday one of the girls Organ Playa was messing with was standing next to me in the choir stand. We were both sopranos. We were in the middle of singing a song, and I do have to admit that the spirit was high. All of a sudden she started shouting. She was slinging her head, waving her arms, and jumping up and down as if she was really trying to shake something evil off of her. When she jumped up, the heel of her right shoe jabbed me in my left toes. I so dearly wanted to push her out of the choir stand directly onto the altar because I knew she was faking. I knew that she had been with Mr. Organ Playa the night before. I just can't stand a fake.

I don't know why women think that pretending to be filled with the Holy Spirit will attract a man's attention. If he is really spirit filled, eventually he's going to find out you are not for real. God will not allow his chosen to be deceived. If you truly are a child of God and are filled with the Holy Spirit, He gives you the power of discernment. And I really hope they don't truly believe that they can fool God. You can't fake forever. Plus when you act one way in church and then act a completely different way once you are outside of the walls of the sanctuary, no one is going to take you seriously. That's why a lot of people are staying away from church now because of all of the hypocrites that they meet when they're there. And, unfortunately, they will find some hypocrites in almost every church that they go to.

Well, needless to say, we did join The Bread, and it ended up becoming a huge part of our lives. We met a lot of good people in that church who we ended up spending lots of time with.

The pastor and the first lady were extremely sweet people. They treated us like we were a part of their family and the pastor often referred to us as his daughters. The majority of the first lady's family members attended The Bread and we were cool with all of them. My mom has always been sort of a pastor's aid type of person, and it was no different in that church. Whatever the pastor and first lady needed, she did.

I remember when we first joined the church, for some reason the pastor called my mom up to sing a solo. Why did he do that? I could see the look on her face when she walked up there, and I knew exactly what was about to come out of her mouth next.

"I would like for my daughter to come up here and help me sing this song," she said.

My heart dropped to my feet and my face turned beet red. I sat there for a few seconds trying to pretend that I didn't hear her. She wasn't trying to hear that. She made this motion with her hands and had this stern look on her face that I dared not resist. I reluctantly dragged myself up to the microphone with my heart racing a hundred miles a minute. I was so nervous that my palms and the soles of my feet began to sweat. I'm pretty sure my face was flushed.

"This is an old song we used to sing at our home church in Florida. It talks about how Jesus gave his life for us for all of our sins. He did not have to make such a huge sacrifice for such an undeserving people, but I'm so very glad that He did. The song is titled 'How Much Do I Owe Him?'"

I was so embarrassed. Not only did I have to get up and sing in front of Mr. Organ Playa, but I had to sing this old, boring song. After we finished singing, I was ready to go home. I could tell by the look on Organ Playa's younger brothers' faces that I was not going to be able to live that one down for a while. After they got to know me, they picked on me about that for the longest. They would always say, "What was the name of that song your mama made you sing?" I dared not tell them.

Jesus Stepped in on Time

When I moved with my mom, she had been in the army for about four years. As an E4, she probably made about thirty thousand dollars a year before taxes. Being a single mom on an E4's salary was not easy, and my dad rarely sent any money to help out with the cost of taking care of me. My mom did the best she could with the little that she had. I knew we didn't have a whole lot of money, so I tried not to ask for too much, but as a teenager, it was hard not to want some of the things that my peers had and often considered a necessity to being cool.

My mom was always going into her secret stash or scraping up change from here and there to make sure I had money for lunch. She would always go without things that she desired in order to make sure we had food to eat, gas in the car, and the items that I needed for sports such as cleats for softball, tennis shoes for basketball, or uniforms for track and cheerleading. We lived on base, so we never had to worry about rent or utilities, thank God.

I remember one time my mom had to go to one of those fast cash places to help get us through. I remember her having to sign away the title of our blue 1985 Chrysler LeBaron with its leaky sunroof and all so that we could have $500. She had to pay the money back in two weeks or else we would lose our car. And Lord knows how much interest she had to pay on that loan, but we had to eat. Those places know they get over on poor people. When you're a mom, you'll sacrifice anything to make sure that your children can eat. Needless to say, my mom was able to pay back her loan and we kept our little car. It wasn't anything fancy, but it was all we had. She had bought the little used car after her other car had gotten repossessed. The white doctor that she had dated up at Fort Bragg had cosigned with her to get a nice red Pontiac Lemans. When we moved to Georgia, my mom sort of stopped making the payments on the car. She knew sooner or later they were going to come and get it but she didn't care. She seemed a little angry at the doctor when she talked about him. I never knew what that was all about. I just know that one morning we woke up and the Lemans was gone just as she had anticipated. That same day she came home with our little LeBaron.

I remember another time when we were low on money, my mom planned to just go to the Quickie Mart after church and buy some bologna for me to make sandwiches for the week and take them for my lunch. When we got out of the car, we headed for the door of the store. My mom was walking behind me. I had almost reached the door to the store when my mom all of a sudden grabbed my arm and said, "Let's go!"

"Why?" I asked confused.

"Girl, don't ask me any questions, just get in the car."

Even though I was confused, I knew to follow directions. When I got into the car, my mom nervously showed me this wad of twenties that she had found on the ground right in front of the store. My mom had snatched the money up off the ground so quick that I had not even seen her bend over. About five different people had just walked into the store right before us and none of them had seen the money. We were in the right place at the right time to receive that blessing. I had money for lunch and we had money for groceries and gas. My mom said she had been praying at church because she didn't know how she was going to get the money she needed to get us through the rest of the month. She commented on how good God was and how He always stepped in for us right on time. No matter how hard things were for us, God always came through. Two little black women from the little town of Callahan, Florida, against the world. We could not lose as long as God was on our side. I agree with David when he said in Psalms 37 that he had never seen the righteous forsaken nor his seed beg for bread. God was always my everything, and I never had to beg for anything, no matter what.

Lead Us Not Into Temptation

As time went on, I had pretty much established myself at Spencer High School. People knew who I was and I began to increase in popularity. More and more boys were noticing my nice shape in the little tight jeans that I enjoyed wearing because of the attention I received. I liked the fact that boys noticed me, but I did not want them to make any sexual comments to me and definitely did not want them to try and touch me in any way.

Through hanging out with my friend Renae, I noticed this light-skinned boy with a curly high-topped fade who was always hanging out with Renae's sister Tonya's boyfriend John. John was a real ruff neck, but Tonya was in love with him. The light-skinned dude's name was Ricky. Renae told me he was checking me out and wanted to know if he could have my number. He was truly the cutest boy who had ever wanted to holla at me, so of course I said he could have my number. He called me that night and we talked for a long time. We talked a little about everything. He seemed like a nice boy, but I could tell that he was used to girls drooling all over him. He had two sisters and one younger brother.

I was a little nervous about being his girlfriend because I had heard rumors about how he had gotten his previous girlfriend to have sex with him and then he had dumped her. I was hoping that he didn't have plans to try the same thing with me. I felt that I was much smarter than the average girl, and if he ever tried to pressure me into having sex, I would just dump him.

He and I hung out a lot together at school. Even though kissing was not allowed at school, we would find nice little places to show our affection for each other. I remember one time as we were walking down the hallway, Ricky noticed this other boy looking at my butt. He turned around to the boy and said, "It's nice, isn't it?" as if to say, "Don't even think about it, it's all mine." The boy didn't even try to hide the fact that he was looking. He just kind of grinned and walked off.

Ricky and I used to meet up at my locker after every class. Eventually he just started putting all of his books into my locker. I was really starting to dig this guy, and I thought that maybe he was the one. Because I could not date, however, the only place I really ever got to see Ricky was at school. Occasionally he would stop by my house for a little while, but it was always when he was on the way to go hang out with John. The two of them seemed inseparable.

You would not believe the number of girls who began to dislike me after people found out that Ricky and I were dating. I remember being at Krystal's one day going through the drive thru. As I was pulling up to the speaker, this girl whom I did not recognize yelled out from the driver's side car window in front of me, "You big faced trick!" I never knew who she was or what that was all about, but I was sure it was somebody who wanted Ricky. Girls would always give me the crooked eye when we walked down the hallway together. None of them scared me, though, because I knew they weren't crazy enough to try anything at school.

The longer I stayed with Ricky, the more curious I became about sex. It was not that he was pressuring me at all. He had not been inappropriate with me in any way. It's just that when I was with him I felt all of these strange sensations and emotions that

I had never felt before. All of my friends kept telling me that I didn't know what I was missing by remaining a virgin. They said that having sex felt better than anything else they could think of. Up until then I just shrugged them off and said, "whatever," but now I was getting a little curious. I seriously began to think about giving it up to Ricky.

On one hand, I was extremely curious about having sex with Ricky. On the other hand, I was scared. What if he did me the same way he did his previous girlfriend and dumped me after I gave it up? What if my mama found out? What if I got pregnant? These were all thoughts that I could not seem to shake. Every time I thought I was ready to do it, one of these thoughts would pop into my head and I would quickly change my mind.

One night I really thought that I was ready. My mom worked shift work as an army nurse, so I was often at home by myself. One Saturday night John brought Ricky by for a visit. When he called and said he was on his way over, I quickly hopped in the shower, lotioned up real good, and threw on some body spray and perfume, taking special care to make sure that I smelled good in all of the right places. When Ricky got there, I gave him a quick kiss and he and John came in. I knew better than to have people over to the house when my mom wasn't there, but that night I was bored out of my mind and really did not care. That was, as long as I didn't get caught.

Ricky, John, and I sat on the couch and talked and watched TV for a bit. After a little while, Ricky and I went back into my room where we talked some more. After we had talked for a while Ricky gave me another kiss and then told me he and John were about to go to a party. *What!* I thought in my head. *You would rather go to a party than to stay here with me?* I'm pretty sure he had no clue what was on my mind because when we started dating I had made it clear to him that I was going to wait until I was married to have sex.

"I hope you have fun," I lied.

I guess this just isn't the night, I thought to myself as I closed the door behind John and Ricky. I would soon appreciate the fact that there was a party for him to go to that night.

My mom and I went home to Florida for pretty much every holiday that she had off. Thanksgiving 1991 was no different. I was excited to go home to see my dad since I had not seen him in several months, and because he did not have a phone, I rarely got to talk to him. It was late the night before Thanksgiving when we got to Callahan, so when we got to Nana's house we basically said our hellos and went to sleep. The next day I had planned to go have dinner with my dad, Mudea, Aunt M, Aunt E, and the rest of the family over at Uncle Jonathan's house. Uncle Jonathan had a good job in Jacksonville, so he and Aunt Emily lived in a nice house on the north side of town over by Ribault High School. I used to like going over there because there were a lot of cute boys in his neighborhood. This time I wasn't studying any of those boys because I had a high yellow boy with a curly high top fade that I was crazy about. Kid from Kid-n-Play had absolutely nothing on him.

Thanksgiving Day was nice. My cousins and I hung out together and walked around the neighborhood. Dinner was excellent as usual. The folks in my family could always throw down in the kitchen. If we could have ever worked together and agreed on anything, we could all have definitely made it rich in the restaurant industry. One of the disappointing things about some black folks is that a lot of times we feel we need to be in competition with each other instead of helping one another. Even people in the same family. We're always trying to outdo the next person. I truly do not believe that is the way God intended for it to be. That's why we as black folks don't ever have anything to pass along to our children. It's because we don't work together to build anything of value. And we are so quick to blame everyone else for what we don't have. My family was no different. We all need to wake up and realize that sometimes you've just got to make things happen. There is no limit to what God can do.

Well, like I said, dinner was good. However the conversation that took place after dinner was no fun for me at all. I honestly felt like all of a sudden everybody's attention had turned to me and that I was in the hot seat being interrogated.

I had told my dad about my new boyfriend earlier that evening. Now all of a sudden it became a very interesting topic to my father and was something that he needed to gain a clearer understanding of. Also, since my parents had gotten a divorce, my dad would always drill me on what my mom had been doing.

We were all sitting at the dinner table talking. My aunt M asked me how I liked living in Georgia and how school was going. I told her that I liked it, I was still making all A's, and that I had a lot of friends. She asked me if I had a boyfriend, and I told her I did and that his name was Ricky.

All of a sudden out of the blue, my dad said angrily, "Every time I talk to you, you have a new boyfriend. Why can't you just stick with one boy? What are you up there doing with them boys? Your mama is always working leaving you at home by yourself. And ain't no tellin' who she got coming in and out of the house. How do I know you're not up there sluttin' around?!"

I think I stopped breathing for a full minute after my dad said that. First of all, I was shocked that he would say something like that to me. And how could he just embarrass me like that in front of everybody? Sluttin' around? At fifteen, I was the only one of my friends who was still a virgin. The only reason I kept changing boyfriends was because I was so afraid that if I stayed with them too long they would be expecting me to have sex with them.

I was so upset with my father at that moment that my chest was hurting. I had so much pressure building up in my head that I just had to get away from everybody before I said something that I would regret to my father. I hopped up from that table so fast that I almost knocked my chair over.

"Danielle, you sit your tail right back down in this chair. I'm not finished talking to you yet."

"Elroy, leave her alone," my aunt M said.

I ran down the hallway to one of the guest rooms in my uncle's house. I laid face down across the bed and sobbed uncontrollably. My aunt M came into the room behind me and put her hands on my back.

"Why are you so upset, Danielle?"

"Because my dad just called me a slut. What did I do to deserve that?" I managed to get out in between sobs.

"Your dad is just a little stressed. I think he really misses you and your mother and he just doesn't know how to show it. He really loves you," Aunt M said.

"Well, he has a terrible way of showing it," I said.

I stayed in the room until it was time to go. On the car ride back to Nana's house, I did not say a word to anyone. I was still very angry with my dad. I may have said a couple of words to Rashawn, but that was about it.

When we pulled into Nana's yard, I just jumped out of the car without saying anything to anyone. As soon as I jumped out of the car I started crying again. I ran into Nana's front door straight past everyone. I just wanted to get to my mom.

"What's wrong with you?" one of my aunts asked.

I did not say anything. I just held my hands over my face and ran to the back of the trailer into Nana's room. My mom was right behind me.

"Girl, what's wrong with you?" my mom asked with this concerned look on her face.

I tried to calm myself down so that I could tell her. "He basically called me a slut in front of everybody."

"What!" my mom exclaimed.

I tried to tell my mom word for word everything that had transpired. The more I talked, the more upset I got. I could see that my mom was getting upset as well.

"I done told him that if he wants to know anything about me he needs to come to me and not put you in the middle. And how dare he talk to you like that?! He's the one that's the slut. That's why we're not together now. As a matter of fact, I'm 'bout to go over there right now and give him a piece of my mind. He ain't fixin' to be bringing you back to me crying like this."

"No, Ma. I don't want you to go over there. He ain't worth it. I'll be all right. I'm just not going to talk to him anymore. There's somethin' wrong with him."

After my mom saw that I was all right, she calmed down. The last thing I wanted was for this to go any further than it had. I definitely didn't want any craziness between my parents. I didn't talk to my dad for a full year after that, and my mom never tried to make me call him. And of course, given the type of person my dad was—never wrong—he never called me either. Oh well.

Father, I Stretch My Hands to Thee

After Thanksgiving weekend was over, it was back to the grind. School, sports, community service, Ricky. I was a busy girl. My mom always used to say to me, "Girl, you can't do everything." If there were more hours in the day and if she would have allowed me, I definitely would have tried.

We had just ended another softball season where we had missed going to the state championship by one game again. We were now into basketball season. I was a sophomore and this was my second year on the team. The previous year I played only junior varsity. This year I was the starting JV point guard and also played in the varsity games when they needed someone quick to get in to steal the ball.

One weekend a group of my friends and I all went down to Cusseta to a "party." The "party" was at one of the little hole in the wall clubs deep down in the country. I was shocked that my mom let me go. I think the fact that she had a male friend come in to visit her from Florida had something to do with her letting me out of the house. My friends used to always wonder why my mom never let me go anywhere or do anything. "You get straight A's and you still can't go anywhere," my friend Renae would often say.

Well, that night I was looking fly as always. I don't know if I realized Ricky was going to be at the party, but he was there—he and John. I honestly tried to act like I wasn't studyin' him because I was sort of mad at him about something that had happened about a week earlier.

About a week prior to the party, John, Ricky, and Renae came to pick me up and we were all going to just go riding around and hang out for a while. Renae had forgotten something at her house, so we stopped by there real quick. When we came back downstairs after getting what she needed, John and Ricky were gone.

"Those sorry fools," Renae said. "How they just gon' leave us like that."

I called Ricky's house, and of course they didn't answer the phone. I was hot. I called back in about five minutes and he answered.

"Hello," Ricky said as if he didn't know who was calling.

"Why did y'all leave us?!" I said.

"John said y'all were taking too long and he was ready to go. He was driving, so I didn't have a choice but to go, too."

"You lyin'. I'll bet y'all got some girls over there, don't you?" I accused.

"Naw. Ain't no girls over here," he stated.

"Whatever," I said. "We're coming over there."

"I'm telling you there ain't no girls over here."

"We'll see," I said. I really think that he thought I was playing. He knew we didn't have a car to get around there so he probably thought that we were just stuck.

"Who can we call to take us over there, Renae?"

"I don't know," she said.

I jokingly said, "Well, let's call Pooky."

"All right," Renae said as she grabbed the phone from me.

Pooky was a guy from school who had a huge crush on me. He was the brother of one of my friends who I had been cool with since the ninth grade. He was a nice guy, but I was so crazy about Ricky that I wasn't really interested in him. Pooky knew that I was crazy about Ricky, but that night I needed some ammunition and Pooky was it.

When we called Pooky, he immediately said that he would come and get us. Within fifteen minutes, Pooky and his cousin Mo were outside to get us. Renae had a huge crush on Mo, who was a star football player in Columbus, so she was thrilled. Mo actually went on to play in the NFL after attending college in Kentucky.

"Pooky, do you mind taking me over to Ricky's house real quick? I think he has some girls over there, and I want to see for myself."

"All right," he said. I think he was hoping Ricky did have some girls over there so that I would break up with him. Then he would have his chance to get with me.

When we pulled up in front of Ricky's house, all of the lights were out. I knew he was home because I saw John's car out front, so I went and rang the doorbell. He didn't answer at first, so I banged on the door. He had already told me that his family was out for the evening, so I wasn't worried about disturbing his parents.

"Open the door, Ricky. I know you're in there!" I yelled.

Finally he peeked out of the window, and he saw Pooky's car out front. That's when he decided to open the door. "What are you doing with him?" he asked.

"I know you have some girls in there. Where are they? You must have let them go out of the back door."

Renae and I looked through the dark house, but we didn't see anyone in there but John who was sitting there with a goofy look on his face.

"Where do you think you are about to go with Pooky?" Ricky asked me again.

"Why do you care? If you really cared, you would not have left us at Renae's house. Now I gotta go," I said.

"You ain't going nowhere with him," he said as he grabbed my arm.

"Let me go!" I yelled.

I kept yanking my arm out of his grasp, but every time I did, he would grab my arm even harder. The more I tried to get away, the harder he would grab my arms. Being that I was very athletic, I was always strong for a girl my size. Therefore, he had a hard time holding on to me. I was five foot two and about 126 pounds with very muscular arms and legs. Ricky was about five foot ten and possibly weighed 150 at the most. He was real skinny. The biggest thing on him was his hair.

Well, anyways, eventually he was able to pin me up against the front door of his house.

"Let her go!" Renae yelled grabbing Ricky by his arms.

I thought about kicking him in the groin, but I didn't do it because shortly after he pinned me on the wall, he let me go. By that time both Pooky and Mo had gotten out of the car and were looking like they wanted to come handle some business. Renae and I ran to the car and hopped in. Pooky asked if I was all right. I said, "Yes," and we drove off.

Pooky took us to his house. For some strange reason, everybody's parents were gone that weekend. My mom was TDY for a few weeks and one of her friends was there staying with me, but she had just taken off for the weekend without letting me know where she had gone. I had no clue when she was going to be back. I kept calling back to the house to let her know that I was with Renae, but I never got an answer at the house.

Oh well, I thought as I made myself comfortable on Pooky's couch. Pooky had a very nice house. He lived there with his mom and his sister. His room was really nice with all white linen and a canopy bed. This was the type of room I wished I had.

"Y'all want a wine cooler?" Pooky asked.

"Naw, I'm all right," Renae said.

I was so upset with Ricky at that moment until I needed something. "I'll take one," I said before I had even thought about it. I had never had anything alcoholic before, so I had no clue what to expect. At that moment, though, I really did not care. My mom was away, my dad wasn't speaking to me, and my boyfriend was trippin'. *Yeah, give me something to drink.*

Looking back on that night, I could easily see how weak-minded people become addicted to alcohol and drugs. When you are feeling so low and disappointed, that's when the devil always presents the perfect opportunity for you to try something you may never have otherwise tried. For me, it was just a wine cooler, but for someone else in that same situation, it may have been cocaine or heroin. Just that one low moment has sent so many people spiraling down the wrong pathway. Thank God for grace because I could have gotten myself into anything that night.

Well, anyways, I sipped on my little wine cooler all night. It was very sweet and actually tasted pretty good. By the time I got halfway finished with it, I was starting to feel a little tipsy. I think Pooky realized that I was tipsy because I kept giggling and talking. He and I kissed a little while on his couch. Renae and Mo were hugged up on the other couch. Pooky never tried to get anything more from me than a kiss. God was really looking out for me that night, because again, there is no telling what I might have done given the way that I felt. I literally just did not care.

We eventually all fell asleep on the couches. When we woke up it was about 3:30 in the morning.

"Oh my gosh! I gotta get home," I said.

"Me, too," Renae said.

Pooky and Mo got up and took us home.

When we pulled in front of Renae's house, all of the lights were on. When she got out of the car, her mom opened up the front door and was standing there waiting on her. She said she really got it that night.

When we pulled in front of my house, I was so nervous that my hands were sweating and my heart was racing. The lights were all still out just as I had left them with the exception of the light on the front porch. I looked around the parking lot and did not see my mom's friend's car. I realized she was not there. I didn't relax, though, until I got into the house and made sure. I checked in my mom's room and the bed was empty.

Boy, did I get away with one, I sighed.

I took my clothes off and hopped into the bed. I slept like a baby.

Well, anyway, back to the "party." By that time, Ricky had apologized and was back on my good side. High school love is so trivial. When I saw him at the party, I was very excited. He was looking and smelling good as usual.

"What's up?" he said as he came over and kissed me on the cheek.

"Nothing," I said feeling all flushed.

"Let's go outside," he said.

"All right."

We went outside and talked for a while. It was early December so it was rather chilly out.

"You want to sit in the car?" he asked.

"Sure," I said.

Soon after we got in the car, Ricky started kissing me. I was cool with that, so I let him. We kissed for a long time, and eventually he was lying on top of me trying to put his hands in my pants. I kept pushing his hand away or squirming in the opposite direction. He kept asking me what was wrong and I said, "Nothing," so he kept on trying. We continued to kiss and I actually put a hickey on his neck. That was my first time doing that. No matter how hard he tried, I was not about to let him get into my pants. He was crazy if he thought I was going to do it for the first time in the backseat of some strange boy's car. I'm not even sure if I knew whose car we were in.

Eventually Ricky realized he wasn't going to get any, so he stopped trying. When we got out of the car, everybody was staring at us and smiling as if they knew what had just happened.

"Well?" one of my friends said as I walked back into the party.

"Oh, we just kissed and touched a little. Nothing more than that."

"That's cool," Stephanie said. "That's usually all I do." Stephanie was a girl that I had recently just started hanging out with. She was a year older than I was and had just transferred in from Germany. She and I played softball and basketball together. She was probably the only other girl I knew besides me who was still a virgin.

"Yeah, I wasn't about to do anything in the backseat of a car. That's gross," I said.

Initially I had agreed with my mom to be home by midnight. At about 11:30 I called my mom and asked if I could just spend the night with Stephanie. Her mom had already said she was cool with that. Again, since my mom still had company, she said yes. I figured with her male company in town she would say yes, and I was right. Normally my mom did not allow me to spend the night with anyone.

The Lord Is My Light

High school progressed as usual. Our basketball team continued to be mediocre. Regardless of whether we won or lost, we usually had fun at our games. We mainly just wanted to get through our games so that we could dress up afterwards and boy-watch during the boys' games. Those were good times. All of our games were fun except one game that stands out from the rest.

Kendrick High School was one of our rivals. There usually was a pretty big turnout, and the game was usually pretty exciting. Our JV girls' game was even good that day. We were tied right up until the end when I stole the basketball and scored the game winning basket. I was always really good at stealing the basketball. I just wasn't that great at converting my steals into two points. After I stole the ball, I would dribble so fast down the court to our basket that I often laid the ball up way too hard and missed the basket. The boy's team always picked at me about that. They often called me the brick layer.

Well, that game I came through. I stole the ball and finished it off with a lay up so pretty I could have kissed myself. I was very high after that game with excitement.

Unfortunately, my buzz didn't last long. After everyone had cleared out of the locker room, my best friend Renae and another friend of ours, Rolanda, were sitting on the bench looking at me with serious faces. Renae told me that they had something to tell me.

"What's up?" I asked trying to lighten the serious expressions on their faces.

"You might want to sit down for this one," Renae said.

"Why?" I asked as I sat down across from them.

Rolanda didn't waste any time telling me what was on her mind. "Ricky slept with Damitra Saturday night after the party."

"What?! He did what?!" I said surprised. At that moment, my heart just sank to my feet. I could not believe what I was hearing. I mean I always had a suspicion that Ricky was sleeping around on me because he definitely had not gotten anything from me, and boys like him always felt like they had to prove their manhood by getting it as often as possible. I had also seen him a couple of times around different corners in school talking to different girls. They would quickly separate when they saw me coming. Then the girls would always be looking at me cross-eyed. I really didn't care because it was me who Ricky walked through the halls with and shared a locker with. It was me who he had attempted to give the eighty dollars to in order to buy my basketball shoes (I was too stupid to just take the money). I just could not believe he had chosen to cheat on me with Damitra.

I thought that he had been acting a little strange and withdrawn when I saw him at school that day. And when I looked at the side of his neck, the hickey that I had put there seemed twice the size of what I had remembered. But, of course, I just brushed those suspicious thoughts away. Dumb me. Always giving people the benefit of the doubt.

Damitra was a Cusseta girl who had played softball and basketball with me for the past year. She was a little older than me and much, much more experienced than I was with the boys. She often bragged about how much she had gotten and how often. "They just can't resist Jane," she would often say. Jane was the name she had given to her stuff. Why Jane, I had no clue.

Damitra was about six feet tall with real short hair and a nose ring. I think that she only came to school for the socialization because I don't think that her grades were that great. I guess they were just good enough for her to play sports and graduate. She was pretty good at whatever she played though. She was tall, slim, and walked like she had just gotten off a horse.

I just could not believe that Ricky would cheat on me, a girl who had everything going for myself, with a girl like Damitra who would most likely just end up working at the chicken factory like the majority of the Cusseta people did. I guess it's true: in high school, boys don't really think about the future. All they think about is getting some. Not just some, but as much as they can, as often as they can, from as many girls as they can.

I was kind of cautious and leery of Ricky even before we had started dating because, of course, I had heard the rumors of how he had used girls to get what he wanted, and then dumped them. The girl that he dated before me was just like me, a virgin. She was really pretty and quiet. I think she was pretty smart, as well. He supposedly dumped her as soon as she gave it up to him. I was determined not to let that happen to me, although I thought about giving it up to him quite often.

The bus ride home after that game was quite interesting. I did not say a word to Damitra about sleeping with Ricky because I knew that she would be ready to fight, and so would the entire Cusseta crew. I wasn't into fighting, but I wanted to slap the taste out of her mouth that night. I realized my issue wasn't with her though. It was with Ricky. He was the one who supposedly loved me. I didn't put anything past Damitra because after hanging out with her, I realized how nasty she was.

I guess Damitra realized that I had found out about her and Ricky because I wasn't talking to her anymore. She immediately took on her ghetto attitude, even though no one had said a word to her. My best friend Renae already could not stand Damitra because Damitra had slept with Renae's sister's boyfriend. They immediately got into it and started yelling and cussing at one another. Renae called Damitra a nasty whore. Damitra tried to bring up some dirt on Renae. It was really getting out of control. Finally I just told everybody to calm down because Ricky wasn't worth all of us getting kicked off the basketball team. Thank God this all went down before the coach got on the bus or we all would have been running suicides until we dropped.

That night I could not sleep a wink. The next day at school, I took all of Ricky's stuff out of my locker and put it on the floor with the picture he had given me of himself sitting on top of the pile. Everyone laughed as they walked by. They were also laughing at him as he walked down the hallways carrying all of his books trying to find another locker to put them in. He should have had one of his other women help him carry them. Where were they now?

Ricky and I didn't speak for days. I guess he was afraid of what would come out of my mouth, and I just didn't want to hear what would come out of his. I was sure that it would just be a bunch of lies. *I was drunk* or *I don't know what happened. I didn't mean to hurt you. Whatever!*

At basketball practice that afternoon, I still did not speak to Damitra. I guess our assistant coach could sense that there was some tension between some of us, so after practice, he called Renae and I into his office to talk. I told him what had happened. He was very understanding and said he didn't put anything past girls like Damitra. He also stated that boys often times only cared about one thing. And they really don't care who they got it from or who they hurt in the process of getting it. High school boys are so self-centered. He also went on to say that girls like me often made the mistake of thinking that if we give the boys what they want then we would be able to keep them. He almost begged me not to make that mistake. I whole-heartedly promised him I wouldn't.

When we left the office, Damitra and her crew were sitting on the floor in the hallway. Of course, when we walked by, she had to make some dumb comment. "Jane got him. They just can't resist Jane," she laughed. I just wanted to kick her in the mouth. But I held my head up high and walked right past her without saying a word.

That day I had decided that I was going to show Ricky what he had missed out on. I went out and bought the shortest, tightest little spandex skirt that I could find and wore it to school the next day. *All eyes were on me!* Every boy in that school was staring at my butt and whistling just as loud as they could. I saw a look of anger on Ricky's face because he knew exactly what I was doing. News certainly traveled fast at Spencer High School because before long almost everyone knew that Ricky and I had broken up. I had all kinds of guys walking up to me asking for my phone number, but I really was not interested in any of them. I was still crazy about Ricky, and being without him really hurt.

Well, anyway, thank God for Damitra, because if it wasn't for her, I may have ended up just like Ricky's previous girlfriend—a statistic. No longer a virgin and heartbroken.

In the end, it was Damitra who got played. She was spending all kinds of money on Ricky trying to get him to be with her, but he didn't want her. He just got what he wanted then bounced. After about a week he started calling me again, asking me to get back with him. I, of course, told him no. Eventually I said we could be friends. Shortly after that, he told me his dad was getting stationed in Germany and he and his family would be moving soon. I was really crushed by this news because I realized we would really never get back together. Even though I had told him I didn't want to be with him, I had only said that because I knew it was the right thing to do. I still cared a lot for him. Oh well.

Rescue the Perishing

Life in my house seemed to be one battle after another. My mom and I could not agree on anything, and I just could not *stand* Keith. He got on my *last* nerve. However, in my mom's eyes he could do no wrong. She thought everything he did or said was so cute, or "he didn't mean anything by that." And he would just sit back with that smug little grin on his big face. He always looked like he was thinking, *I told you, I got her right where I want her. You're no match for me.* If I had ever hated anyone, I would have to say that at the time I literally hated him. *He was always around,* even when my mom was at work. I really felt uncomfortable around him, but it was like she didn't even care. Sometimes I thought she just liked the fact that there was a man in our house. He would even walk into my bedroom without knocking like he was my daddy or something.

One day I was in my room doing my usual, studying, listening to the radio, talking on the phone, and watching TV when in came Keith. He had this dumb look on his face like he wanted to ask me something but did not know how to get it out.

"May I help you with something?" I asked in a smart-alecky tone.

"Well, I was just thinking. Do we need to take you to get some birth control pills?" he asked in a matter of fact way.

"What?!?" I yelled. "You need to get out of my room. You are *not* my daddy!"

Of course he told my mom what happened and she sided with him. "He was just trying to be helpful and look out for you."

"He has no right to ask me anything about my personal life and birth control. He is not my father! You need to tell him to leave me alone!"

I was too through with him after that. I was also fed up with her for once again siding with him. How dare he ask me anything about birth control when I could hear them through the walls almost every night? Living there was almost worse than being in Callahan listening to my dad and his women through the walls. I couldn't find peace anywhere. I couldn't wait to finish high school and be out on my own. Neither one of my parents was impressing me very much. Whatever happened to role models and being examples in front of your kids? Do as I say and not as I do. Yeah right! Kids duplicate what they see their parents do. Mine didn't seem to care at that time. Oh well, I guess I had to find my own way. Now that was a scary thought. A teenager who had never really experienced anything in life before trying to find my own way. Thank God for grace.

Well, anyway, my dad was tripping, my mom's nose was wide open, and I had lost my boyfriend because I wasn't willing to give it up. I felt like my world was about to cave in. Something had to give. It seemed like the harder I prayed the worse things got for me.

Being a teenager was not fun. It seemed like all of my friends were so much happier than me. All of them had boyfriends and seemed to have a lot more freedom than I did. They were having sex and talking about how wonderful it was and how much I had been missing. I was really starting to think more and more about what it would be like to do it. I really had no clue as to what all it really involved, so my thoughts were pretty limited. All I knew was what I had seen on the X-rated movies my dad had left lying around the living room when I was little and in the nasty magazines that I knew he kept "hidden" under the bed in his bedroom. He never knew that I had gone through all of that stuff more than once.

I finally made up in my mind that I was going to do it. I was finally going to see what this sex thing was all about. I, however, did not want to take any chances of getting pregnant. I had already had one scare when I was little, when I thought I was pregnant from hunching. I didn't want to take that chance again. Since I always hung out with an older crowd, I had already been hipped to taking birth control pills. One day when I got home from school, I decided to tell my mom that I wanted to get put on pills to be on the safe side.

On one of the rare days that Keith was not there, my mom and I stood alone in the kitchen together. "Ma, just because a girl gets put on birth control pills, that doesn't mean she's fast, does it?"

"No," my mom said with a puzzled look on her face.

"Well, I'm not saying that I want to have sex yet, but I do want to get put on birth control pills. A lot of my friends say that they take them just so that they will be ready when they do decide to have sex."

"Okay, then. We'll go see Dr. Mee next week."

I was sixteen years old when I asked for birth control pills. At that time I didn't have a boyfriend and really did not know when I was going to have sex. I just knew that when I did I was not ready for a baby.

Shortly after that conversation with my mom, my best friend Renae introduced me to her boyfriend's best friend Deuce. Deuce was short, dark-skinned, kind of skinny but kind of cute. He wasn't nearly as cute as Ricky was, but at that point I didn't care. I was just tired of being alone. I had dated a guy named Stan in between Ricky and Deuce. Stan was tall, brown-skinned, and really cute, but he lived in a low income housing area and his clothes always smelled kind of sour. No matter how hard I tried to make myself like Stan, I couldn't really get into him. He was cute, he was funny, he was popular, but he also liked to drink beer and had a pretty hot temper. Stan would fight in a minute. I didn't have to worry about anybody messing with me, but no matter how hard I tried, I could not make myself like Stan like that. When I kissed him, I felt absolutely nothing.

Needless to say, I broke it off with Stan. Shortly afterward I started dating Deuce. For some reason, I liked Deuce from the moment I saw him. I really don't know what it was about him that made me like him. I think it was the fact that he went to a different high school and I really did not know anything about him. He was sort of mysterious to me. All I knew was what my friend Renae had told me about him.

Things between Deuce and I progressed pretty quickly. Before I knew it, on the Fourth of July 1992, I gave up my virginity to him. My mom was working a three to eleven shift, so I had the house all to myself, as usual. This was one of those days when Keith was nowhere to be found. I was supposed to be going to the Fourth of July celebration on base but decided to have some fireworks of my own right at home.

I was so stupid that I didn't even tell him I was a virgin. For some reason I was embarrassed to let him know. Like being a virgin was something to be ashamed of. How *stupid* was I?

Having sex for the first time was the most *painful* experience of my life. I honestly believe this was worse than childbirth. At least with childbirth you have the option of getting an epidural. I honestly think that I would have preferred to sleep through that entire experience because nothing about having sex for the first time was any fun whatsoever. My friends must have been crazy. "You don't know what you're missing," they would tell me. *Please.* I definitely could and should have waited on this.

After it was over, Deuce had to leave. I was glad because I needed to clear my head. After I walked him to the door, I came back to my bedroom to find blood all over my sheets.

Oh my God! I thought. *I have to get this cleaned up before my mom gets home.*

I took all of my sheets off the bed and washed them. I then made my bed up and when my mom got home I acted as if nothing had happened. I bled for several days after this incident and I was sore from my waist down for about a week. This was probably one of the worst experiences I had ever had. *What fool told me I didn't know what I was missing?* Well, she was right. The problem was that I wished I had kept right on missing it.

Oh well. What was done was done. And in my mind I did not plan on ever doing that again until I was married.

I, of course, called my best friend Renae and let her know what had transpired after it was all over. She, predictably, was extremely excited for me.

"Was it good?" she asked.

"I guess," I said. "You didn't tell me it was going to feel like I was being split in two. I don't think I'm going to be doing that again for a while."

"Girl, you're just saying that because it was the first time. It gets better the more you do it," Renae said.

"Whatever. I'm bleeding and hurtin' all over. I think I could have waited on this."

Renae and I chit chatted about nothing for about a half hour. I finally got off the phone to go and find some food. While I was sitting there eating it finally hit me, I was no longer a virgin. I had given my most precious gift to a boy who I didn't love. I liked him a lot, but I can't say that I loved him. Heck, I barely even knew him. I had not even met his parents yet. *Stupid, stupid, stupid!*

All of a sudden, I lost my appetite.

Precious Memories

It actually took a little longer than my mom thought for me to get in with Dr. Mee. Martin Army Hospital was a pretty busy place. She was, however, able to get my prescription for the pills. Unfortunately, along with the pills came the need to have my first pap smear. Yuck!

What was even worse than the fact that I had to have a pap smear was the fact that Dr. Mee was a man! *A man!*

My mom could tell that I was very nervous about having a pap smear. I think she could also tell that I was kind of freaking out because I had a male doctor.

"He is very nice. He's my doctor as well," she reassured me. "Do you want me to stay in the room with you for the exam?"

"You're not leaving me in there by myself!" I exclaimed.

We waited in the exam room for about twenty minutes before Dr. Mee came in. He was a thin white man with brown hair, blue eyes, and glasses. "Hi, Danielle," he said. "Your mom has told me so much about you. She told me that you are going to the eleventh grade, are a straight A student, and plan to become a doctor."

I was pretty impressed that he knew so much about me. I was starting to feel a little more comfortable around him the more we talked. He asked me a few more questions, then asked if it was okay for my mom to step out of the room for us to talk a little more. I was kind of nervous about this, but I said, "Okay."

When my mom stepped out of the room, he asked the dreaded question.

"Danielle, have you ever had sex?"

I immediately felt flushed and had no clue how to answer this question. Since my mom worked at the hospital, I just knew that he was going to tell her what I said. I seriously thought about lying to him and saying no. However, I was a terrible liar, so I decided to tell the truth.

"I had sex one time, but it hurt so bad that I am not planning on doing it again until I'm married," I said all in one breath.

Dr. Mee looked at me with understanding eyes. He then went on to talk to me about pregnancy, sexually transmitted diseases, and the need to use condoms each time I had sex, unless I was married.

"You can't always just look at someone and tell if they have a disease," he said.

I think I was trying to convince myself more than I was him that I was not going to have sex again until my wedding night. After we finished talking, my mom reentered the room. I then lay on the table for one of the most embarrassing moments of my life. I kept one arm over my face and held my mom's hand with the other throughout the entire exam. It was over in about five minutes and didn't really hurt, but was still one of the most uncomfortable experiences of my life.

Being a woman has never been easy.

Back when I was growing up, as soon as you started taking birth control pills you had to have a pap smear. And everyone had to get a pap once they turned eighteen regardless of whether they were having sex or not. Praise God for modern technology and research. Thanks to the discovery of the link between Human Papilloma Virus (HPV), which is a sexually transmitted virus, and cervical cancer, the recommendations have changed for cervical cancer screening. These days you either get a pap smear three years after the first sexual encounter or age twenty one, whichever comes first. Also, once you turn thirty, if you haven't had anything wrong with your pap smears you can potentially space your pap smear out to every three years. That is, if you are sticking with the same sexual partner. *Whoo hoo!* Being a woman just became a little easier.

In the Valley

Deuce and I continued to talk, and before I knew it, I had given in to him again. This was crazy. Why did I have such a hard time resisting him? I guess when you do it once, it makes it way easier for you to give in again and again in the future. Plus, once you do it, the boy expects to be able to get it from you whenever he wants. The best thing is to not do it at all.

Even though it didn't hurt as bad as time went on, I still didn't see what all of the fuss was about. Well then, why did I continue to do it? To this day, I cannot answer that question.

I was starting to fall deeper and deeper for Deuce. I guess it's true that once you have sex with someone, you are actually giving a piece of yourself to that person. I cared for him in a way that I never did for Ricky. Unfortunately I think our relationship meant way more to me than it did to him. We rarely went anywhere together or did anything other than have sex. We never really talked about much. He never came to any of my softball or basketball games, even when we played right there at his school. I was still crazy about him though. Even after Renae told me she had been seeing him at parties with a big faced mixed girl named Sherrell.

Even though Renae was my best friend, I didn't want to

believe her. I kept telling myself that I had not seen it for myself, so I wasn't going to jump to conclusions. Deuce would go days and days without calling me, but when he did, I was right there waiting. Finally he told me that his dad had come home from Korea and his mom had found some pictures of him with another woman, so things were strained for him at home. He had moved out of his parents' house to get away from his dad after they had almost come to blows over him cheating on his mom. He didn't tell me where he was staying, just that he didn't have access to a phone. That's why he was never home when I called and why he took so long to call me back.

Of course as a gullible dumb-dumb, I believed him.

At school more and more of my friends kept telling me that they had seen Deuce with some other girl. I even found out that the girl was older than me and had about five or six kids by several different guys.

He can't be cheating on me with someone like that, I kept telling myself.

I just refused to believe it, until one night the girl had the nerve to call my house.

"Why are you calling my man?" she had the audacity to ask me.

"What? Your man. How long have you two been together?" I asked.

"Six months," she replied.

"Well, we've actually been going together for the past nine months, so he was my man before you even entered the picture."

"Well, he said he told you it was over but that you still be callin' him and stuff."

"You are so stupid. He has never tried to break it off with me. And he definitely has never mentioned anything about you to me. You know what, he is not even worth my time. You can have his old stupid behind. And heifer, don't you ever call my house again!"

I was so angry I could have spit fire. And what made it so

dog gon' bad was the fact that it was Valentine's Day. I had gone out and bought him some cute little boxer shorts with hearts on them and some candy. I had been waiting for him to call me all day so that we could hook up for me to give him his gift and get mine. I had finally given up on hearing from him when that crazy heifer called my house. I couldn't believe that this was how my Valentine's Day was going to end—in heartache. I had a good long hard cry for about ten minutes. When I realized what I was doing, I wiped my eyes, washed my face, and went in the living room to watch a movie. I was not about to let some stupid boy ruin my night. I had too many other guys trying to holla at me to be worried about his skinny black behind.

About fifteen minutes after I got off the phone with Sherrell, Deuce's best friend Stanley called. "Deuce said that he really loves you. He is going through some tough times right now at home. When his father came home from Korea, his mom found some naked pictures of Korean women in his suitcase. Deuce found out about it, and he and his dad got into it. Deuce's dad threw him out of the house, and the only place he had to go was with Sherrell. He says that this break up is only temporary. He just needs about a month to get himself straight and then things can go back to the way they were between the two of you."

I laughed my head off. "Who in the world does he think he is playing with? I may have been dumb enough to allow him to lead me on up to this point, but having his other girl call my house? Oh no. There isn't going to be anything temporary about this break up. This relationship is *over!*"

"And tell that fool he could have had the nerve to call me himself!" I yelled as I hung up the phone in Stanley's face. I was done.

Once again I had to think of something to do to get back at Deuce. Why can't we women just leave well enough alone? We always have to find a way to get even, and end up making a bigger mess out of the situation. I knew exactly what to do.

His so-called best friend Will had been trying to holla at me for the longest time. I kept ignoring him because I was so hung up on Deuce. Well, now I was going to give him his chance. I was going to use him to make Deuce jealous. Will and I hung out together, went to the movies and to a concert. Will was way sexier than Deuce. He was tall, muscular, had thick wavy hair, and was brown-skinned with a very nice smile. The only problem with him was that he already had a kid with a girl who supposedly was pretty crazy. I wasn't worried about her, though, because I wasn't planning on staying with Will for very long. I just needed him for a short while to make Deuce see what he was missing. Will and I rarely even kissed. He was real fun to hang out with though.

When Deuce saw Will and I together he was on fire. *Ha, ha, ha, who's laughing now?* Deuce and Will fell out for a while. Will said he didn't care. He'd rather have me than Deuce. I felt kind of bad because I knew I wasn't really into Will. Finally, I just told him that I needed some space. He looked kind of crushed, but I had to just leave them all alone. Things were getting way too crazy for me.

I really wanted to see this Sherrell girl that Deuce had left me for. I heard she was not cute at all, but I almost needed to see this for myself. I'm sure, though, with five kids it wasn't her looks he was after. I'm sure she had experience in areas that I was just starting to explore. I was convinced that her experience and willingness to do things that I was not willing to do were what drew Deuce away from me.

I just couldn't seem to get it right. I lost Ricky because I wasn't having sex. Then, even though I was giving it up to Deuce, he still cheated on me. *Boys are so stupid!* I wish they would make up their minds. And guys always say that we females are complicated. Not so. For the most part, if a man respects a woman and makes her feel special, she's going to stay faithful to him. Now, there are some women who cannot be pleased, but that's not the majority. The majority of us just want to be loved, cherished, and made to feel special. But guys, selfish guys, there is just no satisfying them. They just want what they want when they want it, and they will go with whoever will give it to them. And Deuce was no different. Oh well, obviously he wasn't the one God intended for me to be with. I was on to the next chapter in my life.

After a month or two, I was told that Sherrell was supposedly pregnant from Deuce. Better her than me. Thank God for that ram in the bush, because I had too many plans for my life to be ending up with a baby in high school. That was not a sacrifice I was willing to make to try and keep a guy.

Of course Deuce started calling me again trying to get in good. I ran into him a couple of times at the Enlisted Club on post, and he was steadily tryin' to push up on me. I told him he had his chance and that he needed to go home to his family. I was not the one. I don't know why these fools think they can treat women any old kind of way and we're supposed to just let them back in as if nothing has happened. I think part of the reason they think that way is because a lot of us females let them back in too easily. Not me. Once I was done, I was done. They better recognize that they are going to have to come correct or don't come at all. We are not their faithful German shepherds who they can neglect to feed or mistreat and expect us to still be lying patiently at their feet. *No! We are women!* Created by the same God with the same mental capacity to rationalize and realize when a game is being run. It's time out for games. Even in high school I realized that.

And we women have got to step up, say what we mean, and mean what we say. I spent too many years in high school afraid to say what was really on my mind because of fear of rejection or embarrassment. Trust me, I do know better now. I eventually wised up and realized that if they run away from you for speaking your mind, you don't need 'em. A good man will listen to you and give you the respect that you deserve, even if he does not agree with everything that you say.

Yesterday

After I broke it off with Will, I really tried to lay off of guys for a while. I decided to focus on my schoolwork and sports. I made it through my last year of high school softball, again one win away from the state championship. That was a pretty disappointing season because I was the last one at bat against Jordan and grounded out to first base. We lost by one point. After softball season, I decided to try something I had never done before in my life: cheerleading. I wanted to play basketball and cheer at the same time, but my mom told me I had to choose one. Since I had not done that well in basketball the year prior, I decided to just cheer. Being a cheerleader was a lot of fun, and, of course brought even more attention from the opposite sex.

Pretty much all of my best friends were on the squad with me. One of my very best friends, Carlee, was our captain, so when I made the squad, I really was not surprised. We all got along really well.

The funniest thing about our squad was our coach, Ms. Joanne. Ms. Joanne was not a very attractive lady and looked as if she had never fit into a cheerleading uniform a day in her life. She was brown-skinned with mild to moderate acne, black lips, about three hundred pounds, and always wore jeans that were up her butt and looked as if they were cutting off the circulation to her feminine parts. She was a nice enough lady, but what in the world did she know about cheerleading? She always sounded as if she was extremely out of breath, therefore she never made it through an entire cheer with us. My guess is that we just needed a mother figure to be there for us, and she was the only one available to take the job.

It was also during my senior year that some major changes had taken place in my household. During my junior year, my mom was supposed to be getting stationed in Germany. I was all sad because I was going to have to leave my friends. Keith had put Germany on his dream sheet so that he could go to Germany and be with my mom. Fortunately, at the last minute my mom's orders were changed and we didn't go. It was too late for him to get out of his assignment, so it was bye-bye Keith. Praise the Lord! I could not believe Keith was finally gone. I think my mom was pretty glad that he was gone as well. He kept telling my mom that they were going to get married, but he never gave her a ring. We even saw him in the mall one evening hugged up with another woman. He didn't see us, though, and my mom never said anything to him about it. I think after that she lost all hope of them getting married and she knew she had to let him go.

Towards the end of my junior year, my mom started seeing a man from church. The man's name was Gerald. Gerald had been in the military and had been stationed overseas for a while. When he came home, for some reason he was no longer in the military, and his wife decided to divorce him. He was a rather heartbroken man. He and my mom sort of hooked up while they both were busy helping to care for our pastor who for some strange reason suddenly became extremely ill. The pastor was down for several weeks with some unexplained illness. While my mom and Gerald were at the hospital, they connected with one another. When the pastor got better, he told them that the Lord was going to bless the two of them. A month or two later, they were married. I, of course, was my mom's maid of honor. After they were married, my mom told me that the reason Gerald was no longer in the military and why his wife left him was because he had some type of blood cancer. Cancer did not seem like a good reason for his wife to leave him, but I didn't ask any questions. She sort of left it at that.

My senior year was when my mom actually got her orders to go to Germany. I was really sad about leaving my friends then. Since it was my senior year, my mom and I talked about it. We had come to a decision that I would stay behind in Georgia so that I didn't mess up my chances of getting a college scholarship. Plus, I had worked very hard to be ranked number one in my class and was looking forward to being valedictorian at the end of the year. For my mom, leaving me behind yet again was extremely difficult, but again she did what she had to do. I begged my mom to let me stay with Carlee. Her dad had already said that it was okay. I was all set to move in with Carlee and her family when, unfortunately, this lady from my church, Mother Mimso, volunteered to let me stay with her. Initially I was not happy at all about having to stay with this older lady, who I really did not know much about at all. However, my choices were to either stay with her or go to Germany and start all over at a new high school. I chose to deal with living with Mother Mimso.

During one of our basketball games against Kendrick High School, this tall, dark, handsome brother caught my eye. He and I were exchanging glances all night during the game. At halftime my girlfriends and I went to the concession stand. Mr. Tall, Dark, and Handsome followed us out. He came straight up to me and introduced himself. We really did not have much time to talk because we had to go back in to perform a halftime cheer. He gave me his number and I said I would call him the next day. His name was Ben, and it just so happened that he lived right up the street from Mother Mimso. He was nineteen and had graduated from Kendrick the year before. He had a nice money green Mustang and he worked in the mall. After talking to him on the phone the next day, I thought he would be a pretty cool person to hang out with. He and I became pretty tight. He would always come over after I got out of school before he and I went to work.

One night he called me after work asking if I could come pick him up from the mall because he was having car trouble. Of course, Mother Mimso was not too keen on that idea because it was almost nine o'clock. I told her he was cool and that I couldn't just leave him there. We debated the subject for a while and finally I just left. I told her that I would bring him over for her to meet so that she would feel more comfortable about the situation.

After Mother Mimso met Ben, she realized she knew his parents. She told me she was okay with the two of us going out. That was all we needed to hear. After that, our relationship took off and one thing led to another.

As I had feared, living with Mother Mimso was no fun at all. It seemed as if she was very uncomfortable with me being in her house and questioned my every move. No, I wasn't always doing what I was supposed to be doing, and no, I didn't always go where I told her I was going, but what right did she have to question me? One day after I had brought the girls from the cheerleading squad over to change real quick for a game, she questioned me about each of my friends, and then the next day she had a pad lock on her bedroom door. As if I or my friends would want to steal anything from her. I thought she was crazy and made it a point to stay out of her way as much as I could. I felt really unwelcomed in her home. One night she came into the bathroom when I was about to take a bath and told me that I was putting too much water in the bathtub.

"Danielle, you're really using too much water in that bathtub. Why don't you take showers? You would use less water," she said.

I could not believe she was picking at me about the amount of water I was putting in the bathtub. I guess that was something I just was not used to because living on the army post our water was free. And why do people think that taking a shower uses less water than taking a tub bath? If you are like me and you turn the shower on while you brush your teeth, wash your face, and then get into the shower and stay for a while, I guarantee that will require more water than a bath.

This is going to be a long school year, I thought. She was getting on my nerves so much that I decided to get a job to be out of the house more.

The first job that I got was as a delivery driver for this take-out steak eatery called Steak Out. The pay was good, but when I told my mom what I was doing, she got extremely nervous about me going to strange people's houses. She told me that I had to get another job. I did have to admit, some of the neighborhoods I had gone to were not the best and did make me a little nervous. This was probably the only reason I agreed with my mom after her first plea.

I then began talking to some of the kids at school, trying to find out where they worked. One white girl, Tammy, told me that she was working at this restaurant called Country's Barbeque and that she thought they were hiring. I went to Country's that afternoon and put in an application. The next day the manager called me for an interview. He asked me what my plans were after high school. I told him that I was planning to attend college. Since it was February and I only had a couple months left of high school, he told me that he could not hire me because most likely I would only be there for a couple of months before I packed up to leave. I was disappointed, but all I could say was "Fine, I understand."

The next day Tammy asked me how things went. I told her what had transpired. She told me that she was sorry, but she knew that they really needed some help. Well, apparently she was right because that next week the manager called me and asked if I was still interested in the job because they needed more waitresses. I guess there was pressure on him to get the position filled.

That day, after working for only three weeks, I told Steak Out that due to safety reasons I would not be returning as their delivery driver. The manager said she understood, and that was that.

Being a waitress at Country's Barbeque is probably one of the toughest waitress jobs there is. As a Country's waitress, I was expected to memorize the entire menu, including all of the prices, the sections of the restaurant that each waitress was responsible for were huge, I had to carry those heavy trays with all of the barbeque, salads, and sides over my head, sometimes two trays at a time. I had to have tip top waitress skills. I had to serve the food while holding those heavy trays at the same time without spilling anything. It's not like Olive Garden or Red Lobster where I would be able to set my tray down and serve the food (which makes more sense). Also Tuesday nights were all you can eat chicken night, so as waitresses we rotated out as Chicken Lady. As the Chicken Lady, we basically walked around all night with a huge bowl of chicken refilling people's plates at their request. Trust me, my arms got a good workout that night carrying that heavy bowl around for five hours.

Working for Country's really gave me my first experience of having a boss. It wasn't really that difficult for me to be under someone else because of all of the years I spent playing sports and being under my various coaches. It really wasn't a problem for me, but I was not about to let anyone just treat me any kind of way. I remember one Friday night we were extremely busy. One of my customers requested some coffee and it took me a long time to get back to her. Because it took me a while, my head waitress Amy, who was also the manager's girlfriend, took the coffee to the customer. When I came back into the kitchen, she called me out in front of everyone.

"Danielle, I'm tired of having to do your job for you! I think you came out of training too early and need to go back!" Amy said.

Of course, all of the other waitresses were looking at me, and I was completely embarrassed. I apologized to her for having to pour the cup of coffee for me and walked away. I walked away, but I was very upset with the way she approached me, and the more I thought about it, the more it did not sit well with me. I just had to say something to her.

When Amy and I were in the kitchen together, I asked her if I could talk to her for a second. I told her that I did not appreciate the way that she had approached me. If she had a problem with me, she should have pulled me to the side and spoke to me privately. I told her that I did not feel that I needed to go back to training simply because she had to take one cup of coffee out for me. I also told her that I worked because I wanted to work, not because I needed to work, therefore, I was not going to stand to be treated that way.

She apologized for blowing up at me but stated that the day had been very stressful for her and it all just boiled over. She said that I was right and that I did not need to go back to training. Of course, all of the other nosey waitresses were standing right there. They were all so amazed that I had approached her.

"I would never have said anything back to her. I can't believe you went up to her and said that!" one white girl stated.

"Good for you," another waitress stated.

Everyone acted as if I had said what they had been thinking all along. After that day, Amy went out of her way to be especially nice to me. That sort of surprised me because that really was not my goal. I wasn't mad at her though.

For the most part, I enjoyed working at Country's. For a high school student with no bills, the extra money was really nice. I only worked because I wanted to get out of the house and away from Mother Mimso. However, I was able to put away a good bit of money for my transition to college. Plus, if I wanted to go out and do something I could always just say that I had to work. She had no clue what my work schedule was.

I remember one night I had to close, and for some reason it took us forever to get done. When I finally got home, it was well after 1:00 a.m. Of course, Mother Mimso was sitting up on the couch in the dark waiting for me to walk through the door.

"Danielle, where have you been?" she questioned me in a stern voice.

I was tired, I smelled like barbecue, my back was killing me, and I just was not in the mood for this woman that night.

"What do you mean? I've been at work. I thought I told you that I had to work today," I said in an irritated voice.

"I called up there over an hour ago and no one answered the phone. So where were you?" she asked again.

Of course, I was extremely irritated by then. "I told you, I was at work. I don't know where else you think I've been with all of this barbecue sauce all over me. I'm tired and very ready to go to bed. If you want to call the restaurant in the morning, you can ask to speak to Joe. He'll tell you what time I left work. Right now, I am about to go take a shower and go to sleep," I said as I turned and walked away.

I was so angry with her. How dare she question where I'd been? Who did she think she was? My mom was in Germany, and I did not need another one.

I think teenagers are the most conceited people in the world. As a teenager, I must have felt that the world just revolved around me. I didn't seem to care what anyone else thought. All I wanted was what I wanted when I wanted it. I did not want anyone questioning anything that I did. I wanted to be in charge of my life and I did not want to answer to anyone. If I had taken one second to view things from her point of view, I might have realized that she was genuinely concerned about me that night. She may have thought that something bad had happened to me and was probably worried all night. But I was too self-righteous and stupid to realize that. I immediately took a defensive stance, as I often did as a teenager. I'm sure the reason that I was so defensive was because there were several nights that I was not at work and came home late. She could have caught me on any other night, but that night I was actually telling the truth. Needless to say, she didn't question me about coming home late any more after that encounter.

As usual, I was very busy during high school. I was involved in everything that I could get into: Key Club, National Honor Society, Delta Teens, the church choir, working, Beta Club...I have no clue how I kept up with everything that I was doing. If I only had half of the energy now that I had then...

Ben and I continued to see each other for a while. A lot of Mother Mimso's neighbor's were spying on us, though, and were telling her that he was at the house when she wasn't there. She told me she didn't like the idea of me having a boy in the house by myself; but between school, my job, and her job, she was never at home when I was there except at night when we were asleep. When was I going to get to see him? Besides, how was I going to tell him not to come over anymore? Especially when I didn't want to. Ben was cool and fun to be with. The only thing I didn't like too much was the fact that he always smelled like beer when he came over. I thought that was kind of odd because he was only nineteen and it was usually pretty early in the day when he came over. He usually came over right after school was out. I never questioned him about the beer scent though. I didn't feel comfortable enough with him yet to get into that conversation.

A couple of months went by, and Ben and I grew closer and closer. I really enjoyed his company. However, I kept wondering about his drinking. One day Mother Mimso came home from work, and she wanted to sit down and talk about something important. She said something very interesting had occurred at work that day. While she was working, Ben's parents came into her store. She said they began to talk, and she was telling them how happy she was that I was dating their son. They said that he had told them about me, how smart I was, and that I had plans to be a doctor. They were telling her that they really were surprised that he and I were dating and were rather concerned about us being together. They told her how much they loved their son, but that he might not be right for me, and did not want to see him bringing me down. She questioned what they meant. Ben's father proceeded to tell her that Ben had a drinking problem. He said that he got drunk almost every day and was extremely disrespect-ful to his mother. His father said that he was almost to the point of putting Ben out of his house. No matter how much they had tried to talk to Ben, nothing seemed to change his ways. He only seemed to be getting worse. His father did not want to see Ben disrespecting me the same way he did his mother.

I was kind of shocked, but not really. I mean, I was shocked that he handled his mom the way that he did, but not shocked at all about the drinking. When Ben called me later that evening, I told him what Mother Mimso told me. I told him that I couldn't continue to see him because Mother Mimso did not want me to see him and did not want him in her house anymore. He was very angry that I was just going to quit him like that, but one thing I was always taught and seriously believed was that a man who did not respect his mother would not respect any other woman. I could not take that chance. We hung up the phone, and that was that.

After Ben and I split up, I really planned to lay low for a while. *No boys!* My goal was to focus on finishing up school and work. My counselor at school warned me that one of the new kids at school was very close to my GPA and could potentially beat me out for valedictorian. She wanted to make sure that I didn't slack off toward the end of the year. I was told that a lot of the white teachers were making little comments about us "tak-ing over" because seven of the top ten students in our class were black. Oh well. They had better get over that quick because we were making a statement that year.

My senior year was full, yet it seemed like it went by *so* fast. I pondered running for homecoming queen for a while before I actually decided to go along with it. Making the decision to run for Miss Greenwave brought back a lot of memories. I had run for Miss Sophomore, which I did not win. I tried again for Miss Junior. I had done very well that year with my campaigning and was a shoe-in to win. I had managed to keep my nose clean my entire time at Spencer. I had never gotten into any trouble for anything. The day of the vote, I had to go and change all of that.

"Hey, Danielle, you want to go with me to Burger King for lunch?" Francie asked.

I thought about it for a second, knowing good and well that we were not supposed to leave campus for anything. "Girl, we go all the time. It's no big deal," she said convincingly.

"Sure, I'll go," I said, trying to prove that I was down.

The first day everything went just as she said. We were in and out with our Whoppers and back at school before the lunch period was over. Easy as pie. The next day she found me and asked if I wanted to go again. Since the first day went so smoothly, I didn't hesitate to say yes the second time. However, the second time did not go quite as well. Just as we got into line, I saw a school bus pull into the parking lot. *Uh, oh,* I thought. But my dumb butt just stood there. I watched everyone get off the bus, and in walked several of the senior students that I knew. I still stood there. Then it happened. Mr. E walked in. Mr. E was my physics teacher. Of course, he was one of the white teachers. He looked me dead in my face. All I could do was smile. My heart felt like it had sunk to the floor. I still managed to get myself to the counter, order my food, and leave.

When I got back to Spencer, I had no idea what to expect. I think part of me wanted to believe that everything was going to be okay. I mean, I was Danielle, and everyone knew that I was a good student who never got into any trouble. Besides, the only thing that I skipped was lunch. Who cares about that?

Unfortunately, as soon as I walked back into the building I heard my name over the intercom.

"Danielle Swails, report to the library."

Oh crap! I thought. I knew I had to face the music then.

As soon as I walked into the library, I saw them all waiting for me. It seemed like every white teacher in the building was there glaring/smirking at me like they wanted to all say at once,

"We got you now!" Mrs. W had been one of my English teachers and was one of the first ones to speak.

"Danielle, it has been brought to our attention that you were seen skipping school today. Because of this we have to remove you from the homecoming court," she said with her jiggly chin.

"But I didn't skip school. I just went to Burger King for lunch," I tried to explain.

"The student handbook clearly states that no one is to leave this campus at any point during school hours unless they are signed out by a parent or legal guardian," she replied. "I'm sorry, but you broke the rules, and unfortunately you have to suffer the consequences."

I immediately started to cry. I had worked so hard on my campaign for Miss Junior. I immediately began to regret ever running into Francie. It's amazing how when things seem to be going perfectly the devil will always send one of his schemes your way to try and mess you up. He tries to get you to do stuff you know you don't have any business doing. Stuff you never even thought of doing before. And the crazy thing is, we fall for it. We sometimes do some crazy stuff that we know that we are *not* supposed to do. And the only thing that keeps us from doing it over and over again is if we get caught and embarrassed. It's amazing how a little embarrassment can sometimes cure us of our sins.

When she told me that I had been removed from the court, then I knew that I had won the campaign. At that point, the only thing that I could do was walk away defeated with a huge lump in my chest and a smushed Whopper in my backpack.

When I got home that night, I told my mom what happened. Of course she was upset with me for leaving campus. However when I told her how coldly they had informed me that I was removed from the homecoming court, she was pretty upset. She believed in disciplining me for my wrongdoings, but she was not going to let anyone mistreat me. The next day she called and scheduled a conference with the principal to discuss what had transpired.

That meeting was a blur. The teachers and the principal explained to my mom what the school's policy was regarding leaving the campus during school hours. They talked about how it was their responsibility to make sure we were safe while we were there, and that anything could happen to us if we left the campus without permission. They pulled out the student handbook and showed us the policy. They said that because I had broken one of the rules and gotten into trouble during the election period for homecoming I was no longer eligible to be on the court. They talked for a little while longer. In the end, I was still off the homecoming court, so I felt that the meeting had accomplished nothing.

"Well, that was one expensive Whopper," my mom said. "I hope that it was worth it."

She had a point. And the crazy thing was I didn't even eat the Whopper. After being so nervous about what was going to happen to me that day, I completely lost my appetite. That Whopper was still smashed in the bottom of my book bag. When I got home, it went straight into the trash. Stupid, stupid, stupid. That day I learned that if you are going to do something stupid, you better make sure that the apparent prize is worth the consequences of the actions it takes to get it. And I can tell you that a two-dollar Whopper was not worth all of my hard work on my Miss Junior campaign being flushed down the drain. Oh well, next lesson.

Later that day my softball coach pulled me to the side and counseled me on my actions. During the day one of my friends told me that another girl who was running for Miss Junior had gone to McDonald's for lunch. I told this to Mr. Mac and how I thought it was unfair that I got kicked off the court when she was just fortunate enough not to have gotten caught. On top of that, this was supposedly a trend for her to leave campus for lunch.

"Danielle, I'm going to leave it completely up to you. Do you want me to turn her in?"

Of course with me being upset and angry because I had

gotten caught, I didn't want to go down in flames by myself. I thought about it for a minute, then I told him, "Yes, sir. Go ahead and turn her in."

Somehow I felt that getting someone else in trouble would somehow ease my pain. It didn't. Not only did I feel bad about screwing up my chances of being on the court, but now I also was a tattletale, which is something I had never been known as. Of course, no one knew but me and Mr. Mac that I was the reason she was removed from the court. She and I had been friends since the ninth grade, and she would often say to me, "I wonder how they found out I went to McDonald's?" I would just shake my head and change the subject. Sorry, girl.

High school was full of surprises, craziness, and fun. After thinking about it for a while, I decided to go ahead and run for Miss Greenwave. What did I have to lose? The campaign season was fun, yet very expensive. I created nice posters and balloons. I went all out. The crazy thing was that four out of the five of us who were running for Miss Greenwave were close friends. We all cheered together, therefore all of the votes would be split because we all hung out with the same group of people. Needless to say, we all had fun learning how to walk like a lady and playing dress up. In the end, the girl from Cusseta won because all of the Cusseta folks always stuck together. Nevertheless I was still first runner up and got to go out on the football field during the homecoming game. It was cool.

That year I received many awards for my achievements during the school year and was voted "Most Likely to Succeed" along with my boy Kermit. But my biggest accomplishment was when I found out that I was *the valedictorian!* I was so excited. That was something that I had always wanted to be. I was a little intimidated when I first got to Spencer because there were over five hundred students in my freshman class. I never doubted myself though. In the end with all of the transfers and dropouts, we ended up with about two hundred and nine students in our graduating class. *And I was number one!* It was so wonderful being able to stand up in front of all of those people as the valedictorian of Spencer High School that year. My parents were so proud of me. They even bought me a new Hyundai Scoupe.

By the time my senior year was coming to an end, my dad and I had actually patched things up. One night toward the middle of the year, I decided to write him a letter after not talking to him for close to a year. In the letter I stated that one of us needed to break the ice and that I guess it would be me. I told him that he really hurt my feelings when he spoke to me the way he had that Thanksgiving night. Calling me out in front of everyone, basically calling me a slut when I was still a virgin. The reason that I always had a new boyfriend when he saw me was because every time they would start talking about sex I would break up with them. I told him that I really hoped that we could talk and that he would be able to come to my graduation at the end of the year. I told him where I was living and that I was doing fine living with Mother Mimso.

About a week after I sent the letter to my father, he called me. I was very shocked. We talked for a long time. He apologized for the way he had treated me that night. He said that he was going to come visit me in the next couple of weeks. He also said that he had some bad news. "Your aunt M died a couple of months ago from kidney failure. You know she was a diabetic in need of a transplant. She had been on dialysis for a while, but her kidneys couldn't hold on any longer. The worst part about it was that the day after she died we got a call that they had found a donor kidney." Even though I was happy to finally hear from my father after a year, I sort of wished we hadn't talked, because that was the last thing I expected to hear.

The last time I had seen Aunt M was that Thanksgiving night when she was trying to comfort me after my dad had made me feel like a complete idiot. She didn't even look sick then, and that was only a year ago. I could not believe it. And the worst part was no one even bothered to try to reach me, so I didn't even get to go to her funeral.

"We didn't know how to reach you," he claimed. "But I do have some good news. Aunt M left all of us some money. She left Mudea about a hundred thousand dollars, so she is buying herself a new trailer and some land. She left me fifty thousand dollars, so I'm doing okay. Rashawn got ten thousand dollars. And I have five thousand dollars for you. I'll put it in the mail for you tomorrow."

What, five thousand dollars? That was more money than I had ever seen in my seventeen years of life. I got so excited. It's funny how a little money can make all of your sorrows disappear (so we think).

The next week I received a check from my dad in the amount of four thousand dollars. I called my dad and asked for clarification because I was pretty sure he had said he was going to send me five thousand dollars. "Oh, yeah. Your aunt E needed to borrow a thousand dollars to pay their mortgage, so I was only able to send you four thousand." To this day I do not understand why one of those thousand had to come from my five thousand when he had fifty thousand that he could have shared from.

Well, he ended up putting another two thousand dollars towards my car, so I was happy.

When I got my money, I immediately opened up checking and savings accounts. I decided that I was going to put my money away and save it for college. I've always been real good about saving money. When I was younger and my mom first started sending me my stipend check, my aunt M taught me about budgeting. Out of my one hundred dollar check that I received each month, I was supposed to give my dad twenty dollars for groceries, save twenty dollars, use thirty dollars for my lunch money, then use the other thirty dollars to shop for personal items and things that I needed for school. For the most part I did pretty well with my stipend and was able to stretch it out for almost a full month. It's amazing how God can make a little go a long way because one hundred dollars really is not much money for a month.

My high school graduation weekend was very nice. My mom

and Gerald came home from Germany for that week. My dad and Aunt E and all of her kids, including Rashawn, came up. My godmother and godsister came. It was a lot of fun. Our graduation was on a Monday, but everyone came up on the Thursday before for our baccalaureate service. On Friday we went and bought my new car. On Saturday we all decided to drive to Atlanta to go to Six Flags, which was a blast. On Sunday we had a barbecue at Cooper Creek Park. It was small, but we still had a wonderful time. I can still remember the look on my friend Lenda's face when she tasted blue crabs for the first time.

Graduation day was all that I thought it would be. It felt great walking down the aisle in my gold cap and gown with my National Honor Society ribbon draped around my neck. Our baccalaureate service had already sort of set the stage for the big finale. Our service was very emotional. Only two out of the top ten were able to speak without crying. I surprisingly was one of them. My dad said he was proud of me for saying what I had to say and sitting down without crying. The ceremony, however, seemed like it flew by. Four years worth of growth, maturation, good memories, bad memories, friends, rivals, sports, cheerleading, boys, parties, arguments with my mother...all of that was now over. I was about to be grown and out on my own. This is what I had been waiting for my entire life. I could hardly believe it.

Our graduation night was actually kind of boring. My friends and I drove around looking for a party, but they were all kind of dull. I ended up going back to our billeting room on base at Fort Benning and going to bed. My mom said she was surprised that I was back so early. I told her I was bored and tired.

I was glad high school was over. I was going to miss my friends, but I was very excited to be moving on to the next phase of my life. I knew since the ninth grade that I wanted to become a doctor, therefore I knew I had to go to college. The majority of my senior year I was making my plans to move to Atlanta and attend Emory University. Emory seemed to be the perfect choice because I had always wanted to live in Atlanta, and Emory was one of the few schools in Georgia that also had a medical school. My mind was made up. Yes, sir, I was going to Atlanta to attend Emory University.

During my junior year I had considered very much the possibility of attending Xavier University in New Orleans. They sent me letters in the mail almost every week telling me about their school. Xavier was one of the top historically black colleges in terms of getting blacks into medical school. Xavier and Howard University were constantly battling for being able to say that they were number one in that respect.

I was very interested in attending Xavier, so the summer before my senior year, I decided to attend their SOAR 1 program. This was a great program which gave students a feel for college life and prepared us for the SAT. I was so excited to be going to New Orleans. I had never been there before. My mom and Gerald drove me from Fort Benning, Georgia, to New Orleans, Louisiana. It seemed like it took forever to get there. Ten long hours. When we finally got there I was in awe. New Orleans had more bright lights and tall buildings than I had ever seen. We drove through the downtown area to get to our hotel. After we checked in we headed to the infamous Bourbon Street to tour the popular tourist attractions and have dinner. This was totally new to me. People were out everywhere, and jazz music was floating through the air from every corner. There were daiquiri shops and clubs on each side of the street. The only thing that I did not like, and will never forget, was the smell. The air had a putrid odor of alcohol and vomit no matter where we went.

We found this restaurant that served the traditional Creole food. We all ordered jambalaya. It was delicious. It was just as good as my dad had described it from his days of living in New Orleans. Next we went to the tourist mall and tried some beignets. They were good as well. I felt about ten pounds heavier after that night.

The next day we went to Xavier's campus. At first I was like,

"Wow, this is great." However, after we actually got onto the campus, I was a little disenchanted. It was nothing like I had envisioned a college campus to be like. It was way too small. It only had one short street surrounded by about five buildings at the most. There were only about three dorm buildings, two for girls and one for boys. I was so not impressed. However, I made up my mind that I was at least going to enjoy my month in New Orleans.

Even though I wasn't impressed with the campus, I did enjoy my month at Xavier. I had a lot of fun hanging out in New Orleans, and I met a lot of great friends. My roommate was real cool. She was from somewhere in Alabama. I also met people from Wisconsin, Texas, Florida, California, and several other places. I received excellent preparation for the SAT, and I really felt that all of the instructors cared a lot about all of us students.

That month went by fast. Before I knew it, I was back in Columbus. Even though I really wasn't impressed with the campus, I still knew that Xavier was a good school academically. Therefore I went ahead and submitted my application to Xavier as well as to Emory. The application fees for college were pretty steep, therefore I really did not apply to many schools. I couldn't afford to.

My high school counselor, Mrs. G, was always looking out for me. One day she brought me this application and told me that I needed to fill it out because it was free. Alabama State University was not a school that I knew very much about. I had only known one person who had gone there, my godfather's nephew. I had gone to an Alabama State vs. Florida A&M University football game with my godparents when I was younger. That was years before when I was in middle school. All I could remember was that I really enjoyed their band performances.

I went ahead and submitted my application. After that it seemed like they were calling me every week trying to recruit me to come to ASU. They even sent a recruiter, Mr. P, to Columbus to present me with an offer for a presidential scholarship. I was flattered that they were going through all of this trouble for me. I mean, usually you see schools sending recruiters out trying to get athletes to come play sports for them, but I was not used to people being recruited just because they made good grades.

I had a lot of teachers looking out for me, and I think a lot of them had an even closer eye on me since they knew my mom was overseas in Germany. No matter how far away my actual family was, God always had people nearby to look out after me. I was never alone despite how lonely I often felt. It seemed His Holy Spirit was always surrounding me, flowing into the people around me, causing them to do things for me without having any reservations whatsoever.

Like I said, my counselor, Mrs. G, always looked out for me. She and I were pretty close, and I would always go down to her office to chit chat and talk about preparation for graduation and college. That's why it kind of surprised me one time when she felt she had to go through my cheerleading coach to ask me a serious question.

"Danielle, Mrs. G has mentioned to me that she is worried about you, and to be honest, I have noticed that you have put on a little weight as well," Ms. Joanne said.

"What?" I said. At first I had no clue where Ms. Joanne was coming from. Then it clicked.

"I am not pregnant!" I yelled in exasperation. "How could you even think that?"

"Well, Mrs. G said she wanted to talk to you about it, but she wasn't sure how to bring it up. So she asked me to talk to you. You have always been such a tiny little thing. Now you're kind of spreading a little."

"Well, normally I'm playing basketball this time of the year and running a lot more than we do for cheerleading."

"Oh! Woo, I'm glad that's all it is!" Ms. Joanne said with relief. "You know we're all rooting for you, and we all feel it is our responsibility to look out for you since your mom is gone. We just don't want anything bad to happen to you. Mrs. G was just concerned, that's all. Don't be mad at her for coming to me."

"I just can't believe that she wouldn't just ask me. This is embarrassing!" I said.

After Ms. Joanne and I finished talking, I went to Mrs. G's office to talk. We conversed for a while, and I told her I wished she had just asked me instead of bringing someone else into it. She apologized, then we moved on.

Another one of those special God sent people happened to be my marketing teacher, Mrs. Funderburk. Mrs. Funderburk was a very sweet older white lady who taught at Spencer. One day we were discussing my future plans. We started talking about how ASU had offered me a presidential scholarship and how I was actually thinking about taking it. Even though my heart's desire was to attend Emory, I knew that we really couldn't afford it. Emory cost about twenty-four thousand dollars a year at that time. They had offered me about eighteen thousand a year in scholarships for tuition, books, and room and board, and I had received about four more thousand in community scholarships. My mom was a single mom, and I didn't want her to have to come up with any out of pocket expenses, so I was really considering attending ASU.

Mrs. Funderburk told me that if I was considering going to the school, I really needed to visit the campus. She offered to take me up for a visit. Where in the world did this come from? God was looking out for me yet again. At first I didn't know how to respond. However, I knew that she was right and I had no one else to take me. That next Friday morning we were on our way to Montgomery, Alabama.

Of course, that was the weekend when ASU had everything going on. R. Kelly was coming to town, the yard was jumpin', everyone was hanging out on the wall in front of the dorms. This school seemed like it was the bomb. There were posters up for the party that night. This is the image I had of college. Party over here!

After we rode around the campus, we went to the recruitment office to meet with Mr. P, the recruiter. He told me about a program for science majors who planned to attend graduate school that actually paid a monthly stipend. He told me that all I had to do was apply, and with my background I was pretty much guaranteed to get into the program. A full scholarship and a monthly stipend. They were going to pay me to go to school. Oh, yes, I was there. I guess all that tithing I did really paid off.

I think that after that visit my mind was pretty much made up. Carlee had come along with us, and she decided she was going to ASU as well. We were going to be roommates. God did it again. I was an only child who always wished for a sibling. In high school God blessed me with a lot of great friends, and Carlee was one of them. And now we were going to go to college together. Carlee's family took me in and treated me just like one of the family. Her sister had already graduated and moved out, but she and her little brother still lived at home. During the beginning of our senior year of high school, her mom decided that she wanted a divorce, so she was no longer at home. It was just Carlee, Mr. C, and her little brother. Mr. C was so cool. And talk about someone who could cook. That man could throw down. He reminded me so much of my father when it came to cooking.

After graduation we packed up all of my things from Mother Mimso's house and moved it over to Carlee's until we left for college. I was not about to spend another night in Mother Mimso's house if I did not have to.

You Keep on Blessing Me

After graduation I flew to Germany with my mom and Gerald for a few weeks. This was my first time on a plane. I was a little nervous, yet excited at the same time. The flight was about nine hours into Frankfurt from Atlanta. It wasn't nearly as bad as I thought it was going to be. They served us some really good meals and we watched movies. It was nothing like I had expected. I was just amazed, and still am every time that I fly, at how God gave man the knowledge to fly. How on earth can this huge metal object full of hundreds of people and luggage defy gravity? That was definitely beyond my level of understanding. I just know that I pray to God each time I fly to keep birds out of the engines and to keep the air traffic controller awake and alert.

When we got to Germany, I was in awe. It was my first time leaving the United States, so everything was completely new to me. The first thing I noticed were the differences in the way that people looked, smelled, and interacted with each other. It was very exciting. The airport looked a lot like Atlanta's airport except everything was written in Deutsch. It was very easy to get lost. If there were no pictures next to the words, I would not have been able to find my way to baggage claim.

After leaving the airport, I enjoyed my first experience on

the autobahn. I had heard about it, but did not really believe that people could actually drive as fast as they wanted to. Well, everyone was right. It was crazy out there. All I saw was BMW and Mercedes after BMW and Mercedes flying past us in our little Mitsubishi Mirage. It was cool though. I kept thinking that I would see a lot of accidents because people were driving so fast, but I didn't.

While driving from Frankfurt to Heidelberg, I saw a lot of the German scenery. A lot of it was pretty undeveloped, so there were a lot of nice green trees. There were a lot of German houses sitting up on hills along the autobahn. The structure of most of the houses was about the same. They were a lot smaller than the houses I was used to in America. One thing that I thought was really neat was that in the median area of the autobahn there were gas stations. You just pulled to the median, filled up, and kept going. They even had McDonald's at some of the stops which I thought was really crazy. A McDonald's in the middle of the highway.

I felt so blessed to be in another country. When I was growing up in itty bitty ol' Callahan, Florida, riding my beach cruiser up and down those dirt roads trying hard to avoid the mud puddles, I never imagined going to another country. Shoot, I was excited just to get out of Callahan and go into Jacksonville, which was only fifteen minutes away. Now here I was thousands of miles away from Callahan in Europe.

On the way to our apartment, my mom decided that it was time to inform me of something. She told me that Gerald had gotten a job as a bagger at the commissary. When he got there, he of course met a lot of the other dependents who were baggers there also. He met this one particular guy who said that he had moved there from Fort Benning as well. When Gerald asked the guy what school he went to, the guy told him Spencer. So, of course, Gerald asked him if he knew me. He said the guy was extremely excited and said yes he knew me and that we used to date. Lo and behold, Ricky was there working at the commissary with Gerald, and to make it even better, he lived right up the street from where we lived. I was shocked! Ricky was here. Part of me was excited because I still liked him. It would be good for us to see each other again, I thought.

So, of course who knocks on the door the first day I am there? Yes, it was Ricky. We said hello, hugged, and he came in. We sat and talked for a while. It was really good seeing him again, although it felt kind of strange considering how things took place between us back in Georgia. He seemed like a different person, like he was actually very happy to see me again. He invited me to the festival that was going on that weekend. I asked my mom if it was okay for me to go, and she said sure. After that he left.

That Friday night Ricky picked me up. In the car with him were a few of his friends, two girls and two guys. We exchanged greetings and were on our way. The festival was pretty much like an American state fair. There were a lot of rides, games, food stands, and fireworks. We rode the roller coasters, played a few games, and ate corn dogs and fries. After that he took me back home. It felt really good hanging out with him. It's like I completely forgot about how angry I had been with him back in Georgia. We kissed good night, and he told me he would call me the next day. He actually kept his word and called me the next morning. He said he wanted to take me out again. Again my mom said it was okay. *What?* I was *so* shocked she was actually letting me go places. Back in Georgia, I had to plead my case before the judge before I could go anywhere. *I guess she's getting soft in her old age.* My mom was only thirty-six at the time. Actually, she told me that I was essentially grown now. I had completed high school and was on my way to college. What I did from that point on was on me.

Well, the next day Ricky came and scooped me up in his parents' car again. He took me to the castle in Heidelberg. That was my first time ever going to a castle. It was really nice. There was only one thing that I thought was really strange down there. Right next to the castle there was a river that you could see from a very busy street. Well, along the river were a large number of topless sunbathers just laying there as comfortable as can be. No shame whatsoever. Anyone driving along the roads could catch a clear eyeful of boobs as they passed by the river. I began to feel a little uncomfortable.

Ricky had actually brought a little blanket for us to sit on as we watched the water rush by down the river. It turned out to be a very nice day. Again I was shocked.

My first Sunday there, my mom, Gerald, and I went to their church in Manheim. It was a very nice church. The architecture was a lot different than any of the churches I had attended in the States. The pastor, Pastor Boswell, and his wife were extremely nice. The pastor was also an excellent singer and had even recorded a gospel album.

The church congregation consisted of people from all over. There were people from Germany, Africa, and a lot of military people from the United States. It seemed no matter how far around the world we went, we could never get away from God's goodness. Not that we were trying to. And my mom was right there up front working as a pastor's aide as she always was. I really enjoyed myself there. The people of the congregation were so sweet and welcoming. It was an experience I'll never forget.

My first couple of weeks in Germany seemed to fly by. The only problem that I had was that I had a hard time adjusting to the time difference. I wanted to sleep all day and was up all night. My first three nights, I could not sleep at all. I read Alice Walker's *Possessing the Secret of Joy* in its entirety in those three nights. It was a wonderful novel which really opened my eyes to a lot of things.

After about a week, my circadian rhythm was finally in line with that of the Europeans. I was able to sleep when the sun went down and get out of the bed before noon. For the first couple of weeks, Ricky stuck to me like glue. It was almost as if he was trying to make up for screwing up so bad back at Spencer. He took me out to lunch, to the movies, and we did everything together.

He even put his fourteen-carat gold Figaro necklace that he said his grandmother had given him around my neck as if I was his girl again. It was all good for those three weeks. Then one day he just disappeared. He completely stopped coming around. I had no clue what was going on. I knew it was all too good to be true. Guys are so stupid. And I had allowed myself to be vulnerable and trust one again. *Stupid, stupid, stupid!*

Well, my last two weeks, of course, seemed very boring since Ricky stopped coming around. I mean, it was as if he had just vanished from Heidelberg. I kept trying to figure out what in the world I had done but then came to the decision that he probably realized once again that I wasn't about to give it up to him. The strange thing was that it really didn't seem as though he was trying to push up on me like that. I don't know.

Well, anyways, I was ready to go back to the States and start college. Hopefully I would be able to just forget about him. Besides, I had a boyfriend back in Georgia anyway.

Oh yeah, I didn't mention that, huh. Yes, while working at Country's this girl named Nadja introduced me to this guy who was in the army with her boyfriend. The guy's name was Anthony, and she told me he was really sweet, so I agreed to meet him. I figured I didn't have anything to lose at that point. She was right; he was really sweet. Being an infantryman, he was in excellent physical condition. The only problem was that he was short and looked a lot like Jamie Foxx. Now, I have always been rather short myself. I'm five feet two inches, but I have always been really attracted to tall guys. I was usually attracted to guys who were at least six feet tall. I don't know why we short women always fall for guys who tower above us. Maybe it's because men who are tall in stature tend to portray a more powerful image. I don't know. What I do know is sometimes those attractions to physical characteristics will get us into trouble. Sometimes we focus so much on the outward appearances of things that we don't care to find out what's on the inside. By the time we do find out what a person's actual character is it's too late because we're already caught up. Therefore we start compromising and settling for whatever. A lot of times that's why we end up in unhappy and abusive relationships—focusing too much on the wrong thing.

Anthony turned out to be a very nice guy just like Nadja said. He was very respectful and was always a gentleman. He seemed rather shy and kind of quiet, but I didn't mind because I was pretty much the same way. We hung out a lot, and I immediately felt very comfortable around him. He seemed very interested in me as a person and in trying to do whatever he could to make sure that I was happy, which had always been a plus for me. We initially were only able to hang out for about a month before he had to leave for training for about three weeks. Then I left for Germany.

When I returned from Germany, we had about another week together before I packed up for college. I had no idea where this relationship was heading but I was pretty excited about it.

About a week after I returned from Germany, my dad, Aunt E, and the crew came to move me to Montgomery, Alabama, for the next phase of my life. It was almost a shame the amount of stuff I had packed to take with me. Unfortunately when you are a military brat, you really don't have much of a place to call home, so I pretty much had no choice but to keep everything with me.

We had about three cars worth of my stuff to fit into a tiny little dorm room in Bessie Estelle Benson Hall. Even though it was not the Ritz Carlton, I was satisfied with my dorm room. I was finally going to be out on my own, and that's all that mattered.

When we arrived on ASU's campus, I checked into my dorm and we unloaded the cars. After that my little cousin Tisha and I went to a welcoming seminar for freshmen in the Acadome. The Acadome was the basketball arena, and I was thoroughly impressed by how nice it was. The next day my dad, Aunt E, and the crew headed back to Florida, and for the first time in my life I was really on my very own.

Yeah, Yeah, Yeah

College was a wonderful experience, and I was very glad that I had decided to attend a historically black university. I had gotten a good taste of being around my own people in high school, but this was totally different. There were black folks from everywhere at ASU: Florida, Georgia, Alabama, Michigan, California, New Jersey, Wisconsin, Texas. I think every state was represented there. There were also people from Jamaica, Africa, India, and other countries as well. It was quickly very apparent that each state had their own cliques as well. It did not seem to matter that we were all black and originated from the same ancestors. If you were from Miami, you hung with the Miami folks. If you were from Detroit, you hung with the Detroit crew. And each crew had to try and outdo the other crew. In that respect, it was sort of like high school all over again.

Even though the people in college reminded me a lot of high school, I must say that my classes did not. For the first time in my life, I actually had to study. My eyes were opened in that respect following my first biology exam. I read all of the required reading assignments, then glanced over the material once the night before the exam. But that was the extent of my studying. I was used to being able to do that in high school and make A's on just about everything. When I began looking over those questions,

I realized I had not prepared myself well enough at all for that exam. I began to get a little nervous. The first thing that the devil wanted me to think was that I was in over my head. The second thing he put into my head was that I needed to glance over at Carlee's test and see what answers she had. The devil was really trying hard to convince me to cheat. And for a second there I found myself doing exactly what he wanted me to do. I quickly caught myself, though, and decided that I would just do the best that I could on this exam and do better on the next one.

I scored about an 84 on that exam, and of course I was devastated because I was so used to making nothing but A's. I was even more sad because Carlee scored a couple of points higher than me. There goes that competitive spirit in me again. After that I realized that I was going to have to make some major changes in the way that I studied. I was actually going to have to start studying. That night I prayed for the Lord's guidance. As always, He gave it to me.

For me, college was like a roller coaster ride. It had its ups and it had its downs, and sometimes it threw me for a loop and made me dizzy. But overall it was a very positive experience and really aided in my maturation into an adult. The memories are endless.

Anthony and I continued to date. He was at Fort Benning, and I was in Montgomery about eighty-five miles away. It worked out pretty well because he was close enough for me to see him when I wanted, but far enough for me to still be able to do my own thing. Somehow I was able to convince him that it would be okay for me to have other male friends but he still would be my boyfriend. I was surprised at how easily he agreed with that idea. Now that I think about it, it probably meant that he was there doing what he wanted to as well. But anyway, I had my life in Montgomery, and he was there for me in Columbus.

It worked out pretty well for me. I was always upfront with the guys that I dated in Montgomery. They knew that I had a boyfriend in Columbus, and that our relationships would never be more than friendships. Most guys were okay with that initially, but in time they always seemed to want more, and when I reminded them of the initial agreement, they would get upset. Oh well, I just moved on to the next person.

I remember this one guy that I hung out with, T. T was in the air force. I think I met him at the gym on Maxwell Air Force Base. He was short, light-skinned with light eyes, rather cute. T was in the church, saved, and seemed like a really nice guy. His only drawback was that he had a child already, which was something that I always tried to avoid. I never wanted to be in a relationship with a guy with kids because I knew that the mother of those kids would always be in his life. I didn't want the competition. Well, T and I hung out, went to the movies, went to the gym, went to church. We were having fun. He knew I had a boyfriend, and he seemed cool with that. However, one evening we were standing outside of my dorm room by his car. He put his arms around me, which I thought was odd. I didn't say anything though. I decided to just listen.

Then he laid it on me. "God told me that you were going to be my wife," he said looking me dead in the eyes with a straight face. At first I didn't know what to say. Then I backed up a little, hit him on the shoulder, and said, "You are so crazy! Stop playin'."

His facial expression did not change one bit. He was dead serious! Here I was twenty years old, only halfway finished with college, and here he was an airman in the air force with a child already and he expected me to marry him.

"T, I'm sorry but God didn't tell me that I was supposed to marry you and He usually communicates with me on these matters. I think you may be making a mistake. Remember, I have a boyfriend already."

We stood there for another fifteen minutes while he tried to plead his case. Finally I was tired of listening and I told him I had to go. After that I sort of avoided his phone calls until he got the point. I was not about to marry him! I would see him in the gym on occasions. He always had this sad look on his face like I really broke his heart. *I told him I had a man already.*

Another guy, R, that I used to hang out with was real cool. I met him in the parking lot of our student union. My friends and I were walking to the pool hall, and he pulled up beside us in his shiny blue Pontiac Firebird. His car was tight! He had his engine hooked up so that it sounded like a racecar. He also had a huge woofer in the back and large sparkling rims. He was talking to my friend Tiff at first, but I saw him looking my way. He asked Tiff to get my number and I gave it to him.

When he called me, he told me that he played minor league baseball for the Baltimore Orioles but was thinking about trying out for the NFL. He asked if he could take me out. I told him upfront as well that I had a boyfriend. He said he was okay with that and just wanted someone to hang out with until he left for his NFL tryouts. I said fine, but until I got to know him he would have to take me out with at least one of my friends. He told me I could bring whoever I wanted. So about three of my friends and I all met up with him for dinner. It was nice.

R and I hung out for several months. Not once did he try so much as to kiss me. He seemed real content with just going to the movies, going out to eat, going to the gym. He even took me and Carlee to Six Flags over Georgia in Atlanta. That night in Atlanta we stayed at a hotel, but Carlee and I took the beds and he slept in the recliner. He opened car doors for me and paid for me to get my hair done. I was loving this friendship. I thought everything was just fine the way it was. I should have known that something was up, though, when he started taking me home to meet his parents, and they referred to me as his girlfriend. He also had a child. He had a precious little girl with his girlfriend from high school.

Then it happened. He asked me to spend the night with him. My dumb butt agreed to it. My thinking was that we were going to be in the same house as his parents, so no harm in that. Whatever! That entire night I had to keep pushing him off me. Finally

I jumped up out of the bed and said "Take me home!" When he saw that I was serious, he decided to stop trying. He promised he wouldn't try any more if I would just stay the remainder of the night. Since it was pretty late, I agreed.

After that I avoided his calls for a while. When we did talk, all we did was argue. I couldn't take it anymore. Finally I just told him we couldn't be friends anymore. I think I learned an important lesson from this relationship. No matter how nice a guy is to you, if he is spending his money on you, eventually he is going to want something from you. I had managed to convince myself that R was different, but he promptly proved me wrong.

There was even this one guy that I used to hang out with who was a Kappa. I met him when I was a freshman, and we kind of hung out off and on from my freshman to my senior year. He was always the guy that I could call if I was just bored and wanted to go out and do something. He was always real sweet to me. He would take me to nice restaurants or we would just ride around and talk. He was a chef at a local restaurant, so he cooked pretty well also. He would take me to his apartment and make me steaks. His mom was a cardiologist in Birmingham, so I think he was a little spoiled. He also had a child, a little boy. I remember one day while we were sitting in his car going back to campus from eating dinner, just out of the blue he told me that he wanted me to have a little girl for him. Once again I just about choked. *What is up with these guys?! We haven't even kissed. I am not ready for any of this!* I kind of started to wonder if telling guys that I was going to be a doctor was really a good idea because it seemed that once they found that out they were on a mission to somehow make me fall in love with them. Maybe they were all looking for a potential sugar mama. I don't know.

Aside from the growth that I experienced in dealing with the opposite sex, I had a lot of memorable experiences at ASU. Most of them were good; however, it seems like it is always the negative ones that stand out the most.

During our freshman year, Carlee and I met a couple of guys

that we used to hang out with a lot. They were really sweet, so we called them our adopted brothers. There was no dating, no buying us anything. We just hung out. We called them K and K. K and K were from Atlanta and Detroit. I think they met initially when they came to college, but it felt like they had known each other their entire lives.

One day toward the end of our freshman year, it was strangely hot outside. Montgomery, Alabama, was always hot. I remember taking a shower and walking across campus to my first class. By the time I got to my classroom I would be so sweaty that I would feel that I needed to shower again.

Well, this day there was just a strange type of heat going on. It was so hot out until it was just boring on campus. To top it off the sky had an outlandish orange hue to it. Toward the evening Carlee, I, and the rest of our crew went to eat in the cafeteria. On the way back from the caf, which is how we often referred to the cafeteria, we saw K and K and a few other boys from Birmingham sitting on some steps in front of the north dining hall. For some reason K and K had a sort of sneaky look on their faces that I had never seen before. I spoke to them, and something made me just utter to them "stay out of trouble" with a smile. They both kind of looked at me bizarrely, smiled back, and said, "always." After that we headed back to our dorm room.

The next day the campus was buzzing and everyone in our little crew seemed to be in a state of disbelief.

"Girl, you ain't heard?" one of my friends asked.

"Heard what?" I asked dumbfounded.

"Girl, K and K tried to rob Burger King last night. All they got was about thirty dollars. But the bad part is they shot and killed someone."

I could not believe what I was hearing. We had just seen them sitting in front of the caf the night before. That was why they were looking so oddly and responded in the way that they did when I spoke to them.

"What!" I exclaimed.

"Yeah, girl," my friend continued. "They had set it up with one of their boys who worked there. He was supposed to leave the back door open for them after hours so they could come in and empty out the cash register. The friend was just going to call the police afterwards and say somebody busted in the door while he was trying to lock it and robbed him. Unfortunately one of the other guys who worked there came back to the store because he forgot something. K and K got freaked out when the other dude came back and they shot him. They were so stupid. They kept the gloves that they wore and the pistol in their dorm room. They went all the way to Birmingham last night and came back. They could have thrown that stuff out of the car anywhere between Montgomery and Birmingham. But they kept it in a shoe box under their bed. The police came into their dorm room and found all the evidence they needed. I guess the dude who worked there told on 'em."

I could not believe it. We had hung out with K and K almost our entire freshman year, and they killed somebody. Two more brothers going to jail instead of getting an education. As if there weren't already enough young brothers in prison.

Another uncanny recollection that I have from college was the baby that was born in our dorms. Apparently there was a girl who lived several floors above us our sophomore year in the Tower who was pregnant. Everyone who knew her, of course, knew she was pregnant. I never knew who she was. I just heard the story from several of my friends, and later on the news. Well, purportedly the girl went into labor in her dorm room. Her roommate was not there at the time. She allegedly had the baby in her closet. As if that was not freaky enough, after she had the baby she supposedly placed the baby in a plastic bag and poured bleach into the bag to kill the baby and hide the odor as the body decayed. She then proceeded to throw the baby down the garbage shoot. Somehow one of the custodial engineers discovered the lifeless baby's body in the garbage. Shortly after that there was a swarm of police cars surrounding our dorms to collect the body, evidence, and to question people to try to find out who had been pregnant in the dorms. A couple of days later the story ran on the news, and they showed the girl with her mother by her side. Apparently her mother never even knew she was pregnant. She said she just didn't want to let anyone down. Everyone was counting on her to finish college and make something out of herself. When the baby came she panicked. I'm not sure what kind of punishment she received.

She seemed really sorry that she had done what she had. How on earth could anyone bring themselves to kill their own flesh and blood? I have never been able to understand that. That poor little baby. So helpless. Babies depend on their mommies for everything. Mommies are supposed to protect their babies no matter what. Mommies often sacrifice their own happiness and wellbeing to make sure their babies are cared for. How can you kill your baby? There are so many other options. If you can't care for your baby, at least give the baby a chance at life and put it up for adoption. You can drop your baby off at any emergency room or fire department, no questions asked, and they will make sure the baby gets to someplace where he or she will be cared for. Please stop hurting babies!

Another very creepy memory that I have involves one of my softball buddies from high school. Michelle was our third baseman. She was one of the sweetest and smartest girls I knew. I really looked up to her.

She was the valedictorian of the 1993 graduating class at Spencer. She went away to college at Mercer University in Macon, Georgia. During the early part of Michelle's sophomore year at Mercer, my freshman year at ASU, she was found murdered at one of the parks in Macon. Initially no one had a clue what happened. She was at the park with a guy that she was dating and both of their bodies were found near his car. His body in the car, and hers outside of the car as if she was trying to get away from her attacker. Her story was on America's Most Wanted and everything, which eventually led to the capture of her murderer.

Well, after her death all of the local papers said, "Spencer High School Valedictorian Murdered." I received so many phone calls from people checking to make sure that it was not me who had been murdered. That really freaked me out. People actually thought that I was dead. It gave me the chills.

Needless to say, her funeral was extremely sad. How could someone murder such a young, beautiful, sweet person? When everything finally came together, I think they said on America's Most Wanted that the guy who murdered them was actually after her boyfriend and she just happened to be in the wrong place at the wrong time.

Traveling Shoes

The Christmas break of my freshman year, I went to Germany to visit my mom again. Lo and behold Ricky resurfaced. I thought he was coming to take his necklace back, but initially he came by just to drop off a letter. In his letter he felt the need to explain to me why he all of a sudden just disappeared during my last visit. In his letter it stated, "I had got this girl fat in the front. After we talked about it, she decided to get an abortion, so that's not an issue anymore. I would like for us to pick up where we left off. I'm sorry."

That letter frustrated me so much. In one way I was glad that he didn't just disappear because of something I did, but on the other hand this letter just proved that he really had not changed much at all since high school. It was still all about him. He really expected me to just forget all about the fact that he just left me hanging. How crazy was that?

My mom and I were riding in her car while I was reading the letter.

"Ma, why do guys just think they can do whatever they want to do and we'll be right there waiting? Why don't they just leave us alone if they don't really want to be with us?"

My mom had no clue as to what I was talking about. I

explained it to her by telling her what was in the letter from Ricky.

She proceeded by saying that a lot of times guys keep doing what they do because we let them. "As long as they can keep getting what they want from a girl, they'll keep coming back." I saw a look of apprehension in my mom's face as she said this.

"But Ricky has never gotten anything from me but a kiss. I don't know why he keeps coming back to me."

I saw a little smile come across my mom's face. "Well, maybe he knows that you are a good thing and he wants you all to himself. He's probably not been able to find anyone else like you, but he is not ready to settle down and be with just one person. I think young men feel like the more women they have, the bigger man they are and the more status they have."

My mom always had a way of saying things. I think it must have been the evangelist in her. Her statement made me feel really special.

I went out to the movies and to dinner a couple of times with Ricky during that visit. I really didn't have much time for him, number one because I think I was starting to outgrow his games, and number two, because my mom and I spent a lot of my visit traveling to Paris, Vicenza, and Venice.

Europe was wonderful. Everything was within a few hours' drive from Heidelberg, so we didn't have to spend very much money at all traveling to the different areas. We went to Paris first on a day trip. It took us about five hours to get there. We did not plan to spend the night, so we tried to do all of Paris in a single day. It was interesting. Once we finally found someplace to park we decided to get something to eat. None of us spoke any French, so we looked around until we found a restaurant with an English menu. All of us ate spaghetti. It was pretty good.

After we ate, we walked around and found the Eiffel Tower. We also went into the Louvre and saw a lot of the beautiful paintings. Even though Paris was nice, I didn't get a great vibe from the French people. What we found was that a lot of them would pretend that they could not speak English if they didn't want to deal with us. After we would leave their stores we would hear them speaking English, or see them talking to someone else laughing at us.

After we got tired of walking we grabbed some gelato and hopped onto a tour bus. Paris was beautiful. The building architecture was so amazing. The city was so clean and the roofs were made out of gold. Even though we were thrilled to be there, we were also exhausted. My mom and I fell asleep on the tour bus, so my stepdad made us get off the bus because he thought we had wasted his money. I thought the money was worth a good nap.

While I was in Europe, I was determined to find myself a nice pair of black sandals for school. I had looked all over Heidelberg and had not found a pair. While walking around Paris I looked in every shoe store that we came across, but could not find a pair that I liked. Finally we came upon a shoe vendor who was selling shoes at an outside booth. He was trying extremely hard to sell me his shoes. There was a pair that I thought were kind of cute but they had wedge heels which were not in style here yet. When I told the guy that I didn't really like the heels, he told me, "That's because these shoes are for woman, you are just a girl."

I wanted to grab that "woman's" shoe and knock him in the head with my "girl" hands. But I kept my cool, kept my money in my pocket, and said, "whatever" and walked away.

We ended our whirlwind tour of Paris with another trip to our then favorite restaurant for a second round of spaghetti. We knew that we could trust the food and the prices were very reasonable. After we ate we headed back to our car to find a French ticket on the windshield. Apparently we had parked illegally. What a great way to end our trip.

After our quick trip to Paris, my mom took me to Vicenza to visit a friend of hers who was stationed there. The trip was a lot of fun. We drove to Italy from Heidelberg. The countryside was beautiful. My favorite part of the trip was driving through Switzerland. Switzerland was one of the most scenic countries I had ever seen. The grass was very plush and green. The water was deep blue. The mountains were gorgeous with their white crowns of snow. There were waterfalls streaming down the mountain-sides along the highways. The houses were neatly situated along the tops and sides of the mountains. I was in awe.

One of the things that I found pretty unnerving about the drive, besides the fact that every time we entered into a new country we had to pay toll, was the fact that the roads were very narrow and were often along the edge of the mountains. If we looked down out the window there would be nothing but air and water beneath us. I prayed for safe passage. I knew my mom was a little nervous and praying the entire way because she didn't talk much throughout the portions of the trip that we spent rid-ing along the mountainsides. My mom has always had a fear of heights. She hates riding over any bridge, but she especially hates drawbridges. Driving along the edges of mountains turned out not to be a favorite thing for her to do either.

We stopped in a town in Switzerland to get gas. The Swiss people were so nice. They actually did look a lot like the Swiss people I often saw on television. Blond hair, blue eyes, and ivory skin. They seemed very welcoming to black people.

Once we got through Switzerland, we entered into Italy. I think one of the first cities we came upon was Milan. I really was not very impressed by what I saw there. For a city that was sup-posed to be so infamous for its fashion, the city seemed pretty old and dreary. Somehow we got a little lost while we were there, but eventually we found our way. After getting back on the autobahn, we were in Vicenza in no time. It was a very cute little town and my mom's friend had a nice place. We stayed with her for about a week. One of the days that we were there we caught the train and went to Venice. The train ride was really rewarding in that I was able to see a lot more of the countryside. The train had us in Venice in no time.

Even though it was a dreary day with a lot of overcast, Venice was still beautiful. The gondolas, all of the little shops, the food, the music. Everything was really nice. There were people there from what seemed like everywhere. Some of them were nice and clean. Others smelled like they had never bathed a day in their lives. The body odor was not so bad until we got onto a little boat to take us from one part of Venice to another. On that boat there were a lot of people, it was hot and humid, and all of the windows were up. The body odor seemed to permeate my nostrils so strongly that I could taste it. I felt as if I was suffocating. I had to find a way to open those windows quickly. Once I got a window cracked enough for me to stick my nose through it, I was okay.

Although there were all kinds of different people in Venice, there were not many black folks there at all. We were definitely the flies in the milk. But everyone there was so nice. Much nicer than in Paris. The one time we did see other black people was when we were exiting the train at the train station. They appeared to be Africans. We were so happy to see black folks that we immediately instinctively smiled at them and spoke. They looked us dead in our faces, proceeded to turn their noses up at us and utter, "Ooh, Americans." They actually frowned upon us because we were from America. How crazy was that? That was the first time I had experienced anything like that, and it really was not a good feeling. Oh, well.

While in Venice I was actually able to find the black shoes that I had been searching for. They were the perfect pair. So much for that French man.

After our day in Paris we caught the train back to Vicenza. Of course we all fell asleep on the train, so we slept past our stop. I think I woke up first and started looking around. I woke my mom and her friend up to inform them that we possibly had missed our stop. When my mom's friend looked at where we were and reviewed the train schedule, she realized we really had missed our stop. We just got off at the next stop and caught the train going in the opposite direction. It was fine because we did eventually get back to where we needed to be.

After spending the week with my mom's friend and her

daughter, we headed back to Heidelberg. Our trip had been very relaxing. The drive back was pretty nice as well. The only bad part for my mom was that there was a detour on the autobahn. That detour took us all the way up to the top of a mountain. And of course the road that we had to take was very narrow and there were no side railings to keep us from running off of the road and rolling down the side of the mountain.

My mom had a look of fear in her eyes. She even started to hyperventilate. At first I thought she was joking because I had never seen my mom act this way before. She was the type of person who was tough throughout any situation. She was the epitome of the term "army strong."

Because I thought she was joking, I stupidly started laughing at her. "Ma, you are so funny. This is really pretty. Why are you acting like you are scared?"

When I was that age, I was not afraid of anything. Anything, that is, except spiders and snakes. Everything else I was able to tolerate.

When I realized my mom was really scared, I stopped laughing and told her I would drive. We switched places right there on the mountainside. I kept trying to get her to look out and enjoy the scenery, but she kept her eyes closed the entire time.

I thought it was beautiful. At that time I had never been to the mountains before. I was able to see the waterfalls and streams from a closer view. As we got higher, it got colder and there was snow. When we finally made it to the top of the mountain, there was a little shop that we stopped at to use the restroom and get some souvenirs.

Amazingly, when we got to the top of the mountain, my mom reverted to her normal self. She was no longer anxious. While we were on the mountaintop, we walked around and took in the scenery. I was just so amazed at how creative God was. Everything was so perfect. The trees were bright green and plush. The sky was a wonderful shade of blue. The rocks were shiny and gray. The snow was like a thick, fluffy white carpet. The air was so fresh, crisp, and cool. A little too cool for me given we had not packed for snow. I felt so fortunate and blessed to be there.

A lot of people from small towns are afraid to venture out of their city limits. They feel uncomfortable leaving their familiar surroundings. My nana was that way. The only places she would go were the doctor's office and occasionally to church. She was the type of person who was content with getting dressed and sitting in the same spot on her couch. She felt she could have church right in her house with the preachers on TV and on her videos. It was a shame too because when she did get herself dressed to go out she would always look so pretty. My nana was a beautiful lady, and she always smelled so good.

Well, my mom and I definitely did not have small town mentality. We would go any and everywhere that God had created. Just give us a map and some gas, and we were there.

My mom kept her eyes closed the entire way down the mountain, just as she had on the way up. Going down didn't take nearly as long as going up did. Before long we had crossed over into Germany and were back at home. A few days later, I left to go back to school. I think this was the time my mom procrastinated until the last minute to leave and take me to the airport. Needless to say I missed my flight and had to reschedule for the next day. To this day, I still believe that she did that on purpose to spend more time with me. I'm not mad though.

Hide Me

My freshman year of college seemed as if it had flown by. I finished with a 4.0 GPA. Anthony and I were still kicking it on the weekends, and I did whatever I wanted to do during the week. It worked out well for me. I had finally talked him into taking some college classes. He took Math 101 and something else. He really did not seem motivated to get an education. He was content with just being in the military. He would always save his math homework for me to do for him, or he would call me and I would help him over the phone. He would be extremely excited if he just got a C on his exams. I was always trying to get him to set goals for himself, but he didn't seem too interested. He just went along with whatever I said—I think to keep me quiet.

During our sophomore year, Carlee and I decided that we were going to apply to join a sorority. We always said that we would join Delta Sigma Theta if they ever came back on the yard. Well our sophomore year we finally saw the signs that they were having a rush. We immediately decided to go over together to get our application. We started to learn as much as we could about the DST organization.

A couple of weeks after we submitted our applications and letter of recommendation, we found out that we had been accepted. We were so excited. We both went to the ATM to get the money for our dues.

After we got our money, Carlee went to the science building to get something. I decided to go back to our room to cool off. As I was walking up the stairs to get to our floor something happened that just changed everything.

A few weeks prior to that, one of our friends Keke, who was from Cleveland, began having problems with her roommate. Apparently they had gotten into a heated argument about her roommate's friends always being in their room sitting on her bed. They almost came to blows, and Keke came to our room about to cry. Of course, since she was our girl, her problem became our problem.

Every time we saw her roommate, Mandy, she would look at us and roll her eyes. She used to hang with a bunch of heavy-set girls. She was a pretty big girl herself.

She and her big-boned crew would walk in front of us and stop, trying to block our paths. Her crew and our crew would often get into arguments calling each other names. One weekend, Carlee and I were headed to Columbus. I had forgotten something in our room, so I ran back upstairs. On the way back into the stairwell, who did I run into? Mandy and one of her friends. Of course when they saw me they started walking real slow blocking my path. They opened the door to the stairwell then let it slam shut in my face. Then they stopped on the other side of the door sort of blocking it. When I opened the door, it hit the back of Mandy's shoe. Because I knew they were intentionally trying to block my path, I didn't bother to say I was sorry. I just kept walking right past them and made my way down the stairs. All of a sudden, Mandy turned into a mad woman.

"Heifer, you better say you are sorry!" she kept yelling as she ran behind me down the stairs. She walked behind me yelling all the way down the stairs, through the lobby, and out of the front door. When I got to the steps outside the door, I turned around, yelled a few choice words back her way, held my hands up like "what do you want to do?" and waited there for a few seconds. She turned around real quick and ran back into the building. I really let the devil get to me that day.

I don't think I saw her any for a whole week. The day that we found out we were accepted into DST and had gotten our money to pay our dues was the first day that I had seen her since that incident. Of course the devil would resurface on a day that I was feeling good. As I was walking up the stairs, she entered the stairwell behind me.

"Did Ms. Green contact you from the front office?" she yelled.

I had no clue what she was talking about because no one had contacted me. I tried my best to ignore her, so I kept right on walking. She must have thought that I had not heard her because she felt the need to repeat herself.

"Hey, I said did they contact you from the front office!"

I kept walking. I was trying so hard to avoid another confrontation. I was in too good of a mood to have to deal with this chick today. But then she said the words that plucked my heart strings.

"I should have kicked your behind last week like I started to!"

At that point, I stopped dead in my tracks, my heart started beating real fast, and I started breathing heavily.

"What did you say?" I asked.

"You heard me. I said I should have kicked your behind last week for stepping on my shoe!"

At that point I put my wallet down, took off my necklace and my earrings and placed them neatly on the floor, stood up, turned around, and said, "What's stopping you now, ho?"

She looked a little stunned when she realized I was not afraid of her. "You better not call me that again!"

At that point, I was so angry that I did not care what happened. My face was hot and flushed. I'm sure the devil was jumping up and down with excitement at that point yelling, "Fight, fight!" He knew he had me right where he wanted me.

After that all one hundred and eighty pounds of her rushed forward and swung at me. I really don't remember much about what happened next. When I snapped out of my rage, I was sitting on top of her, pinning her to the floor and holding her head down by her hair. She was yelling for me to get off her, but I was not about to let her up so that she could charge at me again. I wasn't even sure how I got her pinned on the floor. She outweighed me by about fifty pounds.

She had her fingernails dug deep into my arms trying to get me to let her up. "Get your nails out of my arms!" I yelled as I grabbed her braids even tighter and banged her head against the floor trying to get her to release the grip from my arms. The farther she dug her nails into my arms the tighter I grabbed her braids and banged her head into the floor.

When I realized what was going on, I got a little nervous. I had actually blacked out. I had never been in a fight before. I had never been that angry before. It was scary what I could have done to her at that point if I had actually had some type of a weapon. I had never seen that side of myself before and I really did not like it. I had always been someone who could maintain control no matter what the situation was. I saw why people claimed temporary insanity when they got in trouble for something. If you get angry enough, you really do lose your mind. I understand now why the Bible says to be slow to anger.

So I had her pinned to the floor. I was definitely not about to let her up. There was no one in the hallway but the two of us. We could have gotten up off the floor and gone to our rooms and no one would have known but the two of us that we had fought. *Lord, what do I do now?* I thought to myself.

At that moment, a girl that I knew named Tracy came out of her dorm room. "What are ya'll out here doing?" she asked.

"She came at me and I'm not going to let her up," I said breathing hard.

Once she realized it was me, she asked, "Danielle, what do you want me to do?"

"Call security."

"All right," she said.

About five minutes later, Ms. Green came running up the stairs with security.

"Danielle, let her up," she said.

"Ms. Green, I can't let her up because she's going to run at me again," I said.

"Mandy, if she lets you up, are you going to run at her?"

"No, ma'am," Mandy replied.

"Danielle, let her up. She's not going to run at you."

After a little convincing, I eased up off Mandy and walked down the hall a little toward my suite. I did not go into my suite because my wallet with all of my money and my jewelry were down the hall in front of Mandy's suite. As I walked down the hall, I saw all of Mandy's braids that I had pulled out during our fight. I felt kind of bad for her. I also felt very fortunate because at the time I had a sew-in weave that she could have easily grabbed a hold of and messed my head up pretty bad.

No sooner had I gotten up off Mandy and headed down the hallway did she start running at me again. Somehow my instincts kicked in and I just started boxing her. I was moving my feet and actually boxing her like I knew what I was doing. Pretty soon I got tired of fighting her, so I just decided to step back and look at her. She was fighting like a typical girl—head down and arms swinging wildly. I don't even think that she realized I was just standing back looking at her.

Finally the security guard grabbed her and took her away. I had to go with another security guard down to the police station for questioning. I thought for sure that I would be kicked out of the dorms for this. I had no clue what I was going to do if I was kicked out.

As I walked through the dorm looking crazy escorted by the security guard, I felt like a criminal. I did not know what was going to happen to me. I just hoped I didn't get kicked out of school.

When we got to the police station, the officer told me to write down my version of the story exactly as it happened. At that time my mind was still racing a hundred miles a minute. I wrote down everything that had happened word for word. After that was complete, he told me to return to my dorm room and await my trial.

After I left the police station, I went over to the science building to let the director of the biology program know what had happened. Part of me hoped that he could help me out in some way. He said he was sure everything would be fine given I had never been in trouble before. I was hoping he was right.

That was the most agonizing few days of my life. I believed this happened on a Wednesday. I was praying that someone would let me know something quick because intake for DST was that weekend. That Friday I was called into the Dean of Student Affairs' office. Ms. W was a light-skinned lady with a full head of thick wavy hair. She was definitely one of the "privileged" Negroes who probably came from a family of uppity black folks.

When I got to her office, she directed me to a seat across from her. In front of her, she was holding the pieces of paper that contained my statement of the events surrounding the fight. She told me that she had read the statement and was shocked at what it stated. She also told me that she was aware that I had applied to become a member of DST. She herself was a member.

This lady, who knew absolutely nothing about me other than what she read on those three pieces of paper, proceeded to tell me that I was not DST material. I wanted to scream at her and ask, *If I am not DST material, then who is? I have been through so much in my life and still managed to break free of my small country town. I was the last virgin among all of my friends, graduated as valedictorian of my high school class, did not curse (unless I was really provoked) did not smoke or drink alcohol, exercised three to four times a week, went to church, volunteered, attended college on a full scholarship, had a 4.0 GPA, was going to be a doctor, had never been in trouble in my life before this single event, during which I was only defending myself, and you're telling me that I am not DST material?* It really did not make any sense to me, however judging from her "I'm better than you" attitude, I figured trying to make a case for myself would probably be a waste of oxygen. I mean, there were several girls who I knew had crossed into DST for whom profanity was their second language. But I was not DST material?

I was pretty devastated by the news. That weekend Carlee packed up her things to attend intake weekend for DST. I felt like crap when I saw her packing her things to go. I could tell that she wasn't nearly as excited about it either because this was something that we were supposed to be doing together. I decided to pack my bags and go to Columbus that weekend. I couldn't stand being on campus any more than I needed to be.

When DST crossed their line of ninety-six girls, I really felt like crap. I was so jealous of all of them. I felt like I was being punished for defending myself. Since Mandy wasn't really involved in anything, she really did not get any type of punishment. We were both placed on probation for a semester, but nothing much beyond that. I knew that I should be grateful because I could have gotten kicked out of school, but I still didn't think that it was fair.

Well, I guess the devil really knocked me down in that chapter of my life. Thank God we don't have to stay down though.

Just Another Day

I ended my sophomore year without any further major mishaps. Since I had been so shaken up by the fight, I decided to really try to keep my nose clean. I decided to bury my head in my books. I finished another year with a 4.0 GPA. That summer I accepted a position to work as an intern at Cornell University School of Medicine in Manhattan performing research in the tuberculosis lab. Even though a lot of times I had absolutely no clue what I was doing, it was still interesting.

If nothing else, I got to learn about various laboratory techniques and what each process was used for. I also got the opportunity to get paid a lot of money to spend three months roaming around New York City. How cool was that? I made a lot of good friends and got to explore several neat places.

That summer, Anthony was at West Point, so he was able to come and visit me a couple of times during my stay. I thought that was wonderful because it did get pretty lonely up there at times. New Yorkers were nothing like the people that I was used to. I had always lived in the South, so I was used to people speaking to me and asking how I was doing. In New York, it seemed as if every man was for himself and himself alone. There were several times when people would just bump into me on the streets and would not even extend the common courtesy to say, "Excuse me." It sort of reminded me of some of the Europeans that I had encountered. A lot of them would look you directly in your face and would act as if you did not exist. In Europe I found that there was no such thing as personal space. People would come and stand as close to you as possible as if to intimidate you.

Well, aside from the people, Manhattan was a wonderful place. Tons of restaurants, places to shop, museums, the theaters. I was extremely excited to be there. At first, I was very paranoid. Coming from a small town, I heard all kinds of crazy things about the big city. Mostly from people who had never even been outside of the city limits. But those stories of muggings and rapes really had me nervous when I first got there. Everywhere I went I was constantly looking over my shoulder and maintaining a strong grip on my purse. Most of the time I was too afraid to even carry a purse, so I just kept everything in my pockets. I never really went anywhere by myself. Throughout the summer I got to where I would walk to the McDonald's on the corner by myself and catch a cab to Harold Square to go to Macy's or the other many places to shop down there. Anytime I got onto the subway, I always made sure there was someone else with me. Preferably a male in the group.

Although I enjoyed myself tremendously, I was very glad when that summer was over. I was ready to go home. By that time, my mom was stationed back in the U.S. at Fort Gordon in Augusta, Georgia. She and Gerald were still hanging tough despite the news she had recently given me about him.

During my last visit to Germany, Ricky was shaping my hairline. When my mom noticed that he was using a pair of Gerald's clippers on me, she sort of lost it. "Girl, don't you ever use anybody else's clippers to cut your hair!" This completely caught me off guard. I had no clue why she was so upset.

When we got to Fort Gordon, I started noticing a lot of little pill bottles under the sink in my mom and Gerald's bathroom. All of the bottles had Gerald's name on them. I sort of recognized some of the names of the medicines. When I saw this, it all made sense to me.

"Ma, what kind of cancer did you say Gerald had?" I asked while we were in the kitchen one day cooking dinner. Gerald was away at work at the time. She sort of looked at me as if she was defeated and had to break down and tell me the truth.

"Danielle, Gerald doesn't have cancer," she said. "He has HIV."

"I already knew that," I told her. "I was just waiting for you to tell me the truth."

I already knew what she was going to say before she even said it. We had studied some of those medications in some of my college courses. When I took cell biology and learned all about DNA and viral replication, we learned about how some of the medications worked to block the DNA replication of HIV. I also knew that HIV was not transmissible through skin to skin contact. That it was only transferred through bodily fluids. Therefore I was not afraid of being around Gerald. I was afraid, though, for my mom who was married to him. I knew they had to be having some sort of intimate contact. I was somewhat relieved by the fact that my mom was a nurse, so she knew all of the necessary precautions to take. I was also relieved that she knew he was HIV positive from the beginning, so it's not like she had been intimate with him first and then found out he had HIV after the fact. She was completely aware of what precautions to take from the very beginning.

She told me that the reason she married Gerald was because she felt very sorry for him. When they started seeing each other, he had nothing. His wife had left him and taken their two kids and the house. He couldn't even afford to keep his little car. My mom paid the five hundred dollars to keep the car from being repossessed and gave it to me while I was in high school. She said initially Gerald was told that he would not live for much longer. He always seemed pretty healthy to me.

After my mom confirmed Gerald's diagnosis for me, I did

start avoiding using the bathroom in their room. Everything else, however, remained pretty much the same. I didn't treat him any different.

After the ending of another event-filled summer, I was off to begin yet another year of college. I was now an upperclassman. After the culmination of my sophomore year, I was determined to make my junior year a more positive one. Things could only get better.

Campus life had not changed much. Carlee and I were still in the same dorm room in the Tower. We always submitted our dorm application really early so we would get the very first room on the second floor. That way if the elevators went out we did not have far to walk.

All of the DST girls were walking around on campus flaunting their crimson and cream attire. I always wanted to go the other way when I saw them. Almost all of them knew that I had also been accepted into DST. Some of them knew the reason I was not flaunting my own crimson gear. Others still questioned the fact. When asked, I always told them that something came up so I wasn't able to do it. They probably thought that I had gotten pregnant and had an abortion or something. At any rate, I still had to face that on a daily basis.

Since I was not a member of the organization, Carlee really did not get into many of the activities. She did go to some of their meetings and participate in some of their events, but she really didn't seem too thrilled by it. I felt really bad because I did want her to enjoy it; it was just hard for me to bring myself to the point of being excited for her. Every time I thought about it, I just wanted to go grab Mandy's head and start banging it into the floor again. I really had to pray for God to help me forgive her. "Lord, please give me strength."

I blamed myself every single day for what had happened. Why hadn't I just kept on walking? I couldn't answer that question. When she threatened me, I just could not keep walking away. My parents always taught me to stand up for myself, and that's what I thought I was doing that day. I was so confused that I didn't know what the right answer was. Somehow I was going to have to forgive Mandy as well as myself. I also had to realize that this was not the end of the world. I think a lot of times we focus so hard on what we want for ourselves that we fail to realize that maybe what we want isn't always what God wants for us. I mean, why else would I have gotten into a fight when after twenty years I had never been in a real fight, other than with my cousins, before in my life? Maybe it was not meant for me to become a member of DST at that point in my life.

I Was There

My junior year was the year that I really had to focus my attention on taking the medical college admissions test. From what I had heard, this test was no joke. It basically covered biology, general chemistry, organic chemistry, physics, and there was an essay portion. I had no idea where to begin studying. After much research and talking to people about how to prepare for this test, I decided to take a Kaplan Prep Course. The course was offered at Auburn University, which was about thirty minutes from ASU's campus. The class was on Saturday mornings. It was supposed to be really good because the instructors taught lessons on the various subjects and there were reading and workbook assignments between classes. They even offered a couple of mock tests with scores to give you a feel for the actual examination. I had planned to take the test in April of 1997, so I began my Kaplan course around January or February of that year. Prior to that, I purchased some books that I began to review on my own during my summer in New York.

During the same time as my Kaplan course, ASU put together a softball team. When I heard about this, I was extremely excited. I had missed softball so much. I immediately went over to talk to the coach. After I told her my softball history, she told me to come on out to practice that day.

That afternoon I reported to the softball field with my glove and my cleats. I was ready. Lo and behold I was in for a big surprise. Guess who was also on the softball team. You guessed it—Mandy. At first my heart started racing because I had not been this close to her since our trial. After that she seemed to avoid me at all costs. Now we would be teammates. When I saw that she was out there, I immediately made up in my mind that this was my chance to truly prove to myself that I could forgive her. I figured if Jesus could forgive me for all of the craziness I had done in my life then I could forgive her for starting all that mess with me and causing me not to be able to pledge DST.

Of course, the first thing that we always did in practice was warm up. It just so happened that everyone had paired up with somebody except me and Mandy. I grabbed the ball and turned to face her to start warming up. I could see a look of disdain on her face, but I smiled anyway.

Every day at practice we always seemed to get stuck with each other for warm ups. I really was surprised at how much it did not bother me. I truly believed God had helped me to forgive her. However, I could see that it was eating Mandy up inside. Eventually she just stopped coming to practice. The coach didn't seem like she missed her much at all. Mandy seemed more like she was in the beginner stages of learning to play ball.

Well, between playing softball, taking my Kaplan courses, studying for the MCAT, studying for my regular classes, being president of a club with over a hundred members, and trying to make time for Anthony on the weekends, I was getting pretty burnt out. I had to let go of something, and as much as I hated the thought, it had to be softball. The reason I chose to let softball go was because a lot of our games were away on Saturdays and my Kaplan course was on Saturday mornings. After paying nine hundred dollars for that class, there was no way I was going to miss it.

When I told the coach that I had to quit, she didn't seem to want to understand why. She told me that if I couldn't make it to all of the games that would be okay because she understood that my education came first. She also told me that I didn't have to ride the bus with the team. I could drive myself to the games if I needed to. She even asked me if there was anything that she could offer me to make me stay. I told her I already had a full scholarship and was receiving a stipend each month, so there really was nothing else that she could offer. Part of me felt that she was trying to bribe me in some way, but my decision was final. At this point, I had to focus all my energy on getting into medical school.

Carlee and I both entered into college with aspirations to become doctors. Entering into our junior year, our plans had not changed. We talked often about preparation for the MCAT. I had made the decision to take the Kaplan course, but Carlee was still trying to figure out what she was going to do for preparation. She seemed to be getting a little discouraged. I kept trying to encourage her and get her to take the Kaplan course with me, but she didn't really seem convinced that taking the course was worth almost a thousand dollars.

Well, I continued to prepare for my test, which I was planning to take in April. I decided to take my test in Atlanta at Morehouse College. Why on earth did I decide to do that? The weekend of my test happened to be the same weekend as Freak-Nic. Freak-Nic was exactly what it sounded like, a freaky picnic. Freak-Nic was the weekend when every single, young and wanna-be young person got together in Atlanta for one big party. Girls came out with their best weaves and shortest-tightest shorts and low cut shirts. Guys came out in their souped up cars with low profile tires, big rims, and loud beats. As usual in the black community, everyone was trying to outdo the next person. All the guys were trying to get with as many girls as possible. All the girls were trying to look their best so that as many guys as possible would try to holla at them only so that they could reject them. It was a freaky mess. There would be so much traffic in Atlanta during Freak-Nic weekend. People would be stopped on the interstate for hours. Eventually everyone would just get out of their cars and start partying in the streets.

Needless to say, concentrating on my test did not happen. My mind was out of the window somewhere wishing I was outside having fun with everyone else. I think that I was sort of defeated from the start on that test. I did not feel as prepared as I thought I would after taking that Kaplan course. I think part of the reason was because the course at Auburn was run by college students. People who were on the exact same level as I was. A lot of times when I would ask a question, I felt that they were just as unsure about the answer as I was. I felt they were just reading from the answer book.

I struggled to finish my test in time. Towards the end, I was just ready to turn my scantron in and go. I already knew that I was going to be retaking the test in August. I was glad to have just gotten the experience of going through the actual exam. I was especially glad that I had decided to take the April exam so that I would have time to retake the test in August.

When I received my exam scores, I was not surprised. I scored a 20. My goal was to score at least a 27 to help me get into Emory. Oh well. I had to study harder over the summer.

It seemed like each year in college, Carlee and I endured experiences that changed us in various ways. College is definitely a time when lots of maturation occurs if you go through it with the right intentions. Freshman year, two of our buddies went to jail for murder. Also one of the guys from Florida that I used to hang with was shot in the head and killed by a group of guys from Montgomery. His situation was one in which his Miami crew was arguing with a group of boys from Montgomery over representing where they were from. The dumb thing is that they were arguing over territory, and none of them even owned any property. It was during my junior year that my Mudea lost her battle with ovarian cancer. That was a sad time for my family. Those experiences really helped me to appreciate how precious life was. Sophomore year I had my fight. I had to learn to hold my head up and keep going even when I felt like things were caving in around me. No matter what we had gone through those first two years, nothing topped what Carlee experienced our junior year.

One afternoon after I had finished class and was on my way back to the dorms, I noticed Carlee's boyfriend and brother-in-law sitting in a car in front of the dorm. I was taken aback wondering what was going on because it was on a Wednesday, and we didn't usually see them until the weekend. I spoke and asked what was up, they just told me that Kera, Carlee's sister, was inside the dorms waiting. I walked into the lobby and saw Kera sitting in one of the seats waiting for Carlee. When she saw me, she hopped up out of the seat and walked toward me. She had sort of a distraught look on her face.

"Where's Carlee?" she asked as if she was barely keeping it together.

"She's in class taking a test. She'll be here in about thirty minutes. What's going on?" I asked.

As soon as I asked her that, she began to cry. "Daddy's dead!" she exclaimed.

"Oh my God," I whispered as my heart dropped into my stomach. I could not believe what I was hearing. Their father, Mr. C, had been like a second father to me throughout high school, so I really did not want to hear what I was hearing.

I immediately grabbed Kera and took her upstairs to our dorm room. The only thing I could think about was getting Carlee's stuff packed so that we could get her in the car before we told her about their dad because if we told her in the room we would never get her downstairs.

"Kera, let's not tell Carlee until we get her in the car. When she finds out she is going to fall out, and we won't be able to get her to the car," I said.

When we got to the room, I grabbed Carlee's suitcase and just starting grabbing clothes out of her closet and drawers. About fifteen minutes later, Carlee came walking in the door. "Kera, what are you doing here, girl?"

Kera looked like a deer caught in the headlights. She had no idea how to respond to Carlee's question.

"Carlee, something happened, and they need you to go to Columbus with them," I immediately said to bail Kera out.

"What happened?" she asked.

"Let's get you in the car first and then they'll tell you," I continued trying to smile to ease her anxiety.

"Will somebody please tell me what's going on?" she said with a nervous smile.

We just continued packing her suitcase. I asked her to take a look and see if there was anything else she needed. She reluctantly looked and then grabbed a few more things. After that we took her and her suitcase downstairs.

When we got downstairs, it had gotten dark and had begun to rain. It had also cooled off quite a bit. After the guys got Carlee's suitcase and other items put into the trunk, they all got into the car. Everyone but Carlee. She just stood on the sidewalk next to the car refusing to get in until someone told her what was going on. At that point, Kera looked Carlee in the eyes trying to hold it together. She then in a very slow and careful voice informed Carlee that their father was dead.

"Oh, God no. Not Daddy!" Carlee yelled in exasperation. She immediately collapsed onto the wet ground with a very loud painful sounding thud. Her boyfriend jumped out of the car and swept her up from the moist ground and placed her into the car. They then headed to Columbus to face what was no doubt the biggest challenge of their lives.

After they left, it finally hit me what had happened. Mr. C, one of the nicest men I knew, was dead. "Lord, why would you let something like this happen to him?" I was so confused. I immediately ran back into the dorm covering my face so that no one could see me crying. Since my shoes were wet from the rain I slipped as I walked across the lobby floor, but I was able to recover without falling and get upstairs to my room. I immediately called my mom and let her know what had happened. She was shocked as well.

A couple of days later, Carlee called me and gave me more information. Her father had been a correctional officer for many years. He and several of his coworkers had gone to Macon, Georgia, for some training. There were about thirteen of them in their van. On their way home from training, apparently the driver of a semi-truck fell asleep behind the wheel and crossed the median and entered into oncoming traffic. The driver of Mr. C's van tried to swerve out of the way but ended up losing control of the van. They crossed the median into oncoming traffic and were hit by another semi-truck. The van flipped over, and four of the thirteen men were killed, and Mr. C just happened to be one of them.

Life after that was changed forever. Carlee decided to withdraw from ASU for that semester so that she could get things done at home. Her dad named her as the executer of his estate, so all of a sudden she had a lot on her plate. She didn't quit school though. She transferred to Columbus College for the semester so that she could remain on schedule with graduation. She was always a well-grounded person who knew that no matter what happens, life goes on.

Encourage Yourself

The remainder of my junior year I spent without Carlee. Since school had already started, I did not get another roommate that semester, therefore I had the entire room to myself. Keke would come down almost every night, so it was almost as if I had a new roommate.

I still saw Carlee on the weekends, because I would still go to Columbus to see Anthony. He had finally gotten a car, so a lot of times he would just drive to Montgomery to see me, and we would get billeting on base. One weekend when he came, he didn't seem like his normal chipper self. I kept asking him what was wrong, but he just kept telling me, "Oh nothing, just tired." Finally that Saturday night he opened up to me.

"Well, sweetheart, they told me the other day that I have to go to Korea for a year."

At first I thought I heard him wrong. Then I looked up and saw his face and realized he was serious. I immediately started to cry. It seemed like the people I loved were always taken away from me for an extended period of time. At that time, Anthony and I had been together for three years. I had really grown to depend on him always being there for me no matter what. Even though we had started fussing a lot, mainly because I wanted him to step up and have more of a "man in charge" attitude, I really did not want him to go anywhere.

He grabbed me and gave me a huge hug and told me everything was going to be all right. He tried to reassure me that the year would most likely go by extremely fast. I was so heartbroken at that point that I did not know what to do. Therefore I just went to sleep, hoping that when I woke up in the morning the conversation would have been just a bad dream.

The next morning he left to head back to Columbus. I went back to campus, went straight to my dorm room, and jumped in the bed. I think the only times I got out of the bed for the remainder of the day were to eat and use the bathroom.

After Anthony told me that he was going to Korea, it seemed that the last few months of my junior year flew by. From the time that he told me about going to Korea, he had been asking me little questions about marriage. I sort of hinted that if he was thinking about asking he would have to get my mom's permission. A few days later, my mom called me on the phone sounding a little frantic.

"Danielle, Anthony just called me and asked for my permission to marry you. I told him ya'll must be planning on a long engagement. You are not even finished with school yet. Do you love him enough to marry him? Are you sure he is the right one for you? You know I always have told you that you need someone who is going to be on the same level as you mentally and educationally. Someone with similar goals in life. I'm just not sure he is the one."

"Well, Mom, I do love him, but I am not planning on getting married anytime soon. I need to have my college degree and my doctor's degree before I marry anyone. If he does ask me, it will definitely be a long engagement," I assured her.

Well, I must say, he did not waste any time. Valentine's Day 1997 we went out to dinner at Ruby Tuesday's in Montgomery Mall. I noticed throughout the entire meal he just seemed real nervous about something. He barely even touched his food. After we ate our entree, I ordered the strawberry shortcake dessert. As the waitress was handing me my dessert, I looked up and saw Anthony drop to one knee.

"Look, he's proposing!" a heavyset white lady yelled.

"Danielle, will you marry me?" Anthony said in a nervous squeaky voice.

At that point, everyone in the restaurant had turned around and started looking at us. To my surprise, I was not nearly as excited as I thought I would be when someone finally proposed to me. In fact, it was almost as if I felt nothing at all. Part of me wanted to tell him no because I really was not ready for this. But, because I did not want to hurt his feelings, I went ahead and said yes. He then placed the ring on my finger and stood up and gave me a hug and a quick kiss. Everyone in the restaurant started clapping. I was completely embarrassed and ready to leave at that point.

After it sunk in a little bit, I was pretty thrilled to be wearing an engagement ring. It felt kind of good telling people that I was engaged. I had a fiancé. It seemed as if everyone noticed my ring when I got back to class. All of the girls asked me about it. They all wanted to know how he proposed. It was cool. A lot of the guys would ask in sort of a smart-alecky way.

"So you engaged now?" they would ask with contempt in their voices.

"Yep," I would say proudly as I held my finger up for them to get a closer view.

May rolled around pretty quick, and before I knew it the time had come for Anthony to get on the plane for Korea. The weekend before he left, I flew out to Arkansas to meet all of his family. He was from a real small country town called Hampton. Hampton, Arkansas, was about as small of a town as they came. When I say only one traffic light, I truly mean this town only had one traffic light. It had one gas station, one country restaurant, one grocery store. It was small. Hampton made Callahan look like a big city.

When I got on the plane to head back to Montgomery, I cried like my world was falling apart. We had never been apart for more than three weeks. Now we were going to be apart for a whole year, and it would be seven months before he would be coming home on leave for the Christmas holidays.

By the time my flight was halfway over I had regained my composure. I realized I was going to be fine. The time that we had apart was going to be the time that I spent working on me. I really needed to focus on getting into med school. I also wanted to get back into shape, so now I would have plenty of time to spend at the gym. On top of that, in a couple of weeks I was going to be heading to Madison, Wisconsin, to begin a summer research program at University of Wisconsin-Madison. Once again God was taking me to another place on His earth that I had never visited before. God is awesome!

After school had finally wrapped up for the summer I packed up my belongings and headed to Augusta, Georgia to visit my folks for a little while before I headed up to Wisconsin. I was very excited because I had not seen my mom in a while. I was also excited because my mom finally had a house of her own. I was at last able to tell my friends that I was going home to my mom's house for the summer. My mom had purchased a new home in a suburb of Augusta called Hephzibah. Hephzibah was a small area where a lot of military and retired military families lived. It was also home to a wonderful restaurant called Hosanna's Seafood. This restaurant made some of the best fried rice and flounder I had ever eaten. We ate there, it seems, almost every day. The owners were a mixed couple. The man was black and his wife was Korean, hence the combination of the fried flounder and the fried rice. They were just as sweet as they could be.

There was not much to do at all in Augusta. All I did was exercise, visit my mom at Eisenhower hospital, go to the mall, and go to church. Because of my mom's extensive military career, she seemed to know people from all over the world. One of the many people she knew led her to a church called Faith Outreach, which was led by Pastor Peoples. Pastor Peoples and his family were extremely nice people. Within a matter of months, it seemed, the church grew from just a few people meeting in a school cafeteria, to a large congregation gathering in their new sanctuary. God really blessed that church. I believe it was because the pastor was truly genuine and was about providing the Word of God for the people of God.

In early June, my mom and I headed on our quest to get me to Wisconsin. We had calculated it to be a fourteen-hour drive, but we planned to make a couple of stops along the way. We left three days before I was supposed to be there just to give us enough time to enjoy our trip. We loved going on road trips to see the countryside. Besides, it was best to drive so that I would not be stuck without my car all summer.

On our trip, we stopped in Nashville, Tennessee. We saw all of the people standing on the street corners with their guitars playing loudly hoping someone would sign them to a record deal. It was in Nashville that I also saw my first real life pimp. There was actually a guy in a super fly suit and hat with a feather in the side driving in a big body Cadillac standing out in front of the gas station. With him was a skinny chick wearing short shorts and a sports bra. The crazy thing was that the girl was pregnant and still out there trying to turn tricks. Truthfully, I thought that stuff only happened on TV. I guess I was wrong about that.

After we had lunch in Nashville, we traveled on to Clarksville, Tennessee, to visit my uncle Fella and aunt Lorraine. We got a hotel room and spent the night there so that we could spend a little time with them. The next morning we got on the road again and traveled all the way up to Chicago. When we got there, we decided to get a room and complete the rest of our journey the next day. That night in Chicago after eating dinner, my mom and I were walking down the streets of the downtown area. All of a sudden we heard a lot of cheering, car horns honking, toilet tissue rolls coming out of windows. All of a sudden it got real crazy outside. "The Bulls did it again!" someone yelled. Apparently the

Chicago Bulls had just won their fifth straight NBA championship. It was amazing being on the streets of downtown Chicago experiencing this.

Chicago was such a beautiful city. There were tons of places to shop, eat, and relax. The Lakeshore Drive area was just amazing. I really enjoyed my stay there, and made it a point to revisit during my summer in Madison, which was only two hours away. Plus, I had a friend who lived in Chicago, and I told her I would visit when I came to the area.

Madison, Wisconsin, was completely different from what I thought it would be. I was not at all surprised that the city was mostly white. There were very few blacks in the area. Although it was small, it was really a nice college town. The University of Wisconsin's campus was so beautiful. The student union sat on a huge lake. In the middle of the campus was a street called State Street that was full of places to shop and eat. The campus was huge. The thing that really surprised me was that the people of Madison were so nice. They seemed as if they were really happy to see black people in their town. They almost broke their necks to talk to us. My mom and I were a little apprehensive at first, because we knew sometimes people would only pretend to be nice to us just to get in our business, but these people seemed to be genuinely nice. I really felt that I was going to enjoy my summer in Wisconsin.

And I did. That summer ended up being a very positive summer for me. Aside from the fact that I almost got kicked out of the dorm after we had a girls against boys battle one night. We were extremely loud and the boys ended up pouring buckets of water under our doors. The security guy actually thought that the girls took turns pouring buckets of water under each other's doors. After we explained to the program director what happened, the guy who actually poured the water was made to move out of the dorms for the summer. That was another scary, stupid, avoidable moment for me. After that I decided to take my summer seriously.

I accomplished more those eight weeks than I had at any other point in my life. I worked on a research project that involved the herpes virus, I worked out every day and ended up losing ten pounds, and I retook the Kaplan course and received excellent teaching by doctors and graduate students. I also got to travel to Milwaukee for Afro-fest and back to Chicago to visit friends and go to the Taste of Chicago, which was a lot of fun. I met Big Les from BET and got the opportunity to take a picture with her. While in Chicago I also got to go to a party on Navy Pier where Kidd Capri was the DJ. It was really a great summer.

At the end of my internship, I felt really wonderful. I was proud of myself for all that I had accomplished. I was healthier and I felt really well prepared to take the MCAT again. My mom flew up to meet me, and we drove back down to Augusta. A few days later I retook the MCAT exam. This time when I walked out of the room, I felt much better about my performance.

A couple of weeks after I took the MCAT, I was back at school beginning my senior year. I was really pumped about being a senior. I really couldn't believe that the time had gone by so fast. When I had gotten to ASU in 1994, four years seemed like a really long time. However, once I had gotten into studying and involved in all of my extracurricular activities, the time flew by.

Being away from Anthony all summer had been hard. I was really glad to be back in school to take my mind off him. A lot of my guy friends were still in school, so I always had someone that I could call when I just wanted to hang out. It seemed that the longer Anthony was gone, the less I actually missed him, which was very strange to me. He would send me all kinds of neat gifts from Korea. It seemed that every week I was headed to the post office on campus to pick up a package. One day while I was in organic chemistry lab, this guy named Al who was a chemistry major asked me what I had in my package.

"Oh, a gift from my fiancé," I told him.

"Oh," he said and turned and walked away.

I had noticed Al around the building, but we had never really held a conversation. I knew that he was a chemistry major and that he was pretty much the smartest chemistry major on campus. He was also very handsome. Tall with smooth brown skin, he was definitely my type. And he had a smile that just took my breath away. Even though he was super smart, he did not look nerdy in any way. He always wore baggy Polo jeans, big Polo t-shirts, and Timberland boots. He was intelligent but dressed a little thuggish. He was just my type. And unlike all the other guys in the science building, he never really tried to push up on me. After that day in the organic chemistry lab, it seemed like every single time I turned around Al was somewhere standing on the wall chillin' lookin' all good. Not only did he look good, but he always had the sweetest aroma. I had gotten to the point where I had actually started looking for him around the building. I actually got butterflies in my stomach every time I saw him. I finally told Carlee that if I did not have a fiancé, I would try to get with Al.

I was really good friends with Al's roommate Lamar. Lamar was from New York, and we had a lot of classes together. He was an Alpha, therefore a lot of girls on campus were always all over him. Every time he came to class, he had a huge hickey on his neck. One day after class Lamar asked if he could call me. I was completely shocked because I had never looked at Lamar in that way. He was always someone that I could joke with in class and fuss at for missing class. It seemed being in a frat was taking its toll on Lamar and he was choosing his frat over his class work. He would always ask me for the notes for the classes he missed, and since we were cool, I would try to help him out.

At first, I did not know that Al and Lamar were roommates. When I realized that they were and that Lamar was trying to get with me, all I could say was, "Oh, no. I am crazy about his roommate."

I kept telling Lamar that I could not get with him because I was engaged, but shortly after that I decided to express my interest in Al. We were standing outside of the science building one day and I just walked right up to him. "So when are you going to cook for me?" I asked him. He looked a little shocked. I had overheard Al bragging about how well he could cook, so I figured I would see what he was made of. He lived in the male honors dorms, and for some reason they had stoves when no one else was that fortunate.

Al looked at me with a straight face and said, "When do you want me to?" He had the deepest, sexiest voice I had ever heard. I was in so much trouble. I was extremely surprised that I had made the first move. That was something I had never done before. I was pretty glad that I had though. I was excited about my dinner date that Friday night.

It's Time

I arrived at Al's room looking and smelling good that Friday night. His dorm room actually smelled like he had thrown down in there. He had cooked some butter beans, rice, fried chicken, and cornbread. Oh, it was *on*. A brothah who could cook! That's what I was looking for. It was not looking good for Anthony at all.

Surprisingly enough I was very comfortable around Al. I was usually very shy when it came to eating around guys, which is the dumbest thing. We all have got to eat, so why is eating anything to be embarrassed about? Anyways, dinner was wonderful and the conversations that we had were really interesting. Finally, a guy who was on my level who I could talk to about stuff that actually meant something to me and he understood. I always felt like I had to hold back with Anthony because without having gone to college he really did not understand what I went through on a daily basis, therefore he could not relate. I definitely could not talk to him about any of my classes. It sort of limited our conversation to a lot of chit chat about meaningless issues. I think it frustrated me so much that I would pick arguments just so that we would have something to talk about.

With Al it wasn't like that. He was a lot of fun. He made me laugh a lot with the things that he said. After we ate dinner

I invited him to come to the movies with my friends and I to see *Soul Food.* Of course, when we got to the movies, his boy Lamar was there. When he realized Al and I were together, he sort of gave us a strange look like "what are ya'll doing together?" I have no clue why he was looking at me strange, because he still had a huge hickey in his neck and was there with one of his chicks. *Soul Food* was an excellent movie. Vivica Fox, Vanessa Williams, Nia Long and everyone else all played their parts very well. We had a really good evening all around.

After that night it seemed like Al and I hung out every day. Visitation began in his dorm at five o'clock. When five o'clock hit I would call Al and ask if he wanted some company. He always said yes, so I headed over to his room to hang out. We would study together, watch wrestling and *Southpark* together, and I would fall asleep on his chest. He would just let me sleep until about twelve forty-five because visitation was over at one o'clock. I would then go back to my room, shower, and then call him. We would stay on the phone until about two or three o'clock every morning, knowing we had eight o'clock classes the next morning. We did the same thing almost every day.

The more time that I spent with him, the more I realized he was exactly the type of guy I wanted to be with. Everything just seemed so natural with him. He was very respectful to me. We talked very little about my relationship with Anthony. Neither one of us really wanted to think about it. With him being in Korea, it was almost as if he was nonexistent. I was very upfront and honest with Al from the beginning about my relationship. I told him that I had been thinking a long time about breaking up with Anthony because I just did not feel we were compatible. He had a hard time understanding why I would stay with someone for four years if we were not compatible. I had a very hard time answering that question. Although I knew the real reason that I had remained with Anthony for so long was for the simple fact that I did not want to be alone.

Al and I continued to grow closer and closer. That October

we went to the Magic City Classic in Birmingham. Al drove, and he let Keke ride with him given Carlee and I were Golden Ambassadors and had to ride the school bus. After the activities for the game were over, Al came to the hotel and picked Keke and I up to go to the hotel where he and his Mobile crew were staying. There I met his mom, sisters, and brothers. It was real nice to hang out with them. I was a little nervous around his mom at first. She was a real nice lady but she did not seem like she played at all. The last thing I wanted to do was to get on her bad side.

When Al and his brother took Keke and I back to our hotel, I went to give him a hug good night. As I hugged him, I looked up into his eyes and he laid the sweetest kiss on me that I had ever experienced before in my life. I literally felt as if I was going to melt. After our kiss, I quickly told him goodbye and went into the hotel. When Keke and I got into the hallway I slid down the wall onto the floor. I could not believe that we had kissed, and I definitely could not believe that a single kiss could make me feel that good inside. I knew at that moment that he had to be the one. I was definitely breaking up with Anthony when he came home for Christmas.

When Al and I had returned to campus after the classic, we continued our usual routine. Eventually one thing led to another, and before I knew it we had taken our relationship to another level. It was definitely a done deal. My relationship with Anthony was over.

That semester turned out to be very busy but fun. I spent a lot of time completing applications for med school, interviewing in various places including Birmingham, Augusta, Memphis, Wisconsin, and Atlanta. I initially had applied to about ten medical schools, but the cost of the applications was so high that I narrowed my list down to five schools when it came time to submit secondary applications. Emory was always my number one choice. When I received my MCAT scores I was sort of satisfied, yet a little worried that they would not be good enough for me to get into Emory. I had hoped for at least a twenty-seven. I scored a twenty-five, which was five points higher than my previous score. I knew I would get into someone's school, but I was a little nervous that I would not get into Emory because it was extremely competitive.

The week after I interviewed in Memphis, I received my first acceptance letter from them for medical school. I was praising God because I knew that even if I did not receive another acceptance letter I was going to be a doctor. This would be the end of struggling. My family would be well taken care of. A couple of weeks later I received my second acceptance from Birmingham. That letter was followed by yet another acceptance letter from the Medical College of Georgia in Augusta. Next I received a letter from Wisconsin stating I had been placed on their waiting list. It really did not bother me, because it was so cold in Wisconsin when I went there in November to interview I pretty much guaranteed myself that I would not be coming to school there. So far I had gotten three acceptance letters, but none of them were from the school I had really wanted to go to. I prayed to God for Emory to contact me.

When I had gone to Emory for my interview, it was totally different from my interviews at the other schools. Emory did a couple of individual interviews, but they also conducted three on three group interviews where each applicant interviews with two other applicants. There were also three interviewers. During my interview, I felt so inadequate because one of the girls in the room with me had traveled all over Africa on humanitarian missions. She also had her Ph.D. and had done tons of things that I had no clue about. I had done a lot of research, volunteer work, was a club president, and a few other things, but I felt like I was in way over my head when it came to comparing myself to her. I thought there was no way I was ever getting in over this girl. I interviewed with Emory in December. I then had to spend the entire Christmas holiday wondering what my fate with Emory would be.

When December came around, Anthony called and said that he was on his way to Arkansas. A few days later he told me he would meet me in Augusta. Part of me was looking forward to seeing him so that I could finally put our relationship to rest. Another part of me was dreading what I was about to do because he had no idea what was about to occur. He still thought everything was cool between us. I was completely honest with Al about Anthony coming to see me over the Christmas holiday. It did not seem to bother him one bit.

When Anthony arrived at my mom's front door, he was all smiles when he saw me. He immediately wanted to hug and kiss me. I gave him a hug and I really was glad to see that he was doing well. He came in the house and got comfortable. We talked about his trip. We all went out to dinner that night. When we got back to my mom's house, my mom and Gerald went to bed, and Anthony and I sat up to get reacquainted. After having spent the past few months with Al, being with Anthony just was not the same. I felt absolutely nothing for him. I had to find a way to let him down easy. The more comfortable Anthony got, the more I realized I had to think of some way to break up with him. I was having a very hard time because we had been together for so long and I never wanted to hurt his feelings.

Gerald was being a little messy as always. He and Anthony had grown to be pretty tight over the four years we had dated. When Gerald decided to reset the answering machine, he wanted all of us including Anthony to state our names on the message. I really did not want his voice on that machine, but again I did not want to hurt his feelings.

New Year's Eve rolled around, and we attended Watch Night service at Faith Outreach. That night during service, something happened that gave me the strength to do what I had to do to get out of my relationship with Anthony. After Pastor Peoples finished preaching, he asked for all of the fornicators who wanted to be forgiven to come to the altar for prayer. I thought about it for a second, and initially thought that I did not want everyone up in my business. However, the more I thought about my situation, the more I knew that I needed to be at that altar. It seemed like the closer I got to the altar the more the weight was being lifted from my shoulders. When I got to the front, I just fell on that altar and asked God to help me to do what was right. I laid on that altar and just cried out for God to guide me. I really needed help. Lord knows I wanted to be with Al, but Anthony had always been there for me and I did not want to hurt him. While I was spread out on that altar, God told me Anthony had to go.

As I was lying on the altar, I felt a pair of arms go across my shoulders. It startled me at first, but then I realized that it was Anthony who was hugging me. I immediately wished he would have just stayed in his seat. I finally just stood up, and when I did a couple came up and started talking to us. They told us about their prior situation. They said that they had shacked up for a few years before they decided to go ahead and do what was right. They were encouraging us not to be afraid; as long as we kept God first everything would be all right. I appreciated the fact that they were trying to help us, but they had no clue what I was actually on the altar praying for. Neither did Anthony.

When we got home after church, I told Anthony that I thought we should take a break from our relationship. He looked a little stunned, but he didn't ask any questions. Once again he just went along with whatever I said. I really wanted to tell him that I wanted to take a permanent break, but I just couldn't bring myself to hurt him like that. I figured I could just email him once he got back to Korea and tell him that we would never be getting back together again. After I told him we should take a break, he said that he had planned to come back with me to Montgomery for another week. I was sort of irritated by that because I really wanted to get back to Al, but once again I thought about the fact that he had come all of the way from Korea and then from Arkansas to see me. As much as I wanted to say no, I really didn't want to hurt his feelings. I reluctantly said okay.

I had talked to Al several times throughout Christmas break. During the first few conversations, he seemed very happy to hear my voice and it seemed like he missed me. Pretty soon he stopped calling, and when I called him he was either too busy to talk or when he did talk he did not seem like he wanted to be bothered. I really did not know what had changed. I was starting to think that once again I had been played. But I really could not understand it this time. I mean, I could really feel that he cared for me while we were at school. I knew he could not have been jealous of Anthony because he knew of that situation before he and I had gotten serious.

When Anthony and I got to Montgomery, we checked into our room on base. I then told him that I had to go on campus for a while. I went straight over to Al's room to welcome him back from the holidays. When I called him to tell him I was on my way over he really seemed like I was getting on his nerves. I went over there anyway. When I got there, he just seemed so bitter to me. I tried to give him a hug, but he just gave me a quick pat on the back and sort of pushed me away. He did not have very much to say to me at all. This really hurt my feelings because all I could think about the entire time we were apart was getting back to Montgomery so that I could be with him. Something had to have happened to make him do a complete one eighty on me like that. When I asked him what was wrong, he quickly said, "Nothing."

After I saw that he didn't want me there I went to my dorm room for a minute to speak to Carlee who was back at school doing well. I then grabbed a couple of things for class and then headed back to the base. I took my shower and went to bed. That whole night all I could think about was the fact that I was losing Al and I wasn't sure why. I swore to myself that I was going to straighten things out so that they could be the way they were before the Christmas break.

At the end of that week, Anthony finally left. He was probably shocked at how quickly I hugged him, gave him a quick peck on the cheek, hopped in my car, and left him standing in the

Shoney's parking lot. This time when he left, it was nothing like the way I was boo-hoo crying when he first left to go to Korea. I was actually happy to see him go. I actually felt like a ton of bricks had been lifted from my shoulders this time. I was off to get my man.

Hold on to Your Faith

It seemed the closer I tried to get to Al after Christmas break, the more he pushed me away. I just could not figure out what was going on with him. When I tried to talk to him about it, he would not give me any answers. He just acted like I was really annoying him. I really did not need this stress in my life. On top of waiting to hear from Emory, it was just getting to be too much. I kept thinking that maybe he was mad at me because of Anthony's visit, but then I told myself that there was no way that was it because I was completely honest about the fact that Anthony was coming back from Korea to see me. He knew I had a fiancé before we even started talking, and he seemed entirely cool with it the entire time.

Al continued to act cold and harsh toward me for the entire month of January. Finally I just asked him if he wanted me to stop calling him and leave him alone. He paused for a very long time and then answered "yes." Because he paused I didn't believe he was being honest. So I told him to actually say the words that he wanted me to leave him alone. He said the words, but I still didn't believe him because I had to prompt them out of him. "You don't mean it," I said and then changed the subject. The next day I called and ask if he wanted company and he would always say yes.

Because he was distancing himself so much from me, I had not bothered to tell him that Anthony and I had broken up. I didn't want him to think I was just telling him something to keep him. On top of that, he had told me that during his Christmas break he had met someone back home. When I asked him what he meant by "met" and if he planned on continuing to see her, he wouldn't give me an answer. When he told me that, I started to feel sick on my stomach. I just could not understand why he was being so mean. Since I did not seem to be getting anywhere with Al, I accepted a few dates with this really cute guy, F, who I had known the entire time I had been as ASU. F was also a biology major and had given me his phone number earlier in the year and told me to call him when it was okay for him to take me out. I had really hoped going out with him would take my mind off Al. Needless to say, the entire time I was with F all I could talk about was Al. Plus, F was rather quiet and shy, which I really did not like. I liked for a guy to talk and make me laugh, exactly the way that Al did. F and Al were supposedly friends, and he knew Al and I had been hanging out, so I felt I could talk to him about Al.

In February my friends and I had decided to go to Mardi Gras. We were initially going to New Orleans to stay with my aunt Ella and uncle Jimmy, but we decided we didn't want to go there. We had heard about the Mardi Gras in Mobile and had decided we would try that one out instead. One night while Al and I were on the phone, I told him that Keke, Carlee, and I were going to come down to Mardi Gras in Mobile. I was pretty shocked when he invited us to come and stay at his house. I told him that we could get a room of our own, but he said that didn't make any sense.

When we got to Mobile, we went to the various parties and parades. Al did his thing and I did mine. We really didn't do very much together because I didn't want to cramp his style. I did not want him to feel like I was in his space. Sometimes when folks get around their own people they start to treat you funny, and I didn't want to give him that chance.

On Saturday night when we all went out together, I really wanted to hang out with him. I just felt that it was so ridiculous for us to be that close to each other and act as if the other did not even exist. We were at one of the parties and he had gone to get a drink. He actually came over and asked me if I wanted something. When he brought my drink back to me, I asked if we could dance together on the next slow jam. He said okay, which shocked me, so I was very excited. He went back over to the side of the room where he was standing with his younger brother. All of a sudden, I saw a couple of girls walk up and stand next to them. One of them was wearing this super tight velvet dress. I saw her looking my way. She then moved even closer to Al who was just standing there grinning all in her face. At that point, a slow song came on. I walked over to him and told him I was ready to dance. He said okay, but did not move. I decided that I would walk over to Keke and Carlee and wait for him. The next thing I know the girl in the tight velvet dress had turned around and was rubbing on her butt right in front of Al while he was standing there staring and smiling even bigger. It was at that point that I had decided my relationship was completely over with him. There was no way on God's green earth that I was going to let any guy disrespect me like that. When he finally decided to walk my way I pulled him into the hallway and told him that when we got back to school whatever there had been between us was completely over. And I have to admit that the words that I chose were not that nice. I then left him in the hallway, grabbed Carlee and Keke, and we went out on the dance floor to have some fun. I did not speak to Al anymore that entire weekend.

Sunday we all went out on Dauphin Street to get Mardi Gras souvenirs. My friends tried to trick me into sitting up front with Al. I just stared out of the window the entire time. I was not about to talk to him anymore because I was not about to let him hurt me again. I had put up with more from him over the previous few months than I had from any other man in my entire life. I really felt like I had been in a constant battle trying to get things back to where they were between us, and I was tired. Something had to give.

After we got our souvenirs, I was very ready to head back to Montgomery. I felt horrible the entire ride back to campus. I was really frustrated with Al because I really had no clue why he would all of a sudden lose complete interest in me. I was also upset with me for allowing myself to fall so hard for him. I had learned from all of my previous relationships to always keep my guard up, but he seemed so different from all of the other guys I had known. I really thought he was the one. No other guy had ever made me feel the way that he did. He was the only guy that I ever made the first move with. I guess I won't do that again.

I think I was in a state of depression those first few days of school. I had gotten so used to hanging out with Al after my classes were over and studying with him. My mind was blown. I had to figure out how to get myself back together. I couldn't eat, couldn't sleep, my appetite was gone; it really sucked feeling this way. I then began to think that maybe I should have just stuck with Anthony. I didn't know what to do. All I could do was pray for God to remove that empty feeling from my stomach.

I dragged myself through the beginning of the week. After class I went to the gym and worked out for about two hours, which is what I did before Al and I started hanging out. It made me feel a little bit better. My friends and I went to the mall, which always relieved my stress. It helped a little as well.

That Wednesday night I had come from class and gone to the gym again. Just as I was getting out of the shower, my phone rang. I just knew that it was someone that I did not want to be bothered with. I slowly walked over and answered it.

"May I speak to Danielle?" a deep voice asked.

My heart immediately skipped a beat, and I all of a sudden became really nervous.

"This is she," I answered.

"I just wanted to call and apologize," Al replied. "I was wrong. I thought about what I did the entire time I was in Mobile and I realized I needed to tell you I was sorry. That girl was just doing that to make you mad. My mom told me I probably hurt your feelings. I understand if you still don't want to be bothered with me."

I just could not believe what I was hearing. This dude had basically dogged me out for the entire month and a half that we had been back to school, and the moment I tell him I'm done, he calls me and tells me he's sorry. I was totally blown. I was not expecting that. The only thing I could think was God is good, because He knew I really wanted that man in my life.

"Well, I'm glad you called. That was pretty wrong how you treated me. I forgive you this time, but it better not ever happen again."

During that conversation, it seemed as if once again a ton of bricks had been lifted off my shoulders. I finally told him that Anthony and I had broken up. He couldn't understand why I had not told him sooner. Maybe I was wrong, but at the time he didn't seem to care anyways. He finally told me that the reason he had flipped on me was because over Christmas break he had called my mom's house and heard Anthony's voice on the answering machine. He said at that point he thought he was being a fool to think that I was going to leave someone that I had been with for four years for him.

We talked for about three or four hours that night. After that conversation we picked up right where we left off before Christmas break. A few weeks later on March 23, 1998, we officially declared ourselves a couple. It felt good.

Even though the semester started off rough, it ended up being a pretty good close to my senior year and my college career. In early March, I had gotten an acceptance letter from Emory. Once again God had come through and answered my prayers. On top of that, I had received a scholarship from the United States Air Force, which paid all of my medical school expenses and gave me a stipend each month for bills. God's favor was never-ending. After that, I was certain that there was nothing that God could not do.

My senior year had been filled with a lot of drama. On top of all of the stuff I had already mentioned, my father began to go through what appeared to be a midlife crisis. After he had received the insurance money from my aunt M's death, he decided he did not need to work anymore. I'm not sure how long he thought that he could survive without working with forty thousand dollars in the bank. He started hanging out with a pretty bad crowd, and even had some pretty negatively influential people living in his house. His house became a hang out for a lot of messed up people, who really began to drag him even further down a path of destructive behavior. We would go weeks at a time without talking. People would call me all of the time telling me how bad my dad looked and about all of the craziness that was going on in his house. It's so funny how I could get a phone call from people to report something like that, but never could get a call from them just to say hello or to see how I was doing.

One day the craziness got out of hand, and one of the young addicts who hung out at his house got upset with my father and hit him in the head with a bat. My dad was supposedly knocked unconscious. The guy stole some stuff from my dad's house and then ran away. Thank God he only hit him one time because he could have easily continued to hit him and cause some serious brain damage or even death.

One time when I had gone home to visit my family, my dad hid from me the entire weekend. I had called him and let him know that I was coming down from college. He sounded all excited about me coming home. I even called him when I got down there and told him exactly when I was coming over. Again, he said he couldn't wait to see me. When I got to his house, he was nowhere to be found. I called several times that weekend and he never called me back. I felt terrible. But, given his past behavior and the things that I had been hearing about him, I was not surprised.

So when my graduation date came, I was not at all surprised when he was in jail and could not make it to my college graduation. I was the first person in my family to graduate from college, and my father was not even there to see it. It caused me to be sad when I thought about it, but I didn't allow it to spoil my day. I had plenty of other people there to help me celebrate, including Al, who graduated Summa Cum Laude right along with me. We made the perfect couple.

It Will Work Out

The summer after college graduation was very busy and exciting for me. Al and I had gone to find places for us to stay. I found a cute little apartment in Atlanta. We then went up to Chapel Hill, North Carolina, where he would be attending graduate school to find him an apartment. My mom and I went to Ochos Rios, Jamaica, to celebrate my graduation. It was so beautiful and relaxing there. After our week in paradise, I came back to attend Commissioned Officer Training School for four weeks in Montgomery. After that training, I flew to Vegas to spend a week with Al who was out there working for the summer. Before I knew it, I was in Atlanta preparing to take my first medical school course, embryology.

I was excited about med school, but I was also very nervous. Everyone I had talked to told me how hard it was going to be, which I expected. I mean, I was going to be responsible for people's lives. I wouldn't expect that to be easy.

And, boy, was it hard. When I tell you I had no life outside of studying, that is exactly what I mean. I was surviving on four to six hours worth of sleep every night with really no time to hang out with any of my friends. I studied more than I had ever studied before in my life. My first class was only a two-week class to help us get our feet wet. I studied my behind off for that class and ended up with an 89 average. One point away from an A. I was so disgusted. And, of course, I immediately began to feel like this was going to be too hard for me. It seemed like my entire first year no matter how hard I studied I always ended up with B's. This was just not me. I was used to getting A's and nothing but A's. When I was at ASU, one of my biology instructors, Dr. O, told me that I was at the top at ASU, but when I went to med school not to be surprised if I was in the middle. When he told me that, I was like "whatever." During my first year of med school, I began to understand what he meant. All of us had been at the top at our previous schools.

I really do believe that during my first year of med school, I was operating in a state of depression. I was stressed, I had piles of work to study every day, my boyfriend was six hours away in North Carolina, my mom was overseas somewhere again, and I had dropped to become a B student. There were so many nights when I would sit in my lonely one bedroom apartment at eleven o'clock at night looking at the thick pile of lessons that I still needed to study before the next day. A lot of times I would start to feel discouraged and wonder if the stress was worth the end result. There were times when I would just sit on my couch with my notebook on my lap and books and papers scattered all over my floor. All of a sudden, I would start crying uncontrollably asking God to give me strength to handle it all. Once I got my cry out, God would tell me that at that very moment there was someone else sitting in their living room on their couch feeling the exact same way. I was not alone. All I had to do was continue to trust that He would give me the strength to conquer that pile of work and it would be done. After my cry, I would put on one of my gospel CDs and keep on trucking. I would usually stop studying at about one a.m. so that I could get at least six hours of sleep to be ready for all of the information my brain would be flooded with the next day.

My mom would call me a lot to encourage me. I think some-times I freaked her out because I would get so stressed that it would sometimes induce anxiety attacks. I would tell her that I wasn't able to sleep at times because my heart would be racing extremely fast. I told her one day that I just felt like jumping off my balcony. Mind you, I lived on the first floor, and my balcony was only a foot off the ground. She got real nervous then.

"Danielle, just take a deep breath. It's going to be all right," she said.

"Ma, I know. I'm just talking."

Having Al in my life was probably the best thing that ever happened to me. Even though he was far away, he really helped me get through med school. With him being in graduate school getting his Ph.D. in organic chemistry, he really understood the stress I was under, and vice versa. We were really there for each other. He would stay up all night with me, just holding the phone to help keep me awake while I was studying. We didn't even have to talk. Just knowing that he was on the line for me was a big relief. When I felt like I needed to take little catnaps, I would tell him to call me and wake me up in twenty minutes and he would.

Every free weekend I had I spent driving or flying to North Carolina to see Al. My friends in Atlanta would get so mad at me because I would never stay in town to hang out with them on the weekends. I told them they had their men right there with them, so they were just going to have to be mad at me.

After my first year of med school, things seemed to get a little easier. I really don't think that the work load decreased at all, but I just got used to the intensity of it all and by then I had developed my study habits. I finished my first year with a couple of A's and the rest B's. I learned to be thankful for what I had, because I could have done a lot worse. There were a few people in our class who had to be placed in the decelerated program because they had not done so well that first year. I was very thankful that I was not one of them, because I wanted to move quickly past that portion of my life.

At that point, Al and I had been dating for about two years.

We often talked about God, and he knew that my faith was strong and that I always went to church. He was very impressed by how well I knew the Bible. To me, I didn't know enough. He had been raised Seventh Day Adventist, but he really did not attend church very much at all. In college, we both liked to go out to the club, hang out. I drank a little bit, but he really liked to indulge in Hennessy when he was trying to relax. He also liked to smoke little Indian cigars called bidis.

Of course, the first thing that had to go was the bidis. Every time I would kiss him, it would taste like smoke. I told him I couldn't keep kissing him if he kept smoking those bidis. Surprisingly, he threw them out of the car window right then.

Even though Al did not go to church on a regular basis, any time I invited him to go with me, he went. For some reason, even though I was always taught that you should not be unevenly yoked, I was not worried about the fact that: number one, Al was raised Seventh Day Adventist and I was not; number two, Al was not in the church; and number three, Al liked to drink. God had already told me that He had a plan for both of our lives and for me not to worry. So I didn't.

Al and I often talked about marriage. Of course, I always brought it up. To my surprise, he never shied away from the subject. One day while we were lying in bed, I brought the subject up again. I was really joking about it at the time.

"So, when are we going to get married?" I asked.

"When do you want to get married?" he said.

"Whenever you ask me," I replied nonchalantly. I was completely caught off guard by what he said next.

"Will you marry me?" he said with a serious look on his face.

"Stop playing," I said as I punched him in his arm.

"I'm not playing. Will you marry me?"

I laughed at first, but then my laughter turned into tears as I realized he was serious.

"*Yes!* Of course I will," I yelled as I grabbed him and hugged him. I could not believe what was happening. I immediately noticed the huge difference in the way that I felt when he asked me compared to when Anthony asked me. Even though he didn't have a ring to give me at that time, I was still thrilled that he had proposed to me. True love was there; the ring, which was only a symbol of that love, could come later. I really loved this man. Of course I was going to marry him.

That next day I called my mom in Macedonia and gave her the news. She initially voiced concern about us being so young and needing to finish school. I told her that we were more than ready. After we talked for a while, she was convinced and was excited for us. We planned to have our wedding that following July.

I began planning everything immediately. Planning our wedding was actually a wonderful break from all of the stress I endured in school. Having my wedding to look forward to really motivated me to get through my second year. On top of planning my wedding, though, I had to prepare to take the first step of my medical boards. I was determined to get through it all, though, and with God's help, I did.

By the time my mom came home from Macedonia, I had my entire wedding planned. I had picked out my dress, the reception hall, the cake. She did get to help me with the bridesmaids' dresses and the decorations. We decided to go home to Florida for a few days to visit my nana and so that I could see my father who was back in jail again. I have never really been a fan of visiting jails. I would go to hospitals, nursing homes, anywhere but the jails. I just did not feel comfortable there. But that was where my dad was, and I wanted to see him to make sure he was okay. When we got to the jail, one of the guards directed us to the counter to verify that my name was on my father's visitor's list. I quickly walked over to the counter watching mine and my mom's backs the entire time. The guard asked me what my name was and I told him. He looked up and down the entire list. He then asked if there was any other name it could be under. I was a little surprised, but since I went by my middle name, Danielle, I figured maybe he put it under my first name, Tomeka. He looked for that name as well and then looked up at me and shook his head.

"I'm sorry, miss, but your name isn't on the list."

"But he's my father, and I drove all the way from Atlanta to come and see him," I pleaded.

"I'm sorry. There's nothing I can do. He didn't put your name on the list," he said as he stared at me with a blank look on his face.

My heart sank to my feet. I tried to keep a straight face as I turned around and walked out. My mom tried to reassure me, but I could tell that she was getting angrier and angrier by the second. I knew that she was getting really sick of this man hurting me. He had gotten three months in jail this time, and since my wedding was two months away that meant that he wouldn't be able to walk me down the aisle. Once again my earthly father was not there for me. Oh, well. Hold your head up, girl, and keep steppin'.

After that, I couldn't wait to get out of Florida and back to my life in Georgia.

With everything that was going on, my second year of med school flew by. I finished with a few more A's that year than I had my first year and was feeling pretty confident in my knowledge base and skills. During the summer, I studied really hard and took my boards. I felt confident that I had at least passed when I was done. After my boards, I had three weeks to get ready for our wedding.

When God Gave Me You

Our wedding day came so fast I could hardly believe it. On Saturday July 15, 2000, it was one hundred and six degrees outside in Columbus, Georgia, and the sanctuary of Bread of Life Christian Center was packed. Everyone was awaiting the union of Mr. Albert Eugene Russell and Miss Tomeka Danielle Swails. We had planned for about one hundred and fifty guests. Several people showed up who had not RSVP'd, but accommodations were made for everyone. Albert's family and friends actually chartered a bus to the wedding. They always rolled deep. I often wished that my family was that tight. I had a few family members who came up from Florida for which I was grateful, because I really had not expected anyone from Florida to come except my aunt E and her crew. The majority of people who were there to support me were friends from Columbus. My goddaddy came up to walk me down the aisle in the place of my father. I called him up and asked, and without hesitation he agreed. Ever since I was a little child, he has always been there whenever I needed him.

When our wedding day came around, of course almost everything that could have gone wrong did go wrong. Our candles all melted from sitting in the car too long. Our photographer, my cousin, went to jail on the way to the wedding for driving on a suspended license. Our videographer broke his camera and did not tell us until the night of our rehearsal. Someone erased all of our wedding songs from the CD because he hit the wrong button. About three months before our wedding, the preacher, my pastor during the time I was in high school who supposedly considered me as one of the daughters he never had, informed me that he had to go to a family reunion. I was fit to be tied. However, one thing that being in med school had taught me was that no matter how bad things seemed, just take a deep breath and press on through. I figured as long as Al and I were there and there was a minister available to administer our vows we were going to be married no matter what. We managed to rush to Wal-Mart to get more candles, we got our music back together, the church had a video camera we could use so one of the church members videotaped, we bought a bunch of disposable cameras and took our own pictures, and both of my parents were preachers, so my new step-dad performed the ceremony.

When my mom and I were in Jamaica, she met someone who excited her and made her feel special. During this trip, she really came to grips with the fact that she was not happy with Gerald. Therefore, while we were in the airport awaiting our flight back to the U.S., she told me that she was leaving Gerald. She said she was tired of being the one always having to provide for them and that he didn't seem to appreciate her. She said she didn't feel guilty because he was actually a lot healthier than she thought he was, even though he was HIV positive. I told her I wasn't shocked and actually knew what she was about to say before she even said it. Three months later, she had divorced Gerald, and she and Dean were married.

Well, Dean performed our ceremony, which was pretty interesting. I think he was more nervous than we were because he kept calling me Tomeka knowing good and well that I go by Danielle. Plus he was fumbling over a few key words. We just laughed about it later.

Despite all of our pre-wedding drama, everything turned

out really well. I walked down the aisle to Whitney Houston's "I Believe in You and Me." My bridesmaids marched to Eric Benet's "Spend My Life with You." I managed to make it through our entire wedding without crying because I did not want to mess up my makeup. After we lit our unity candle, we did a tribute to our mothers. We played Patti Labelle's "You Are My Friend" and gave each of our mothers a bouquet of roses. It was at this point that Albert began to cry. When he hugged his mom, they both began to sob uncontrollably. Everyone in the sanctuary began to cry along with them. I was standing behind him fanning my face trying hard to dry my tears before they rolled down my face destroying my mascara. After our tributes, everyone clapped.

We ended our ceremony with "The Lord's Prayer" being sung while we knelt holding hands asking God to bless what He had ordained. By no means was anyone or anything ever going to come between us. The scripture on our program was "A cord of three strands is not easily broken," and we knew that as long as we kept God at the helm of our marriage, nothing could tear us apart.

After our prayer, we jumped the broom and that was that. We were introduced as Mr. and Mrs. Albert Eugene Russell. Again, everyone cheered as we marched down the aisle hand in hand.

Our reception was beautiful. My mom had poured her heart out into the decorations, and it had definitely paid off. Our wedding colors were lavender and platinum and those colors looked very beautiful together. Since I was a commissioned Air Force officer, we held our reception at the Officer's Club on Fort Benning. We decided to have a buffet dinner. I was very shocked because I did not expect to have servers, but we had waiters and waitresses. It was very nice.

We had way more people than what we paid for, but to my surprise the people at the club just brought out more tables, more chairs, and more food. They were so understanding, and the food was excellent. All of the guests really seemed to enjoy themselves.

After we ate, we did the traditional cake cutting, bouquet toss, garter toss, and first dance. We danced to Case's "Happily Ever After." I just love that song. Everything felt so right for us.

Everyone got up and danced when Jagged Edge's "Let's Get Married" began to play. We, of course, did the traditional Electric Slide, which got everyone up out of their seats. It reminded me so much of the reception scene in *The Best Man*, which came out only a few months before we got married.

Our wedding day was definitely one of the best days in our lives. It was a day that we will never forget. Our wedding night was even more unforgettable! I really wished I'd saved myself for my husband. He would have been well worth the wait.

Since we were struggling students, we went on a poor man's honeymoon to Disney World. Our hotel was free because we had gone to some presentation a few months prior. We ate well though. Because we had been given about seven hundred dollars in cash, we used that to really enjoy ourselves, so we ate one hundred dollar meals every night that we were in Orlando.

I Smile

My third year in medical school was supposed to be *the* year. This was the year that we actually went into the hospitals and learned actual doctor skills. This was the year that we got to actually see all of the diseases and injuries that we had been reading about for two years. This was what we had all been looking forward to. And, of course, I had passed my boards, so I was allowed to enter into that phase of my training.

Grady Hospital in downtown Atlanta was a world of its own. You can imagine being in a downtown metropolitan area that it had to be pretty interesting. And since this was the place where everyone who did not have insurance came, you can imagine some of the stuff that we saw. Grady was also a Level 1 trauma center, so we saw some of the worst-case scenarios when it came to accidents and trauma. It was great training, but it could be a little scary at times, even for those who were the best prepared.

The emergency room at Grady was a place of utter chaos. On any given day there were beds lined up all along the sides of the hallways. Urinals hung from the sides of makeshift beds. People throwing up, bleeding, cussing, crying, moaning; it was pretty crazy. I really enjoyed it though. That was how I knew that I had chosen the right profession. None of that bothered me at all.

Because a lot of those people never went to the doctor, we

would see a lot of diseases at their worst possible state. We saw a lot of cancers, tuberculosis, heart attacks, automobile accidents, and needless to say, gunshot wounds. Pretty much all of the gunshot victims were very young black males. Whenever I would ask them what had happened, the textbook answer was "They tried to jack me for my rims." I think they all got together and rehearsed that line before they came in, because none of them ever said, "This was a drug deal that went wrong" or "I tried to rob somebody" or "I tried to shoot somebody but they shot me first." I guess they figured if they said they got robbed and the person was wearing a mask, they wouldn't get into trouble and no one could make them snitch on the person who shot them. I figured they were going to try to handle that themselves when they got out, and pretty soon I would be meeting either that same patient or their enemy/victim in the trauma bay.

One patient that I will never forget was a young dude who was about twenty-three years old and came in with a gunshot wound to his face. His story, again, was that someone had robbed him. For some reason I believed his story. The bullet had gone in through his right upper jaw and come out through his left lower jaw. It had completely shattered both bones. His face was very swollen and blood was just dripping out. Every time he spoke, his teeth were just flapping around in his mouth with no support because everything in his mouth was shattered. He was so frightened. All he kept saying was "Please don't let me die. Please don't let me die..." as he looked at me as if I was his last hope. All I could do was hold his hand and tell him to remain calm. I tried so hard to reassure him that he was in the right place and that everything was going to be all right, but I was pretty nervous for him myself. I had never seen anything like that in my life.

He was taken to the operating room by the ENT specialist and a plastic surgeon, who managed to reconstruct his face. Although his mouth was wired shut for a long time, he did recover. God really had his hands on that young man that night, because if that gun had been angled sixty degrees higher that bullet would have definitely gone through his brain and he probably would not have made it. I really hope he took that as a wakeup call that God was giving him a second chance at life.

One thing that I noticed about living in Atlanta was that there was a very large gay community. There were places that we would go and I would wonder if I had just stepped foot into Greenwich Village or San Francisco. The Cheesecake Factory on Peachtree Street was one of those places. And that happened to be one of my favorite restaurants.

Given that Atlanta had such a large number of gay men I was not all at surprised by the fact that a very large number of my patients at Grady were HIV positive. Young, beautiful black men all with HIV or even AIDS. It saddened my heart so much every time I walked into a room and looked into the eyes of these patients. They never had any family members with them. They were just alone, and a lot of time had given up on life. They had stopped taking their HIV medications, they were depressed, they were angry, sometimes they were violent. A lot of times they just did not care anymore. For some reason I would always go spend more time with them throughout the day than I would any of my other patients. I always tried to talk to them and encourage them that they did not have to give up. I was very optimistic with them that there may someday be a cure for their illness, and if they just held on, then maybe they could recover. I often shared the story of my ex-step dad and how healthy he appeared. There was one patient who had HIV neuropathy, and he would get really bad pain in his hands and legs. The only thing that gave him any relief was when someone would massage his hands for him. He always seemed to cheer up when I walked in the room because he knew that I was going to spend a few minutes massaging his hands for him.

I also remember one of my patients, whose name was Kobe. Kobe was from South Carolina and had been in Atlanta for several months. He was formerly in the army, but had voluntarily separated. He was HIV positive and had actually progressed to

AIDS. Kobe did not admit to me that he was gay, but I could tell by his mannerisms and when he spoke of his prior sexual partner that he was referring to another male. Kobe had been in and out of the hospital for several months with various infections. He had come into the hospital about a week prior for really bad headaches. I was on the psychiatry service at that time, and we were consulted to see him for depression. As I interviewed Kobe, I had learned that he was all alone with no family in Atlanta. His mother was still in South Carolina, and she did not even know that Kobe had HIV. She had no clue that he was sick and in the hospital. He also told me about his time in the military and how much he enjoyed it.

After a few visits with Kobe, I finally convinced him to call his mother. He was very nervous, but I told him it was something he needed to do. He gave me her number and I dialed it for him. I even introduced myself to his mother, let her know Kobe was in the hospital, and then gave him the phone. I then left the room to let him tell his mother what was going on with him. Later I came back and checked on him, and he had a look of relief on his face. He said even though she could not come and be with him, he felt much better after letting her know what was going on. That was something that he knew he needed to do, but had not been able to bring himself to make the phone call. He was thankful. A few days later, he was released from the hospital.

I always thought that it was strange how God brought all of the HIV positive people into my life. Maybe He knew that I would be compassionate toward them, not try to judge them, and not be afraid to touch them. Or maybe He knew that HIV would really touch home for me in the future and He was just preparing me for a future challenge.

Being in the hospital was a lot of fun. It seemed every rotation I was on I really became interested in becoming that type of doctor. All of my rotations, with the exception of one, were positive experiences. The only rotation I had any trouble out of was my general surgery rotation at Grady. I had done general surgery at the VA hospital with an all female team and loved it. Even though it was long hours, I really loved being in the OR with my team. I had never even dreamed of being a surgeon before, but that rotation really had me thinking about it. I was with them for about two weeks before I switched over to the trauma team at Grady. Again, it was mainly a female team at that time, and to be honest, even though that was supposed to be one of the most difficult rotations of medical school, it was my favorite.

I didn't have any problems until my last two weeks on my surgery rotation when I was on the team with Dr. Rowe. Dr. Rowe was one of the few black male residents that I had gotten the opportunity to work with. Initially he seemed cool, but then he just jumped on my case about every little thing. He chewed me out or cut me off every opportunity that he got. I had absolutely no clue what I had done to this guy to make him behave so rudely toward me. My fellow teammates would often look at me trying to figure out what was going on between the two of us. One of them told me that if he didn't know any better, he would think there was something going on between us, because when I got sick of the way he was talking to me, I starting talking back to him in the same tone he used towards me. I hated being on his team. Finally, I just lost all interest in surgery, and did whatever I could to stay out of the OR with him. It's such a shame that the only issue I had with anyone I rotated with had to be with another black person. It was like he was intentionally trying to make me look bad.

I managed to make it through the remainder of medical school with a pretty decent grade point average. It wasn't nearly as high as I would have liked for it to be, but I figured a 3.3 GPA from medical school at Emory University was pretty good. I could have done a lot worse. By the time my last year began, my dad had made a major turnaround. He had gotten out of jail at the beginning of my third year. Very soon after he was released he began working at the mulch plant in Callahan. Within a year, he had actually been promoted to a supervisory position. My dad was actually a very smart man, and when he got into doing something that he really liked he was actually very good at it. I was so happy and so proud of him because for a while I was always very worried that one day I was going to get a phone call saying that someone had found him dead someplace. On my graduation day from Emory, he was right there by my side looking as proud as he could be. And, of course, Aunt E and her crew were there to support me as always.

I was very happy to have my family there for such an important event. I was finally going to receive my doctorate degree. I was going to be a doctor. The little nappy-headed girl from a small country town who a lot of people thought wasn't going to ever get out of Callahan was now in Atlanta, Georgia, about to get her doctorate degree from a very prestigious university. That weekend was almost perfect.

The reason I said almost perfect was because this was the weekend that I had to come to grips with something that I had been in denial about for a long time. I came to the realization that Rashawn was actually pretty sick. I had been hearing rumors that he had been sick, but of course I just brushed them off. I had even heard that he was in hospice once. However, one thing that I had learned from dealing with my family was that they had a tendency to take the smallest bit of information and sometimes blow it out of proportion. They tended to overreact a lot about a lot of different issues, but especially when it came to someone being sick. I really did not believe them because Rashawn had not told me he was sick and neither had Aunt E. However, when I saw him during my graduation weekend, I realized the rumors were probably true.

My mom had tried for years to convince me that Rashawn displayed characteristics of being gay. I, of course, refused to believe this about the very boy that I considered to be as close to me as the brother I never had. I would get so angry with my mom when she would make comments about his sexuality that it would often bring me to tears. Finally, I would just quit talking to her. I would totally ignore the flaming gay friends he would bring to my grandmother's house with their little shorts on, or the guys with the pastel colors on who talked with a twang and gestured with a little too much wrist action. I refused to see what was right before my eyes. A couple of years prior to my graduation, one of my cousins on my mom's side tried to tell me that she heard Rashawn had HIV, but again I hated rumors, and it seemed there was always one floating around Callahan. I just ignored what she said and changed the subject. I had seen Rashawn a couple of times since then, and I had begun to notice that it seemed as if he was wearing foundation to try and cover up some skin lesions that he had. Again, I just wanted to believe that they were acne scars that just would not fade. While Rashawn and I were on the phone making the plans for everyone to come up for my graduation I noticed that he would take a very long time to say what he was trying to say, or would often lose his train of thought mid-sentence. I, naively, just laughed at him and told him he was getting pretty old. He would often comment that his head had been hurting him a little as well.

When they came for my graduation, my heart sort of sank to my feet when I saw Rashawn. He had always been small, but his body just looked so frail, and it looked as if he had started to apply even more foundation to try and cover the spots on his face. Rashawn had always been such a handsome person, and this really caught me off guard. Don't get me wrong, he was still handsome, but he was really starting not to look like himself. I also noticed that he was moving a lot slower and seemed to get tired very easily. He also held his head a lot as if the noise was causing him to have a headache. It was at that point that I realized my cousin, my brother, was dying. At twenty-eight years old Rashawn was dying.

Despite how terrible it seemed he felt, he was trying to hang in there and have a good time for me. That was the kind of person he was. He never wanted to spoil anything for anyone. The first day there, we all went to the Martin Luther King Museum, then later to the ESPN Zone for dinner. He actually left dinner early to go home and rest. That night while I lay in bed I cried extremely hard, praying for God to forgive him and to heal his body. I just prayed that He would give Rashawn a second chance. As I prayed, God kept telling me that He had already given Rashawn peace; that everything was going to be all right.

The next day we had a huge barbecue for a few of the students and our families at Stone Mountain Park. It was also Mother's Day, so we had a large cake and I gave words of thanks on behalf of all of us to our mothers for their love and support. It turned out really nice, and Rashawn seemed to have a good time. Again, he mainly just sat during the entire barbecue, but he seemed content. That night he began having really bad headaches again. I was really worried that he had some type of brain infection or tumor from his HIV. I went over to their room and lay on the bed beside him, laid my hands on his head, and prayed a silent prayer for God to heal him of whatever was going on. It was at that point that I began to feel really bad about laughing at Rashawn's inability to complete a full sentence without pausing a few weeks prior.

Graduation was actually that Monday. It was a long day full of activities, but it was very enjoyable. Rashawn made it through that day and the celebration dinner apparently fine for which I was thankful. My dad cried when I walked across the stage and accepted my degree. I wondered if this made him think about all of the things I had experienced that he had not been able to support in the past. At any rate, it was a wonderful day and I was glad that he was there.

That next day everyone packed up and left to go home. My dad, Aunt E, and Rashawn stood talking to me as if they did not want to leave. I was extremely happy that they had spent the extra time saying good-bye because this was the last time I would get to see Rashawn alive. About two days after they returned to Florida, Aunt E took Rashawn in to the emergency room because his headaches had gotten way worse. Apparently he had either a

CT scan or an MRI which revealed the presence of a tumor in his brain. It was felt that he had lymphoma due to his body's inability to fight off cancer cells given his white blood cell count was so low due to his HIV/AIDS infection. It's amazing how joyous occasions can so quickly be over shadowed by sadness.

He remained in the hospital for several weeks. I called him multiple times trying to check on him, but he was on such a high amount of pain medication that a lot of times he was too groggy to hold a full conversation. I would just tell him that I loved him and encouraged him to get some rest. Sometimes I would call and I could hear a male voice with a "girlfriend" twang in the background. That just annoyed me so much, but at least he had someone there to hold his hand and keep him company.

I was shocked when I called the hospital one day and the nurse told me that Rashawn had been released to go home. I immediately called my father to see what was going on. Aunt E and her crew were temporarily staying with him in Callahan at that time, and he told me that Rashawn had come home on hospice. He was talking a little more and was able to eat, but was still requiring large doses of morphine at times to control his headaches. Apparently while in the hospital they had tried to radiate the tumor, but it was making Rashawn so sick and really did not seem to be shrinking it any, so he told them to stop.

At this point, I had begun my residency in family medicine up at Andrews Air Force Base in the metro D.C. area. I had really hoped to attend residency at the University of North Carolina in Chapel Hill where my husband was, but I guess the military had other plans for me. Because I was all of the way up in Maryland, I was very far away from everything that was going on back at home with Rashawn. That was kind of eating me up inside. Plus, as an intern there really was not any time outside of my training for me to focus on anything else.

One weekend I decided I just had to go down to Florida to see Rashawn before it was too late. For some reason I just all of a sudden developed this sense of urgency that I really needed to get down there to see him. I booked my flight two weeks in advance. Those two weeks seemed to drag by. I had finally made it past the first week, and I was getting excited because I only had one week to go. However on Saturday, six days before I was supposed to leave, I received a phone call from my dad. "Rashawn died last night."

I really did not believe what I was hearing. I was too late. I didn't even get to tell him good-bye. I was too late. I was too late. All I could think about was the fact that I didn't make it there to see him in time. I was too late. I tried to be strong on the phone with my dad, because I could tell that he was having a hard time. He said that Aunt E had tucked Rashawn in and everything seemed to be going well the night before. She had even gone in to check on him once during the night and everything seemed okay. But he said when she had gone in to check on him that morning that he had stopped breathing. He slipped away peacefully during the night.

I was grateful for the fact that he seemed to have a peaceful death. I always said that if I was able to choose the way that I die I would prefer to just sleep away. No struggling, just a peaceful slumber.

After I stopped crying, I realized I had to do something to express my feelings toward my cousin. Ever since I was a little girl, I had always loved to write poetry; therefore I immediately decided I would write a poem especially for Rashawn. My poem's title was "Young Angels" because I was convinced that Rashawn had asked God for forgiveness and that God had forgiven him of his sins. In fact, one of his coworkers gave me confirmation of that when she told me at the funeral that she and Rashawn often prayed together, and she felt he had resolved a lot of his "issues." I knew that Rashawn would be up in heaven watching over us as a young angel. My tribute to Rashawn was as follows:

Young Angels

When I think about young angels, I can't help but wonder why

Why did their time on earth so quickly pass us by?

Why does their book of memories seem so unnecessarily short,

And this difficult life's journey they so suddenly had to abort?

Why are they blessed with talents that they never really get to use?

Why are they blessed with such brilliant minds that they prematurely have to lose?

Why are they such wonderful people, so loving and so kind?

Your sibling, your child, your cousin, a best friend that was so hard to find.

But then the thought occurred to me, that this place is not our home.

We are all here but for a moment before our number is chosen and we are gone.

Just how long we'll be here, none of us really know.

That's why it's important that every moment our love we do show.

So why does God need young angels, although it seems unfair?

He needs ushers, musicians, and choir directors that don't all have gray hair.

He needs that sense of innocence that young angels can provide.

He needs that energy and fresh ideas that young angels have locked inside.

Young angels have a place with Him where they will no longer experience pain,

Where their talents, their spirits, and their brilliant minds can so freely live again.

So why does God need young angels? It's all so simple, you see.

God needs young angels that still have good vision to look after you and me.

When I finally made it down to Florida, we went to the funeral home so that I could view the body. I could not make it to the wake on Friday night, but my aunt made sure they did not close the casket on Saturday until I had a chance to view his body, because it was going to be a closed casket ceremony. When I walked into the room, I looked at the body that was in the casket, but I immediately turned around and walked out thinking that I was in the wrong room. My step dad quickly turned me back around telling me that I was in the right place. My cousin did not look anything like himself. He was so thin and dark that he looked like a totally different person. His cancer had started to consume parts of his nose, so the funeral director had to perform a lot of reconstruction of his face to hide everything. That was part of the reason he looked so different. I immediately began to cry again.

Despite how different he looked, everything was so perfect for him. The cream suit he wore was sharp, his cream casket was beautiful, and the floral arrangements brought everything together nicely. They really memorialized him in an honorable way.

During the funeral, I had a hard time getting through the poem that I wrote because every time I thought about the fact that my cousin was lying in that cold metal box in front of me, the sadness almost consumed me. I did not let it though. I managed to finish the poem and return to my seat.

The church was jam-packed for his funeral. Since he had been a choir director for many years, he was well-known throughout various churches in the Jacksonville area. The good thing about the way his illness played out was the fact that he pretty much got to plan his own funeral. He was able to tell my aunt E exactly what he wanted and who he wanted to sing. He chose the location of the funeral, his coffin, the suit that he wore, and everything. It takes a very strong person who is at peace with God to be able to do that.

The funeral service started out wonderfully. The choir that

he had previously directed sang to the glory of God. They definitely made it feel more like a celebration of Rashawn's life than a mourning of his death. Everything seemed to be going great until the show began. On the right hand side of the church, in the first few rows of pews, were several young men who displayed those same excessive wrist action gestures that my cousin had displayed. And it seemed as if they wanted to compete on who mourned the loss of my cousin the most. Pretty soon it turned into a dramatic scene which really started to get on my nerves, and I could tell that it was starting to get on the pastor's nerves as well. It was definitely beginning to make my husband sick on the stomach. One of the guys got up and grabbed the microphone stating that he just had to say something. He introduced himself as the pastor of some unknown church and then commanded the musician to put him in E flat. I was like, *Oh Lord, somebody please get him from up there.* This guy was up there singing like he was sho nuff doing something and could barely even hold a tune. After he finished singing, he had this smug look on his face like he had just knocked one out of the park. I was so glad when he sat down.

Finally Pastor Charles got up and pretty much put everyone in their places. He spoke to the people who were talking bad about Rashawn behind his back. A lot of people in the church had gotten upset with the pastor for continuing to allow Rashawn to direct the choir despite his history. They must have conveniently forgotten the scripture "Judge not lest ye be judged" because I know that they were not all perfect. He talked to the homosexuals telling them that God despised their behavior. He talked to everyone else who was in sin and told them it was time to straighten up. He said that if no other lesson was learned from Rashawn's life and death, we should all learn that it was time for us to straighten up. God was coming back soon and we all needed to get ready because He was coming back for a church without a spot or a wrinkle. He also reiterated the fact that we needed to learn to love one another despite all of our shortcomings. Instead of trying to bring each other down and run folks out of the church, we needed to love one another into reaching our fullest potential.

A lot of toes were stepped on that day, but if that's what the Lord wanted him to say, then that's what he had to say, regardless of what the event was.

It seemed as if the entire group of guys who were sitting on the right side of the sanctuary totally missed the point that Pastor Charles was trying to make, because immediately after the service they were all gathered together in front of the sanctuary like they had just left some sort of show. None of them showed even a hint of sadness or remorse. The so-called *pastor* that thought that he had *thrown down on stage* was right in the middle of them all.

"Ya'll going to that party tonight?" one of them asked.

"I don't know, chile, I might be too tired," one of them replied with the infamous wrist action for emphasis.

I just wanted to go slap all of them across their faces and yell, "Be a man!" I was so glad to climb into the limo and get away from them. After witnessing that scene, I was not at all shocked that the HIV rate in Florida is so high now. I think the statistics show that one in four or five black males in Florida has HIV or AIDS. I always tell people now that if they date someone from Florida they better make sure they get tested for HIV before they are intimate, because you never know who is infected.

We buried my cousin in the Callahan cemetery next to my Mudea and my aunt M. After the repast, we all hung out over my dad's house for a while. Then Albert and I went back to my mom's apartment to get ready to fly back up north the next day. Once again I had had my fill of Callahan for a little while and was ready to go.

Sovereign God

It has always amazed me how God sends a comforter during your time of distress, and how the cycle of life continues. In November of 2002, we buried my closest cousin. In December of 2002, I found out that I was pregnant with our first child. I was too ecstatic for words. I was working at Children's Hospital in D.C. when I found out. When I got to work the next day, I told everyone. Even though I had only known the people on my team for a couple of weeks, they were all extremely excited for me.

Life continued to progress for Albert and I, and before long it was time for me to head to Chapel Hill for Albert's graduation from graduate school. He was about to obtain his Ph.D. in organic chemistry. We were both about to be doctors. It was all so exciting. We were about to be like the Huxtables for real.

We had a lot of family and friends who traveled from a lot of places to be there for him. We were all so proud of him, and I could tell that he was really proud of himself. He had gone through a lot to earn his Ph.D., and he truly deserved it. Things were so perfect that weekend. We had a great time together with everyone jammed into our three-bedroom apartment. I should have known that if things were going well for us, something bad was bound to happen.

At the time of Albert's graduation from UNC-Chapel Hill, I was twenty-six weeks pregnant with Donovan. That night after things settled down, I started getting slight cramps in my back. I tried to lie down and relax, but it seemed like I could not get into a comfortable position no matter what I tried. Pretty soon my cramps got a lot worse, and I had to pee every five minutes it seemed. I thought that I must have been developing a urinary tract infection or something. I tried lying still and drinking lots of water. I told Albert that my back was hurting; therefore he came and gave me a massage. I then tried to lie down and go to sleep. I slept maybe thirty minutes before I was back up going to the bathroom. I probably woke up about once every fifteen minutes until about four o'clock in the morning. It was at four o'clock when I decided to watch the clock and see how close together my back cramps were. I timed them out to be about five minutes apart. It was at that point that I realized that I was having contractions. I immediately started to get nervous because I knew it was way too early in my pregnancy for this to be happening. I told Albert that he needed to take me to the emergency room. The only good thing about the situation was that I had worked at UNC's hospital while in medical school, so I knew that I would receive excellent care because they had wonderful doctors.

When I got to the ER, they immediately put me into a wheelchair and sent me up to labor and delivery. When I got up there, the triage nurse asked me how far along I was and what was going on. I could tell by the look on her face that she didn't really believe that I was contracting when I told her that was the reason I was there. It was probably because I was still able to smile when she greeted me. It wasn't until after she had put me on the monitor and noticed the contractions every four to five minutes that she really looked concerned.

"You're really contracting," she said.

Duh, I was thinking. *That's what I told you when I came in.*

She immediately went to get the doctor, who ended up being a young intern. I explained to her what was going on. She then said she was going to check my cervix and try to figure out why I was contracting so early in my pregnancy. She did her exam and reassured me that my cervix was still closed. I was so thankful. I didn't care how much I contracted as long as my cervix did not start to open up.

I was at UNC's hospital for a couple of hours. They had called up to Andrews and had gotten a copy of my OB record, so the people back at Andrews knew what was going on with me. They ran a couple of tests on me, treated me for what they thought was a yeast infection, even though I had no symptoms, gave me a shot of a medication called terbutaline to try and slow my contractions down, which it did not, and then sent me on my way. I was still contracting about every five to seven minutes when I left that hospital, but my cervix had not changed, and they had performed a fetal fibronectin test on me, which was negative. This test told them that I was probably not going to deliver within the next two weeks.

Since they released me, we decided to head on back to Maryland. That was the longest ride ever. What was normally a four-hour trip took us six hours because it was raining very badly, the traffic was heavy, and we had to stop every ten to fifteen minutes for me to pee since those contractions were squeezing on my bladder. When we got back to Maryland, I went straight in to the hospital where I worked and told them I needed them to stop my contractions. My back was hurting me so bad.

I praised God that night because my favorite doctor and my favorite nurse were working. They took excellent care of me. Dr. De came in and tried to reassure me. She then rechecked my cervix, which by the grace of God had still not changed much. She did tell me that it possibly could have gotten a little shorter, and that was why she wanted me admitted for observation. I was then transferred to Bethesda Naval Hospital.

That had been one of the longest days of our lives. I had been up since about four a.m., had gone to three hospitals, and had vaginal exams by four different doctors by the time the night was over. I was started on a medication called magnesium sulfate to try and stop my contractions, and that mag had some of the most uncomfortable side effects ever. I was also given more doses of terbutaline to try and stop my contractions throughout the night. This made me feel slightly jittery.

By the time the sun came up, my contractions had spaced to about every eight minutes. I felt like I had really been put through the ringer. Yet another doctor came in and checked my cervix, and once again, no change. I just praised God.

They released me from the hospital that morning. I went home and continued to contract. I was told to remain on bed rest for three days, and that's what I did. However, my contractions just continued. I was so uncomfortable, and no matter how hard I tried, I could not sleep. I called my doctor, and I could tell that she was nervous as well. She wanted to do everything she could to prepare me for a preterm delivery just in case Donovan came early. I was so scared at times that all I could do was cry. I prayed, prayed, prayed for God to stop my contractions and protect my baby. I knew he had to be getting tired of getting squeezed on by those contractions. But he kept on kicking and moving as if to let me know that he was doing just fine in there.

One night I had tried everything to get comfortable. Nothing worked, so I decided to get into a warm bath. While in that bath I prayed, prayed, prayed for God to help me. I could not stop crying. God then told me to read Psalms 32 as if He was trying to relay a message to me. I did not hesitate to read it. "Oh, Lord my God, I cried to you for help, and you have healed me..." After reading that I was able to fall asleep in the bathtub and rest peacefully for about an hour because I knew that everything was going to be all right. And it was. On August 8, 2003, Donovan was born full term with absolutely no complications. He was the most beautiful five pound thirteen ounce little boy I had ever seen. And for me, aside from getting stuck in my back eight times for my epidural, childbirth had been one of the most enjoyable experiences I had ever endured. My Albert was right by my side holding my hand throughout the entire event. He was the best husband God could have ever given to me. *I loved our little family!*

Once again, God had come through for me in a mighty way. He protected both me and my baby from what could have turned into a very delicate situation. He continued to protect us, and Donovan grew stronger and stronger every day. When I felt like being a resident along with being a breastfeeding mom and a wife was getting to be too much for me, He renewed my strength daily so that I could continue to journey on despite how weary I got. He proved over and over again that He was able to do exceedingly and abundantly above all I could ever ask of Him. He blessed us with a great daycare provider, a great church family, a great neighborhood to live in, and we always had everything that we needed. He was truly a sovereign God.

Before long I had completed my residency training, and it was time for us to move on to the next phase of our lives. We had asked God to send us back to Alabama to be closer to our families, which He did. We had asked God for another baby, and about a month after we got back down to Alabama I found out that I was pregnant again. I asked God for a little girl, and Genesis was born on my birthday, April 19, 2006. I had similar preterm contractions with her, and I also developed severe preeclampsia when I was thirty-six weeks pregnant with her. However, no matter what Satan threw my way, I was never worried because I knew God was in control of the entire situation. He had kept me through so much in my life, and I knew He was not about to leave me then. Genesis came out just as strong and beautiful as she could be, weighing in at five pounds and two ounces. She was the most beautiful baby girl I had ever seen. It was at that point that I felt that our family was complete.

Revelation

Never Would Have Made It Without You

"I'm stronger; I'm wiser, I'm better, much better..." My life's experiences have definitely made me a stronger person. I went through so many things while growing up that a lot of times I thought I was going to lose my mind. I just wanted to run away from it all. Without God on my side, I have no clue where I would have ended up. I was around so much chaos that I'm sure the place that I could have ended up would not have been pretty. The devil has been trying to take me out my entire life, but he has not been able to. No matter how hard he has tried, like Celie said in *The Color Purple*, "I'm here! I may be black, and I may even be ugly, but I'm here!" I am still standing on the promises of God. The devil has nothing on me. Yeah, I messed up a few times, but God's grace has cleansed me from my sins. He has given me another chance to make it right. Every day is a new day to try not to make the same mistakes that were made the day before.

The reason I believe the devil was not able to take me out was because I know I had a whole lot of people praying for me, especially my mama. There is nothing like a mother's prayer for her children. It can protect us even if we go into places that we know we have no business being in. More mamas need to pray for their children today. The world is hard. It's especially hard for children. They are facing a lot of madness that we never had to face when I was growing up. They are dealing with a lot of issues that their little brains aren't even mature enough to understand. Because our world is so distorted, I pray for my children all of the time that the Lord will keep them covered from all evil, and that His angels will constantly stand guard against anything that may try to hurt them. And I am convinced that He will do it. He did it for me.

I pray that same prayer for each of you reading this book. May God bless and keep you and yours always! I also want to encourage each of you to pray. *Pray without ceasing!*

Every time a child walks into my office, I pray for God to give me something to say to them that will keep them from making bad choices. I particularly remember this one fifteen-year-old whose father brought her in for an evaluation. He said that she had gone from an A/B student to a D/F student in a matter of months. When I asked her what had changed, she initially just put her head down and stared at her shoes. I explained to her that from my experience, when a student all of a sudden stops trying, something had to have happened to make them quit. Either a relationship problem at home, drugs, being bullied; people don't just make drastic changes like that for no reason. After I explained that to her, she looked up at me and said, "They said I ain't gon' be nothin'."

"What!" I exclaimed. "You're going to let what somebody else says about you determine your outcome in life? Girl, people are going to talk about you. There are always going to be haters in your life. The only way that they can win is if you let them."

I then asked her what her plans were after high school. "I wanted to be a lawyer, but that's all messed up now."

"Girl, if you don't stop defeating yourself you will never be successful," I said. I then asked her if she went to church and whether she was a part of the youth group. She said yes.

"Well, what does the pastor tell you every week?" I asked. She just looked at me. "Don't you know that you are created in God's image? And is God a failure?"

She looked at me and smiled and said, "No."

"Well then, how can you fail? God equipped you with the same exact tools that he equipped Johnny Cochran with, so if he became a lawyer, so can you."

I then gave her a business card with my contact info so that she could contact me with any questions. I also told her that I would get her a copy of my book upon its completion. She seemed relieved after our conversation, and I was very glad that God had given me the opportunity to minister to that young lady.

It was at that point that I realized that I did not go through all that I went through in life simply because God was trying to be mean to me or because God did not care. My entire life God has been building testimony after testimony for me to share with others to help bring them into a relationship with God. He truly sanctified me. He set me apart for a special purpose, and I believe telling my story is a part of my purpose. I thank God that, in spite of all that I have gone through thus far, I am still standing! I know that my story is going to help others to persevere and not give up when times get hard, knowing that if a little nappy-headed girl from the small country town of Callahan, Florida, can make it, so can they.

That's why *I praise God for my story and I pray that it will touch thousands of lives!* You should praise God for your story as well! *Amen.*

The End of the Beginning

Divine Forgiveness
By Dr. T. Danielle Russell

"Girl, you better push that baby out! I can't do it for you."

"But, Granny, it's just too hard. I'm tired. I can't push anymore," Deanna cried.

Having a baby was a lot harder than she thought it was going to be. After having an effortless pregnancy with absolutely no complications whatsoever, she thought she was going to go into that hospital and show those doctors and nurses a thing or two about how to have a baby. Initially she said that she wanted to have her baby "all natural." No medications whatsoever. Her granny and mom tried to tell her that as long as the baby came out of her vagina that was a natural birth, but she didn't want to listen. They told her that she had better take advantage of modern medicine because when they had their kids there was no such thing as an epidural, so they knew what true labor pains felt like. Deanna thought she was tough, though, and didn't need help from anybody. She had always been that way in almost every aspect of her life—very independent and headstrong.

Deanna Moseley was the daughter of Edward and Sandra Moseley. Her father had been a hard working merchant marine her entire life and would often be gone for months at a time. That left Sandra at home to care for Deanna and her younger brother Samuel all by herself the majority of the time. When

Edward was home it was almost like he wasn't there because he rarely said anything or interacted with the family at all.

Sandra Moseley was also a hard worker. She was a licensed nurse practitioner who for years had worked at an assisted living facility down in Mobile, where Deanna and her brother were born. She limited her work to three days a week so that she could be there for Deanna and Samuel as much as possible. She did all that she could to keep Deanna and Samuel off the streets and in church learning about the goodness of God. Even if Edward didn't go to church with them, Sandra, Samuel, and Deanna were in church every Sunday and Wednesday night.

Deanna had always been a special child. Aside from her independence and self-confidence, she also possessed a gift that set her far above all of the other kids that she grew up with. That girl could *sing*. She had the most beautiful voice in all of Mobile County. People would travel from miles around to fill the pews at Mount Calvary Full Gospel Church just to hear that child sing. When she opened her mouth, it was as if angels flew out of her vocal cords and filled the sanctuary, ushering in the Holy Spirit. And in no way was she afraid to use the gift that God had given her. She enjoyed the attention she received for her melodious voice.

Not only could Deanna sing, but she was also a very pretty girl. Her grandmother was biracial with long, curly hair and green eyes. She and her mother inherited a lot of her grandmother's features. Deanna's hair was thick, jet black, and naturally wavy, and she had hazel eyes, which also caused her to get a lot of attention. She was also rather petite, standing only five feet tall and barely weighing a hundred pounds. She was always a dainty young lady who loved to sing and dance. She competed in just about every talent show there was in her city and won them all. She was also very involved at Mount Calvary. She sang in all of the choirs and participated in all of the youth functions. She was always at church. That's why when she ended up pregnant at the young age of sixteen, everyone was completely surprised. Her parents tried as hard as they could to figure out how this happened, but no matter how much they questioned themselves or Deanna, they could not come up with an answer that made any sense to them. Deanna always told them she had no idea how she got pregnant. As far as she was concerned she was still a virgin and was in no way able to explain to them how she got pregnant. She told them she had no idea who the father of the baby was. In her mind this had to be an immaculate conception just like when Mary was pregnant with Jesus. Therefore, she knew this baby was going to be special. In a way she was scared, being only sixteen and about to be a mother, but in a way she was excited and thankful that God had chosen her to carry this special gift into existence. Now she was finally about to meet the special little person she had carried inside of her for the past thirty-eight weeks.

• • •

"Girl, pull those legs back and push as hard as you can!" Sandra yelled.

"I'm trying, Mama. I'm trying!" Deanna whimpered. "It's just so much harder than I thought it would be."

"Well, child, that's why they call it labor. You got to work hard to get this baby here. You can do it, though. You strong just like your old granny," her grandmother reassured her as she rubbed on her forehead.

At that point, Deanna grabbed the back of her legs, took a real deep breath, and pushed as hard as she could.

"That's the way I want you to push," the doctor said excitedly. "Your baby's head is right there. Two more big pushes and he or she will be out. Come on, you've done a great job so far."

Deanna didn't feel that she had done a great job at all. She actually felt like a failure because she really wanted to have a natural birth with no anesthesia at all. About two hours into her labor, however, she realized that her labor pains were a lot more intense than she had ever imagined. She felt like someone had taken a vice grip and placed it around her back and stomach and was trying to make a pancake out of her. And this was one type of pain that prayer did not change. She was very disappointed in herself when she had to ring the bell for the nurse to tell her that she had changed her mind and wanted to get an epidural. The nurse reassured her that there was nothing wrong with pain relief. It actually made the labor process more enjoyable, and in some cases made it go by a little faster. After her epidural, Deanna was definitely a lot more relaxed and was even able to get a couple of hours of rest while they waited for her cervix to dilate.

"Your baby is right here! Push, push, push!" the doctor yelled.

Deanna grabbed her thighs one last time, filled her lungs with air, and *pushed!*

The next sound that Deanna heard was the most beautiful voice she had ever heard in her life. She thought this voice was way more special than even her own. Even though she was exhausted, she tried hard to lift herself up to look between her legs to see her baby as the doctor finished pulling it out. She was trying hard to see the little miracle baby that God had given to her. She wanted to make sure that it was okay. She wanted to hold it and tell it that she loved it and that Mommy was right there. Even though she had not even seen her baby, her heart was filled with so much love. It was also filled with much sorrow because she believed that every child needed a mother and a father to raise it. Even Jesus had an earthly father to look after him. She then began to question God about why He would put this precious being on this earth to be raised without a father. It was at that moment that she was able to see the wonderful little creature that she was now responsible for.

"It's a boy!" the doctor exclaimed.

Deanna really didn't care what it was. All she knew was that this was her baby and she was going to do her best to make sure he had everything he needed. Even if she had to work and go to school at the same time, her baby was going to be well taken care of. She honestly believed that this was the reason God had placed her on this earth—to bring into the world this special little being who was going to one day change the world. And she was going to make sure that he fulfilled his mission.